COMPELLED TO WRITE

COMPELLED TO WRITE

Alternative Rhetoric in Theory and Practice

DAVID L. WALLACE

UTAH STATE UNIVERSITY PRESS
Logan, Utah
2011

Utah State University Press
Logan, Utah 84322-3078

ISBN: 978-0-87421-812-1 (paper)
ISBN: 978-0-87421-813-8 (e-book)

Manufactured in the United States of America
Cover design by Barbara Yale-Read

Library of Congress Cataloging-in-Publication Data

Wallace, David L., 1960-
  Compelled to write : alternative rhetoric in theory and practice / David L. Wallace.
      p. cm.
  Includes bibliographical references and index.
  ISBN 978-0-87421-812-1 (pbk.) — ISBN 978-0-87421-813-8 (e-book)
1. English language—Rhetoric. 2. Discourse analysis, Literary. I. Title.
  P302.W35 2011
  401'.41—dc22

                          2010054021

For my parents,
BETTY AND RON WALLACE
with gratitude for all the important things you taught me

CONTENTS

ACKNOWLEDGMENTS

This book, like all books, is the creation of more than just the person whose name appears on the cover in the author slot. As odd as this sounds, the people who helped me the most with this book were the baristas at the Starbucks in my building. Lisa sometimes had my tall nonfat latte ready to hand to me when I reached the head of the line in desperate need of caffeine to clear the morning cobwebs before I pulled out my laptop and forced myself to write for at least an hour before the day could continue to other activities. Danny most often made the half-caf evening version when I needed a little boost for a second round of writing after a long day, and he topped it with a smile that was just as big a boost as the caffeine. And there were many others who ground the beans and steamed the milk without complaining that I sat at a big table with my laptop and books for a couple of hours at a time.

Jonathan Alexander helped me reconceive chapter one and much of the structure of the book in more interesting terms, and Robert Brooke brought his unerring sense of what is newsworthy in our field to bear in ways that helped improved chapters one and six dramatically. Michael Spooner is the editor everyone should want to work with for many reasons, but, in this case, because he understood why this book needed to say some out-of-the-ordinary things in out-of-the-ordinary ways.

My friend J. Blake Scott read and listened; Linda Flower made me think more about how James Gee was relevant to my project; my dear departed friend Wendy Bishop modeled alternative rhetoric for me before I knew what it was; and my dean, José Fernandez, always had a sympathetic ear and wise advice when the pressures of writing this book while chairing a big English department drove me to the limits of my endurance.

You will meet the others who helped me write this book in its pages: queer scholars such as Judith Butler, Eve Sedgwick, and Michael Warner, who helped me see that a different approach was possible; students in my writing classes who wrote hard things that changed my teaching; and many rhetoric and composition scholars who have challenged me to see the limits of my own understanding of what it means to teach and learn writing.

1

DEFINING ALTERNATIVE RHETORIC
Embracing Intersectionality and Owning Opacity

*A central insight to keep fully present in our thinking, rather than on
the periphery, is the necessity of resisting a tendency to view discourse
(language in particular use) as a disembodied force within which we
are inevitably, inescapably, innocently swept along.*

Royster, 2002

The norms by which I seek to make myself recognizable are not fully mine.

Butler, 2005

Could it be that we just don't know ourselves? That the very words we use
to speak ourselves to others obscure as much as they elucidate? That we
emerge only in the cracks when words fail to perform as we have come
to expect them to?

Could it be that we fail words by forgetting they are not/can never
be disembodied but continue to exist only as we speak/write/display
them? That we suffer from the illusion that when we speak we have not
already been spoken?

Some of us are compelled to write because we cannot escape daily
reminders that words define us as different, as other. Some of us are
swept along, free to speak, write, text, sing, shout, live with invisible
words that allow us to lie with the herd.

This book is about those who are compelled to write: those who don't
need Jacqueline Jones Royster's reminder that words are not innocent
neutral tools, those who do not need Judith Butler to tell them that
words they cannot control are used to label them as freaks, queers, others—dismissible. I explore what it means to speak with cracked voices,
to use words, language, and rhetoric in cries and rants, teases and taunts
that refuse to accept the status quo.

But this book is for all of us, too—all of us who are willing to look at the
limits of our own knowing and accept that we have responsibility for what
falls outside our experience, all of us who are willing to reject the myth of

objectivity and embrace our subjectivities, all of us who are willing to see language as discourse and to own the implications of that insight.

Of course, I am hardly the first to note the need for a different understanding of rhetorical agency and its implications. At least since we began reading de De Saussure, Bakhtin, Vygotsky, Foucault, and others, rhetoric and composition scholars have understood that language is not a set, value-free tool. By consequence then, neither is rhetoric. Rather both language and rhetoric are always socially, culturally, and historically situated and dependent on actual practice for their continued existence. The underlying principle here is that language and rhetoric are both constitutive in that meaning making is based on the existence of these sociocultural systems that serve as the basis for shared understanding, but also in that these systems themselves have no existence independent of actual practice. Indeed, language and rhetoric are in a very real sense themselves reconstituted with each communicative interaction.

One of our field's chief problems has been how to translate our understanding of the theoretical complexities amongst language, culture, rhetoric, and individual identity into rhetorical theory, practice, and pedagogy that moves substantively beyond the presumptions of current traditional rhetoric that language and rhetoric are largely neutral tools and that, once mastered, they can be wielded equally by all as the means to economic and other kinds of power. I bring a queer twist to this problem, proposing that the concepts of intersectionality and opacity used in queer theory can help us sort out the knotty problem of negotiating identity in rhetorical theory and pedagogical practice.

As Royster argues in the opening epigraph, the discursive nature of language and rhetoric must be at the center of any understanding of rhetoric and composition that takes postmodernism seriously, and discourse must be understood as an embodied force that has real consequences for real people. My most basic argument in this book is that defining some kinds of semiotic exchanges as *alternative rhetoric* can help us sort out both the ways members of some groups have been systematically marginalized by dominant discourse practices that pretend neutrality and the means those who have been so marginalized have used to challenge the discourses of power. In this regard, I begin with two critical assumptions: (1) personal identity is intimately bound up in the practice and pedagogy of rhetoric, even if that identity is not always immediately apparent to all involved, and (2) fundamental components of culture, language, and rhetoric are complicit in systemic inequities in our society in ways that have real and daily consequences for those they marginalize.

Of course, at some level, defining *alternative rhetoric* is dependent on understanding what it is an alternative to, and defining rhetoric is a task that has kept scholars debating for 2,500 years. Rather than reviewing that long history, I explore in the first section of this chapter more recent attempts in our field to sort out the problem of accounting for the social identity of the writer as a means of illustrating the need for alternative rhetoric as I define it. In doing so, I begin with the assumption that rhetoric becomes alternative when it engages the individual's subjectivity rather than attempting to erase it and accounts for the positioning of that subjectivity within the discourse of power that enfranchise some and marginalize others. In this sense, I argue that *alternative rhetoric* is a meaningful term only if it is grounded both theoretically and practically in a recognition that the effects of engaging in discourse are, to some extent, always beyond our capacity to understand and control and yet, paradoxically, that we are also responsible for those effects. This seeming contradiction is actually a generative place from which to redefine alternative rhetoric in ways that move beyond the presumption that engaging in responsible rhetorical agency requires only that one have a reasonable control of dominant discourse practices as well as the usual sense of what it means to take the kinds of moral action that usually attend those practices. However, taking advantage of this generative position requires an understanding of self that recognizes that one always stands in relationship to the discourses of power in multiple ways and that knowledge of the self and its relationships to others is always incomplete. In short, we must embrace and explore the multiple intersections of identities with the discourses of power, and we must own our opacity.

I draw the terms *intersectionality* and *opacity* from queer theory in the service of exploring how alternative rhetoric can help us move us forward in our attempts to sort out how to account for the social position of the writer and speaker and of the student and teacher of rhetoric. *Intersectionality* is critical to work in queer theory, which argues we must get beyond binary notions of identity. For example, Karen Kopelson (2002) argues that when we allow ourselves to be identified by a single axis of difference in our society we help perpetuate those problematic binaries (a version of the subalternity problem that Gayatri Spivak brought to our attention). Borrowing from Kimberlé Williams Crenshaw's (1993) work that illustrates how major features of identity such as gender and race are not mutually exclusive categories, queer theorists have argued for a notion of identity as multiple and operating in complex interactions that make being an Asian American different from being an Asian American woman and different still from being an Asian American lesbian.

The concept of *opacity* comes from queer theorist Judith Butler's 2005 *Giving An Account of Oneself* in which she explores the moral implications of the fact that complete self-knowledge or self-definition is not possible because we are all reliant on social norms beyond our control not only for our understanding of ourselves and our position in the world but also for the means to engage with that world in meaningful ways. Coupled with an intersectional understanding of identity, Butler's understanding of this basic opacity—this fundamental incompleteness of knowledge of both the self and the other—is the foundation for a new approach to rhetoric that seeks not to minimize or eliminate this basic incompleteness but to embrace it. Butler argues, "If we are formed in the context of relations that become partially irrecoverable to us, then that opacity seems built into our formation and follows from our status as beings who are formed in relations of dependency" (20). Inherent in Butler's opacity argument is the notion that the impossibility of complete knowledge of self, the other, or the full consequences of the values and discursive practices that make meaningful interactions possible does not make agency or moral responsibility impossible. Rather she argues that building an informed moral basis for rhetoric requires a new understanding of the basis for that responsibility: in short, I read Butler as calling for us to own this fundamental opacity both in ourselves and in others as fundamental to rhetoric that seeks to substantially account for difference and to create the possibility for morally responsible rhetorical agency.

In the body of this chapter, I explore how five principles from queer theory that feature *intersectionality* and *opacity* are critical for developing an alternative to rhetoric that sees its main job as persuading the other to one's own position. However, before I do so, I pause to explore some important attempts in our field to deal with the complexities of social identity in language and rhetoric to set a clearer basis for the need for alternative rhetoric.

EMBRACING IDENTITY: WHY WE NEED ALTERNATIVE RHETORIC

Our field has struggled to understand the implications of the social identity of the author both in our approaches to pedagogy and in our conceptions of rhetorical theory. For example, Joseph Harris has rightly argued that, too often, the primary goal of progressive pedagogy devolves into the unseating of particular social inequities. As Harris argues, it is dangerous for our field to settle for approaches to rhetoric and pedagogy that seek simply "to influence [students'] present attitudes (which strikes me as a kind of intellectual canvassing for votes)" rather than to "help them learn to deploy more powerful forms of reading and writing" (2003, 578). Certainly, we cannot substitute leftist political leanings for the more substantive work of rooting out how traditional rhetoric is complicit in the many faces of oppression. However, as Royster argues, we must also be careful to guard the tendency to assume that traditional approaches to rhetorical theory and composition pedagogy provide a fair means for all to exercise agency in our society. As Patricia Bizzell argued more than twenty years ago, we must move beyond our field's nostalgia for supposedly simpler times in which language and rhetoric were seen as neutral tools with which we equipped our students to use as they wished, to a new understanding of the relationship between rhetoric and morality that provides a more substantive basis for pedagogy (1990, 665).

In recent rhetorical theory in our field, an important aspect of the struggle to understand the implications of the social identity of the author can be seen in Sidney Dobrin's chapter in Christopher Schroeder, Helen Fox, and Patricia Bizzell's 2002 collection exploring alternative discourse. Dobrin argues that the concept of *hybrid discourses* makes little theoretical sense because postmodernism has taught us that all discourse is hybrid and subject to change in the process of continual reconstruction. Dobrin rightly reasons that determining what counts as "alternative" or "hybrid" is a theoretically complicated task and that we must be careful not to underestimate the power of dominant cultural practices (even those in the supposedly liberal academy) to simply swallow up and neutralize nontraditional discourses in a shallow form of multiculturalism. For my purposes, the value of Dobrin's argument is that it highlights the basic discursive function of language and rhetoric: all human interactions are complex semiotic negotiations, and we would be foolish to pretend otherwise. However, because he does not explicitly account for the operation of systemic oppression within language and rhetoric, Dobrin's argument could too easily be reduced to the position that the underlying discursive nature of language and rhetoric makes it nonsensical to call out any set of discursive practices as having problematic consequences because all language and rhetoric are by nature discursive and subject to change.

Both Dobrin's argument about theory and Harris's argument about pedagogy implicitly call out the question of whether or not it is incumbent upon those who teach rhetoric and composition to deal with the social identity of the author, particularly in the extent to which we account for how our theory and pedagogy perpetuate the discourses of power that enfranchise some and marginalize others. As is likely already apparent, I believe it is morally incumbent upon us as individuals and as a discipline to do so. As a gay man who has experienced various forms of marginalization on a daily basis, I have a vested interest in this belief. However, as a white middle- to upper-class, physically abled man from a Christian background, I have also experienced considerable privilege in educational settings, and I understand the difficulties of sorting out our privilege within the discourses of power in higher education as well as how frightening it may be to contemplate changes to the rhetorical traditions and discourse practices that many of us hold dear. Before I suggest some ways queer theory can help us understand what it means to engage in such identity negotiations, I provide some historical context for this problem by exploring three principles our field has used to deal with the problem of the social identity of the writer. The principles roughly follow the history of our field on this issue, beginning with commonsense calls to provide nonmainstream students with access to the discourses of power and moving toward calls for explicit transformation of the discourses of power.

In sketching this version of our field's history, I argue that we have not gone far enough in addressing our complicity in maintaining the discourses of power that marginalize groups within our society. However, I also want to acknowledge from the outset that there is sense and value in each of these principles; they have been proposed by thoughtful scholars and often are enacted by caring, sensitive teachers in ways that benefit students. However, my concern is that if we enact these principles without understanding our individual and collective intersectionalities, and without accounting for our individual and collective opacities, we sell our students, ourselves, and our discipline short of the potential to be a force for social justice, and we risk contributing to the status quo that systemically marginalizes some groups in our society. We owe it to our students and ourselves to engage in the full potential of our field.

Principle #1: An Important Part of Our Institutional and Societal Mission Is to Help Provide Students with Access to the Discourses of Academic, Professional, and Cultural Power

More than thirty years ago, ground-breaking composition pedagogical theorist Mina Shaughnessy made the commonsense claim that our field needed to provide access to the discourses of power for all students in a manner that respected their home discourses. Shaughnessy, among others, called for a radical new understanding of our field's mission, rejecting the notion that we should serve a gatekeeping function and embracing our role in helping students whose language backgrounds and experiences do not match well with the discourses necessary for success in the academy and in professional contexts. One of her most telling observations on this front is that "a person who does not control the dominant code of literacy in a society that generates more writing than any society in history is likely to be pitched against more obstacles than are apparent to those who have already mastered the code" (1977, 13). In his seminal article, "Inventing the University," David Bartholomae made an argument that had similar implications for how we understand our function as a field when he argued that teaching college writing is in a very real sense an exercise in asking students to reinvent the university and create a place for themselves in it. In making this argument, Bartholomae proposes a notion of a writer's purpose not as a wholly intellectual thing that he or she creates ex nilo but as, to some degree, bound up in discourse itself "with its projects and agendas that determine what writers can and will do" (1985, 139).

Taken together, the challenges that Shaughnessy and Bartholomae laid out for our field invited us to take up a new understanding of the kinds of identity negotiations we place before our students. Put simply, we needed to understand that our students bring sophisticated grammars and discourse practices with them and that the sets of discourse practices we attempt to teach them require identity negotiations that are much more difficult and complicated for some than others. Engaging in what I will call this "discursive" understanding of our field's mission has been more difficult than understanding the need to do so. As I have argued elsewhere (Wallace 2004–05), our field too often embraces "the Shaughnessy party-line that the best we can do is be culturally sensitive to students' diverse literacy backgrounds as we assimilate them to our understandings of academic and professional discourse" (14). We have become very adept at walking the line between our complex theoretical understandings of the varied implications that learning dominant discourse patterns have for our varied students, but we often fall back in practice on more sophisticated versions of seeing our role as providing students with access to discourse practices that will empower them.

Perhaps the most thoughtful articulation of a discursive understanding of composition pedagogy that seeks to limit the extent to which our field must substantively address the identity issues inherent in our mission is Harris's argument for writing pedagogy that takes as its primary focus teaching the practices of writing. He says, "Our first job is to demystify the actual working of academic discourse" (2003, 578), and he proposes that doing so involves seeing writing as what Sylvia Scribner calls a "practice." Harris is certainly justified in his concern that shallow forms of consciousness-raising pedagogy can distract from the difficult business of helping students develop writing abilities. However, I am concerned that a shallow form of his argument could amount to an updated version of a writing-as-a-neutral-tool stance and to a shifting of the responsibility of dealing with the inequities inherent in academic discourse to students:

> Imagining critical writing in these more mundane terms as a "method of doing something," much like growing rice or sewing trousers, has for me the appeal of rooting our teaching in the actual labor of drafting, revising, and editing texts. And as in teaching someone to farm or sew, our job in teaching writing is to help students gain more control over their work. Their challenge is to make writing work toward their own ends. (591)

My concern with Harris's and Scribner's position is that it underestimates the underlying identity negotiations inherent in seemingly mundane tasks in that, as Butler argues, the very norms by which we make ourselves intelligible to the world are always, to some extent, outside our control. In my experience, it is not a simple matter for a man to learn to sew a pair of trousers or for a woman to slide under the chassis of her Ford F-150 pick-up and loosen the nut on the oil pan with a long-handled chrome ratchet—there are names for men and women who do such things, and the same basic connection with identity also operates in the acquisition and use of discourse practices.

Principle #2: Expanding the Range of Discourse Practices that We Include and Accept in Our Writing Courses Helps to Expand the Canon of Acceptable Discourse More Generally

A second important approach to dealing with the problem of the discursivity of language and rhetoric calls for an expanded range of discourse practices that allow for writers to be more personally present in their texts and for inclusion of a wider range discourse practices, particularly the genres, vocabulary, dialogue, and syntax often used by members of marginalized groups. These calls to expand the linguistic and rhetorical canon have been an important step in helping us understand how our field might do things differently, particularly how personal presence, genre hybridity, and code-switching can work to make the experiences of the oppressed more visible within the discourses of power.

One strand of this work takes the basic position that being personally present in one's writing shuns traditional notions of objectivity and provides a means for embracing one's fundamental subjectivity. For example, Jane Hindman argues for an "embodied rhetoric" that requires a move away from the presumption that academic discourse is and must be "impersonal, detached, objective" and toward rhetorical practice that "gestures to the material practices of the professional group *and* to the quotidian circumstances of the individual writer" (2002, 103). Similarly, Wendy Bishop argues that we need to invite students to become ethnographers of their own experiences, that in composition "[s]tudent writers are creating places to stand, negotiated cultural identities with which to approach and understand their worlds" (2003, 270). Often, scholars arguing for embodied approaches work out of feminist perspectives on language and rhetoric, calling for the use of personal narratives as a means of being personally present in one's writing (Bishop 2003), for including the experiences of women in dominant discourse (Kirsch, 1993), and for telling untold and taboo stories (Daly, 1998).

Such work is important because it has helped our field begin to develop genres and discourse practices that have the potential to provide the means by which we can answer Butler's call for giving an account of ourselves.[1] However, engaging in discourse practices that make one present in discourse does not guarantee that one is accounting substantively for one's position within the discourses of power; as

---

1. See especially Bishop's 1997 collection on alternative style.

Butler argues, "Telling a story about oneself is not the same as giving an account of oneself" (2005, 12). For example, in an article exploring the place of creative nonfiction in composition, Bishop (2003) includes much autobiographical information; however, she does not substantively account for her own position as a heterosexual mother telling a story about her daughter or explore how telling such stories would likely be a more difficult business for those whose sexual identity or other aspects of identity complicate the usual conceptions of family relationships. Thus, for alternative rhetoric as I define it, *embodiment* must be more than autobiographical self-revelation or other rhetorical and stylistic innovations; it must bring the operation of culture into relief in a way that accounts for the interlocutors' positions not only within culture at large but also in relation to each other in the immediate context.

The other major strand of work that seeks to expand genres and conventions of acceptable discourse has its roots in the experiences and language practices of marginalized groups in American society. For example, in the 1960s and 1970s, scholars such as William Labov and Geneva Smitherman pioneered work that helped our discipline understand that African American Vernacular English was not a degraded form of Standard Written English, but a well-developed linguistic system with its own syntax and genres. Similarly, scholars such as Mina Shaughnessy and Mike Rose challenged the notion that those who spoke and wrote from discourses marginalized by dominant culture should be seen as having inferior language abilities. Later, scholars such as Victor Villanueva and Keith Gilyard complicated overly simplistic notions that assimilation to the discourses of power is the obvious path to enfranchisement for groups who have been marginalized because of race in American society.

More recently, a number of scholars writing in the two major collections exploring alternative rhetoric and discourse in rhetoric and composition (Gray-Rosendale and Gruber 2001; Schroeder, Fox, and Bizzell 2002), as well as other venues, have argued more explicitly for discourse practices intended to disrupt dominant discourse and its attendant cultural values. For example, Jeff Schonberg argues that literacy may be disruptive to cultural systems rather than simply providing cultural capital within such a system: "Literacy can disrupt social order, threaten established religious precepts or stimulate unemployment" (2001, 235). Many of the discussions in these volumes suggest that such disruptions can be facilitated through the use of new or underemphasized genres[2] or different rhetorical strategies.[3]

As I have already mentioned, the work of these scholars is important because it identifies some important genres and discourse practices that can help us conceive of rhetoric more broadly. However, I am concerned that this work underestimates the underlying need for change and in the end can too easily support a fairly conservative model for change that assumes (1) that people can learn to switch among codes, (2) that contact with unfamiliar discourse practices is critical for creating a sense of distance from one's home discourses, and (3) that this distance is necessary for understanding the socially constructive nature of language and helpful for learning secondary discourses. For example, Paul Kei Matsuda argues that in the dominant assumptions about language in the United States, "practices that seemed to deviate from the 'norm' had been treated simply as errors or incoherence, if not signs of carelessness or cognitive deficiencies" (2002, 192). He suggests that one way to address this problem begins with the recognition that "everyone in the U.S. academy needs to reassess their assumptions about discourse practices in the academy as they come into contact with unfamiliar discourses" (194).

Matsuda's position is reminiscent of linguist James Gee's argument that everyone can benefit from the experiences of learning what Gee calls a secondary discourse no matter how well or how poorly his/her primary discourse matches up with the discourses of power. In fact, Gee sees metacognition as dependent, to some extent, on lack of fluency within a discourse: "When we come across a situation where we are unable to accommodate or adapt (as many minority students do on being faced, late in the game, with having to acquire mainstream discourses), we become consciously aware of what we are trying to do or are being called upon to do" (1989, 12). Matsuda further argues that dominant discourse cannot be ignored: "Somewhat paradoxically, we also need to better understand dominant discourse practices and their boundaries as perceived by the audience in various contexts of writing

---

2. See Dehann (2001) on immigrant letters, Killoran (2001) on personal home pages, George and Salvatori (2008) on holy cards, and Gray-Rosendale (2001) on children's stories.

3. See Killoran (2001) on irreverence and parody in personal home pages; Collins (2001) on escaping agonism; Ouyang (2001) as well as Powell (2002) on tricksterism; Schroeder (2002) on narrative as well as DePeter (1997) on fractured narratives; and Tobin (1997) on double-voiced discourse in Bishop's earlier collection (1997).

because alternative discourses are always defined in relation to dominant discourses in a particular context" (2002, 195–96). Peter Elbow suggests that one practical way to deal with the ubiquitous Standard Written English (SWE) is for students to engage in a kind of code-switching when we invite (although do not require) them to do some of their writing in vernacular dialects, although he also argues, "I think we should require a good number of assignments to be in SWE, but that needn't be the goal for *all* assignments" (2002, 131).

The attractions of this code-switching/consciousness-raising model of rhetoric/discourse are that it requires very little change for those whose home discourses match up well with the discourses of power and that it allows for an additive model of change rather than one that requires the transformation of the discourses of power. Even the recent calls for a more globalized approach to rhetoric and composition rely on an underlying additive model that does not explicitly take up the need for transformation of dominant discourse practices and the cultural values they support. For example, John Trimbur's vision for composition within a broader notion of American culture explicitly proposes

> an additive language policy whereby all students as a matter of course speak, write, and learn in more than one language and all citizens thereby become capable of communicating with one another in a number of languages, code-switching as appropriate to the rhetorical situation. (2006, 587)

My concern here is that additive models of progressive rhetoric make it too easy to envision goals that do not make the unseating of inequity a primary goal. For example, LuMing Mao argues for a different, non-Western sensibility in rhetoric: "One central mission for Confucius was to restore a rich culture of the past, and to bring back harmony and ritual propriety to his time" (2002, 118). The part of me that knows it is too driven and too Western and that has trouble lying quietly in savasana (corpse pose) at the end of my yoga classes is attracted to the idea of rediscovering harmony. But the part of me that fought through years of homophobia, heterosexism, and self-loathing to find a voice, an identity that let me accept and articulate myself as a gay man, is gravely suspicious of any attempt to return to a "ritual propriety" without careful examination of the underlying values of those proprieties. Because of these experiences, I feel compelled to articulate what I see as missing in the attempts we have made in good faith to understand our complicity in reproducing the discourses of power within the theory and practice of rhetoric and composition while also recognizing underlying value of this important work. In short, this body of work moves beyond the theoretical understanding that language and rhetoric are discursive to a position that explicitly calls for an expansion of the linguistic and rhetorical canon that dominates academic and professional discourse. However, too often, the focus of this work has been on adding to the existing canon rather than explicitly seeking a fundamental transformation of dominant discourse practices and cultural values themselves.

Principle #3: Rhetoric Needs to Unsettle Problematic Dominant Cultural Values and the Discourses of Power that Support Them

Alternative rhetoric, as I define it, must seek transformation not only of dominant sociocultural values that disenfranchise groups in our society but also of its own theory and pedagogy because rhetoric itself is intimately bound up with systems of oppression that operate in our society. A number of scholars in our field have been calling for this kind of transformational approach to rhetorical theory and practice and to writing pedagogy, and these calls often come from those writing from positions of racial marginalization. For example, Royster sees one of the primary benefits in engaging in alternative discourse as that doing so may help "to dismantle the mythology of *rightful stronghold* and *invading hordes* that has been so militaristically rendered in our field" (2002, 26). Malea Powell sees alternative discourse practices as essential "to write our bodies into text and reinvent our writing in another voice, another language" (2002, 21). Similarly, Jonathan Alexander and I (Wallace and Alexander 2009) have argued that rhetoric and composition needs a queered understanding of rhetorical agency that will not only bring LGBT people and experiences more visibly into our discourse but will also allow for many kinds of difference to be addressed more substantively in our rhetorical theory and practice and in our writing pedagogy. This model requires a substantive accounting of the ways in which our field has been a tool of oppressors, and the active deconstruction of our dearly held belief in the generosity and benevolence of our own theory, practice, and pedagogy. For example, in discussing a course in which she attempts to make connections to students' lives and provide an opportunity for questioning social reality, carmen kynard states that she "refused to summon up literature and the arts as a warm and nurturing world that redeems our humanity" (2002, 41).

These perspectives hint that limiting the practice of alternative rhetoric to transgressive techniques and genres would be an oversimplification; as Mao argues, "there is nothing inherently alternative in, for example, performing a genre-mixing speech act or in speaking indirectly" (2002, 120). Even the intent to break out of traditional discourse patterns does not guarantee one will engage one's interlocutors with substantive issues of difference that inform the discourse practices used. Indeed, several factors must be considered in assessing the discursive nature of any act: the intent of the originating interlocutor, the conventional or transgressive nature of the discourse practices themselves, the contexts for the act, and the varied perspectives and experiences of those who see/hear the act.[4] Thus, the value of calling out this third principle is largely in that it moves beyond recognizing that sociocultural history sets the stage for any act of alternative rhetoric to explicit calls for unseating the systems of inequity in both the culture at large and in our own disciplinary practice. Two recent books by scholars writing from positions of racial marginalization illustrate the kinds of sweeping change that will likely be necessary for developing rhetoric that fully understands this complexity but also the danger in limiting one's view to a single axis of oppression when one does so.

In his 2008 *Mestiz@ Scripts, Digital Migrations, and the Territories of Writing*, Damian Baca makes a case that the Eurocentric fallacy needs to be unseated not only in culture at large but also in our own discipline. One of Baca's most insightful critiques of our field's participation in the aftermath of the colonialist Western European claim to occupy the pinnacle of civilization is his call to reconsider Robert Connors's linkage of American rhetorical traditions to ancient Greek ones. In essence, Baca argues that our discipline needs what he calls Mestiz@ rhetorics because we must begin detaching ourselves from colonialist history, culture, and values; he asks:

> When does the American history of rhetoric begin? What should educators do with rhetorical traditions unique to the Western Hemisphere, with beginnings suggested by the memories of Mesoamerica rather than of Greece or

---

4. It may seem that I am reinventing a four-part version of Kenneth Burke's pentad here. And, indeed, Burke's notions of scene, act, purpose, agency, and actor are certainly relevant. However, what is missing in most uses of Burke's pentadic method is the explicit recognition and accounting of systemic power imbalances. Indeed, getting beyond the neo-Aristotelian notion of discourse as neutral is the critical basis for alternative rhetoric and for substantive accounting of discursive subjectivity.

the Aryan-Germanic Enlightenment? How, when, and under what circumstances might "Indigenous Chicanos" enter the imaginary of composition history? (2008, 119–20)

Like other scholars writing from racially marginalized positions,[5] Baca argues that enacting such a thorough change will require revision of the curriculum of rhetoric and composition.

Baca's contributions to the difficult task of deconstructing Western dominance in American history, language, and rhetoric range from a basic pronunciation guide to help Anglos and others unfamiliar with the history and the *Nahuatl* terms and a chronology of the history of Mesoamerica to more complicated analyses in which he unpacks how the Western alphabetic bias worked to deemphasize Mestiz@ culture by devaluing pictorial codices—arguing, "The sixteenth-century European bias that Mexicans lack true writing and history continues today" (2008, 76). As I discuss further in chapter 4, one of Baca's most important contributions to alternative rhetoric is his insistence that Gloria Anzaldúa's challenges to dominant culture and discourse practices necessitate a broader deconstruction of culture and the very discourse practices our field propagates. For example, he argues:

> Yet, rhetorical episodes such as Gloria Anzaldúa's *Borderlands*, for example, will be persistently misunderstood, mistranslated, and misappropriated unless comprehended as "new" rationalities and practices that emerge from the conditions created by colonial legacies. (124)

Ironically, Baca's discussion of how the work of Gloria Anzaldúa could contribute to such a revision reveals two limitations of his own contributions to alternative rhetoric, at least as I define it here. First, Baca's reading of Anzaldúa focuses almost exclusively on race. While this work is important because it helps deepen our understanding of Anzaldúa's roots in race issues, he ignores how her lesbian sexual identity and the hormone imbalance that plagued her childhood also contributed to the sense of distance she felt from dominant culture, and he only acknowledges briefly her emphasis on Mestiza spirituality and its challenge to traditional Western rationality. Also, Baca does not as substantively account for his own subjectivity along the axes of difference in American culture as does Anzaldúa. A reader can easily intuit his affinity with Anzaldúa on the basis of race, but he is largely silent about how

---

5. See particularly Lyons (2000).

such factors as gender, sexual identity, physical abledness, and religion/
spirituality function in his reading of her work. Thus, like many thoughtful scholars writing about difficult race issues in rhetoric and composition, Baca's call for a more thorough critique of dominant culture and
discourse, and his work to explore the historical and ongoing effects of
those biases, make important contributions to rhetoric that takes seriously the unseating of systemic marginalization. However, his failure to
look much beyond race and to account in much substance for his own
subjectivity limits the usefulness of his contributions.

A similar pattern can be seen in Morris Young's 2004 *Minor Re/Visions:
Asian American Literacy Narratives as a Rhetoric of Citizenship*. Young is
much more forthcoming than is Baca about how his own experiences
with racial discrimination illustrate the kinds of challenges faced by
those in racially minoritized positions—in Young's case being seen as
an Asian American. Indeed, as a mainland Anglo, I found it fascinating
to read about the colonial history of Young's native Hawai'i, particularly
the linguistic paternalism of the English Standard Schools and the truly
multicultural, multiracial nature of the Hawai'ian culture. In a very real
sense, Young practices what he preaches about the value of autoethnog-
raphy and language memoirs, and further, Young's autobiographical
accounts of such experiences as feeling like a racial minority for the first
time in a New Orleans comic book store illustrate what it means to be
what he calls a "minor subject." As a white gay man interested in understanding the problematic operation of race in our society in more detail,
I am grateful to learn from Young about experiences of marginalization
that differ from mine, particularly to understand how as a visible racial
minority, Young's identity is often immediately overdetermined by others' perception of his race. Also, I feel a kindred sense when he writes
about how dominant culture seeks to marginalize and control those it
places in minority status: "So if a minor subject cannot be rewritten in
order to fit the cultural script of the story, then the minor subject must
be explained away as unassimilable or even as a threat to the community" (29). Yet, I also find myself disappointed that, like Baca, Young
rarely looks beyond race, nor does he consider how other aspects of his
identity position him in possible positions of privilege in the very culture
he finds problematic on the basis of race.

My purpose in this admittedly brief and incomplete review of recent
scholarship in rhetoric and composition that addresses difference
substantively is not to malign the important work done by scholars to

whom I owe a considerable debt. Nor do I want to suggest that my own approach provides the magic bullet that others have missed. Rather, my intent is to situate my contribution in this ongoing discussion in terms of the important insights that have emerged from previous work and to suggest something that has largely been missing because our field, even in its most informed and progressive work on difference, has not paid sufficient attention to the queer.

OWNING OPACITY: HELP FROM QUEER THEORY

So what more do we need to do? We have acknowledged that the discourses of power are not god-given, natural, or linguistically and morally superior to other discourses. We have taught critique and metacognition, seeking to demystify the complexities of language, genres, and discourse communities. Some of us have worked hard to open the academic and professional canons to new practices that include the personal and the multicultural, trying to make good on the commitment our field made over thirty-five years ago to respect students' rights to their own languages. As I will argue in chapter six, we need to rethink our basic goal for writing pedagogy; instead of trying to ensure that all of our students meet some minimum set of standards, we need to help them understand what it means to be in conversation with the discourses of power and help them to gain some new tools for doing so. I don't mean to suggest here that application to pedagogy is the only way for our field to think about the need for alternative rhetorics; however, it is an obvious one in that so many of us are engaged in the business of teaching first-year composition, and it is an important one because we need alternative rhetorics that work in practice. In this section, I build on the principles already at work in our field to take up the difficult issue of addressing the sociocultural implications of rhetorical practice and pedagogy for individuals who often have very different experiences with dominant culture and the values and discourse practices that support it. First, I argue that we must embrace our individual subjectivities by owning our own opacity, and then I propose five additional principles from queer theory to provide means for doing so.

As I have already argued, this work begins with owning the basic opacity that Butler sees both as preventing us from a full knowledge of self and other and as making the very terms by which we know and are known in the world always outside our control to some extent. Butler explains that responsible action cannot be tied to the conceit of a self fully transparent to itself. Indeed, to take responsibility for oneself is to avow the limits of any self-understanding, and to establish these limits not only as a condition for the subject but as the predicament of the human community. (2005, 83).

My most basic argument then is that owning this fundamental opacity allows us to begin finding middle ground between two extreme positions in our field. On the one hand, traditional approaches to rhetoric assumes that gaining control of dominant discourse practices and genres allows everyone to have the kind of agency usually enjoyed by straight, white, physically able-bodied, middle- to upper-class, Christian men. On the other hand, an extreme postmodern perspective sees identity as so complex and inherently individual that there is no reasonable stance from which to articulate how any kind of rhetorical agency is morally different from another. If we fail to address our own opacity both individually and collectively as a field, we are likely to remain in the muddle created by our laudable commitment to rhetorical theory, practice, and pedagogy that is equitable to all and our difficulties in sorting out what such a commitment means in practice.

To illustrate the perverse nature of this muddle, I use an example from Ellen Cushman's recent article "Toward a Rhetoric of Self-Representation: Identity Politics in Indian Country and Rhetoric and Composition." I chose this piece because I believe that in it Cushman provides one of the most substantive examples of a scholar in our field sorting out her own subjectivity and because her discussion lays bare a real challenge for our field: accounting for the differences that lie among us without pitting one experience of difference against another. Using the cases of her own and Native scholars' attempts to claim their racial heritage both in tribal and academic contexts, Cushman teases out important differences between self-identification, "a claim about one's identity that needs no other evidence," and self-representation, "an identity claim that includes evidence of identity markers valued by multiple audiences" (2008, 323). Cushman seems motivated to make this distinction both by scholars of color in our field who have questioned her status as a person of color and by Native scholars who have questioned her commitment to the Cherokee nation. One of the points she comes to in this analysis is that Native scholars often face a different kind of identity challenge than do other scholars of color because they often have to prove their race legally. "This is not to imply that other scholars of color have an 'easier time' with identity politics than Native scholars, but it is to say that the rhetorical exigencies in creating self-representation are quite different" (326).

Cushman's description of the different kind of rhetorical exigence faced by those of us whose membership in groups traditionally marginalized in American society is not immediately visually apparent rings true with my own experience as a gay man. Having one's membership in a traditionally marginalized group immediately and unmistakably present in all of one's interactions with dominant culture is not something with which I have direct experience, and, like Cushman, I want to acknowledge and understand that status as different is more difficult for some to escape than it is for me. However, as I argue later in this chapter, I think Cushman is right that those of us whose difference from the expectations of dominant culture is, at times, closeted, should also expect that others will acknowledge and seek to understand the types of marginalization we face. However, I take a different lesson from Cushman's example.

Cushman claims that the cases she presents "illustrate the ways in which all rhetoricians might begin to engage in a rhetoric of self-representation when composing identity" (2008, 356). Specifically, she wonders:

> What would identity politics become if white, black, Asian, and Chicano/a scholars began to reveal their family and community authenticity markers and means of accountability? Perhaps we could begin to understand what makes racial categories neutral or complicated; we could begin to understand better the systemic ways in which racial categories circumscribe us all; we might begin to find tangible ways in which we can identify with each other; and we can begin to work toward commonly shared goals for writing and knowledge making for the public good. A rhetoric of self-representation places on all rhetoricians the burden to state and support our identity claims. (357–58)

My disagreement with Cushman is not over her principle that a rhetoric of self-representation is necessary and that all are implicated in the need for it. Rather, I am concerned that she has essentially given us a monochromatic tool for doing so. By failing to address aspects of her identity beyond race, Cushman's contributions to the difficult underlying problem she works so hard to tease out is limited; worse, when she moves to applying her proposals more broadly, she fails to consider how she herself could be creating the very bases for misunderstanding with those who experience other kinds of marginalization that lead her to tease out differences between Native scholars and other scholars of color. For example, her call for other scholars of color "to reveal their family and community authenticity markers" is based in her interesting observations about kinship in Native communities: "Finally, kinship relations matter a great deal as demonstrations of radical indigenism; being for Indians has everything to do with lineage, family, and clan" (2008, 357).

My concern here is that Cushman fails to consider how claiming identity features not based in kinship (like gender, sexual identity, and physical abledness) may require breaking traditional kinship relations. For example, Alexander and I (Wallace and Alexander 2009, 794) argue that kinship relations, particularly those related to traditional notions of the nuclear family, often function in problematic ways for LGBT people because of the operation of heteronormativity in our society. Indeed, LGBT people often risk traditional familial relationships by coming out, and we also must often create new kinds of families for ourselves. In this regard, I think Cushman is absolutely right to challenge our field to engage in a more substantive rhetoric of self-representation, and I admire the personal risks she takes in trying to tease out one aspect of self-representation that has not received enough attention. However, I propose that we must find ways to do so that account for more than one kind of difference at a time or we risk getting so mired in identity politics that we will not be able to develop means for addressing each other in ways that acknowledge and understand the differences that lie among us in concert with the experiences that have the potential to unite us.

As I have already indicated, my contribution to furthering this deeper accounting and further understanding begins with five principles I have drawn from queer theory. To be sure, these principles and my comments about them are largely rooted in my homosexuality; however, I base my efforts in calls from queer theory to embrace intersectionality as a means of owning opacity, so that even though I recognize that I cannot account for the experiences of all, I can make a good faith effort to account for the limitations of my own understanding as I seek means for us all to press forward.

Principle #4: Engaging in Responsible Rhetorical Agency Must Be Rooted in an Understanding of Identity that is Both Multiple and Contested

Central to the practice of alternative rhetoric as I define it is accounting for the differences that fall along the major axes of oppression in our society. However, such accounting must be done in ways that both account for how groups are enfranchised or marginalized according to those issues and require that we recognize individuals can never be defined by a single axis of difference. Both elements are critical; if we focus singly on contested aspects of identity such a gender, race, class, sexual identity, and the like, we run the risk of engaging in identity politics that can divide us by our differences in the service of unseating inequity. However, if we focus only on the plurality of identity, we run the risk of erasing critical differences used in our society to unfairly oppress some groups and enfranchise others.

Even in the broad terms used to define identity in Western culture, each of us speaks and writes from a complex position, and nearly all of us exist in both positions of privilege and disenfranchisement in at least some aspects or situations of our lives. In one sense, this position simply restates the postmodern dictum that all acts of agency are iterations in an ongoing social-cultural-historical web of incredible complexity and that one's ability to take action depends not on some independently existing self but on one's relative position in that web in any given situation. What alternative rhetoric requires is a notion of agency that goes beyond the usual sense that one is responsible for what one intends and accounts for one's positionality within the webs of meaning that make communication possible. Butler argues that accepting our inherent subjectivity and the ongoing iterative nature of all meaning making require unseating the notion that we are only responsible for what we intend and embracing a different basis for responsibility:

> On the contrary, I am *not* primarily responsible by virtue of my actions, but by virtue of the relation to the Other that is established at the level of my primary and irreversible susceptibility, my passivity prior to any possibility of action or choice. . . . Rather, my capacity to be *acted upon* implicates me in a relation of responsibility. (2005, 88)

Like most postmodern theorists, Butler argues that accountability is not impossible because identity is bound up in subjectivity and agency in ongoing processes of iteration: "This ethical agency is neither fully determined nor radically free. Its struggle or primary dilemma is to be produced by a world, even as one must produce oneself in some way" (2005, 19). What Butler adds to this general understanding is that the beginning of moral responsibility is acknowledging that because we are all always and already implicated in social networks for our identity and the means to take agency, none of us can fully know ourselves nor can we expect such full knowledge of others. Two points are critical here. First, we are always personally implicated in the very discourse and social systems by which we understand ourselves and our actions; echoing Foucault, Butler says, "Any relation to the regime of truth will at the same time be a relation to myself. An operation of critique cannot take place without this reflexive dimension" (2005, 22). And, second, we must accept that just as we cannot fully understand or articulate ourselves, this opacity does not eliminate the possibility of responsibility. Rather it relocates the basis of responsibility from the self to relations among self, other, and the discursive practices and social mores that make meaningful interaction possible: "Our responsibility is not just for the purity of our souls but for the shape of the collectively inhabited world" (2005, 110).

One important thing to keep sight of in all of these postmodern wranglings is that the vast majority of those in Western society do not recognize the inherent subjectivity of identity nor the discursive nature of language and rhetoric. Particularly in American society, there is a presumed and persistent belief that society is fair and that the systems of values, language, and education supporting that society provide equal opportunity for advancement to all. Further, this blindness serves the interests of those in dominant positions, allowing those in positions of unearned privilege to imagine they have achieved this status solely through their own merit.

The lion's share of the work of alternative rhetoric will, for the foreseeable future, revolve around exposing systemic inequities in our society and the means by which traditional approaches to language and rhetoric support those inequities. However, given that identity is multiple and that expression of the self is necessarily incomplete, it is important to also recognize that those of us who speak from marginalized positions must also be careful to sort out how our positioning of ourselves and our messages within culture at large and the particular occasion for articulation makes claims about problems in society. Such accounting is critical if we are to practice what we preach. An example from our disciplinary discourse illustrates what this accounting might mean in practice. I believe it is important to be critical of those who write from positions of relative privilege who do not delve deeply enough into the implications of postmodern understandings of identity, agency, and social responsibility; however, it is equally important to examine the practices of those writing from the margins who, too often, presume an unarticulated moral stance. For example, the oft-cited opening claim of Eve Kosofsky Sedgwick's seminal *Epistemology of the Closet* claims that examining how and why nonnormative sexual identities are marginalized in Western society is critical for all people, because "virtually any aspect of modern Western culture must be, not merely incomplete, but damaged in its central substance to the degree that it does not incorporate a critical analysis of modern homo/heterosexual definition" (1990, 1).

For me, the underlying moral basis of this claim does not need explication because I face nearly every day the broad range of cultural tools that dominant culture uses to reinforce heterosexuality as normal, and homosexuality, bisexuality, transgenderism, and transsexualism as unusual, aberrant, or, in some cases, immoral. For me, Sedgwick's claim that heteronormativity subverts and perverts society needs no data, warrant, or backing because my life experience testifies to the veracity of the claim and the implied call for change. However, I can easily imagine that such a basis is not so immediately self-evident for those who occupy positions of heteronormative privilege. Indeed, my own experience trying to come to terms with the privileges that accrue to me because of my maleness and my whiteness suggest to me that heteronormative privilege may seem so natural to those it enfranchises that it is largely invisible to them. I want to be clear, though, that the difficulties of seeing beyond our own privilege do not excuse us from the need for doing so; instead, to be responsible postmodern rhetors and rhetoricians we must educate ourselves in the theory and practice of alternative rhetoric.

Principle #5: Identity is Performative and Thus Changeable

Inherent in the principle that identity is both contested and multiple is the presumption that identity is not fixed, natural or god-given, rather it is performative. Thus, the second principle I draw from queer theory suggests that we can begin to address the difficulties of the individual and collective owning of our opacity by understanding difference as based not in fixed identities but in our continual performance of our identities in discourse. One of my favorite class activities to help students understand how identity is performative begins when I ask my students to take off a shoe and hold it up. Then the class votes on who has the most butch and who has the most femme shoe, and the two winners get a prize (it's amazing what most college students will do for a Snickers bar). My point in this activity is to help students begin to understand that our genders are something we literally put on every morning when we get dressed, and the difficulty we have in classifying some shoes as either butch or femme illustrates that although gender expressions are often thought of as discrete categories, there are considerable gray areas. For example, once I tried to win a Snickers bar by wearing the most butch shoes I owned on the day I had planned this activity, but I could not compete with Sarah, a butch lesbian who proudly held up her scuffed black combat boot.

From the standpoint of a performative understanding of identity, gender, race, class, sexual identity, religious identification, physical or mental/emotional abledness, and other markers of difference can be seen as identity shorthands that govern relationships in such fundamental ways as designating which people can use which restrooms and who is allowed to marry whom. In some sense, such shorthands are necessary for the functioning of society, yet, left unexamined, they are also the basis for forms of systemic marginalization that often go unarticulated. The clearest explanation of this basic performative nature of identity in rhetoric and composition is Karen Kopelson's 2002 *College English* article "Dis/Integrating the Gay/Queer Binary: 'Reconstructing Identity Politics' for Performative Pedagogy." Kopelson builds on Judith Butler's argument in *Gender Trouble* that gender and sexuality are not fundamental truths, not preexisting categories in any ontological sense. Rather, such identity features are *performative*, that is, the very categories are continually recreated through "performative speech acts" (17). Further, Kopelson argues that the field of composition has been slow to embrace this basic principle: "[D]espite the continued 'center-stage' status and interdisciplinary, international circulation of these and similar claims, Butler's theory of performativity has only recently begun to creep *backstage* in composition studies" (18).

There are several challenges in taking up this more complex understanding of the discursive nature of identity performance. First, a shallow version of performativity might too easily be reduced to the notion that identity is something that can be performed at will, that one can simply put on an identity by performing the discourse practices and social values that typically mark a particular identity. Of course, identity is never that simple. For example, early in her unsuccessful primary campaign for the Democratic presidential nomination, Hillary Clinton attempted to adopt a version of Black English Vernacular in her March 4, 2007, speech to an African American audience commemorating the Selma, Alabama, civil rights march. Her awkward performance on this occasion lead to criticisms that she was performing in blackface, and despite her intent to identify with an historically disenfranchised group and her attempt to use a nondominant discourse, it was clear that she did not command this voice because she had not lived it. More than a century earlier, critiques of Frederick Douglass's fluent use of the discourse of power (see chapter 3) were used in attempts to erase his identity as a former slave; even abolitionist colleagues such as John A. Collins (who, incidentally, first encouraged Douglass to speak) urged: "Better have a *little* of the plantation manner of speech than not; 'tis not best that you seem too learned" (Douglass 2003, 266).

Another challenge in understanding how performativity is useful in alternative rhetoric is accounting for the discursive nature of identity performance without erasing the real effects of systemic oppression. One of the most important values of a performative understanding of rhetorical agency is that it makes explicitly clear that change is possible: we can choose to perform our identities in ways that break social expectations and flout discourse conventions. However, as I have already argued, the use of unconventional discourse practices and the intent to be transgressive do not fully determine how any performance of identity will be read. Indeed, queer theorist Michael Warner argues in his 2002 *Publics and Counterpublics* that *publics* are never individual creations and much of the process of their creation remains "invisible to consciousness and to reflective agency;" also, *counterpublics* "are defined by their tension with a larger public" (56). What is important for my purposes in Warner's public/counterpublic distinction is that he attempts to create tools for considering identity in relation to discourse practices that acknowledge difference without presuming there must always be a binary relationship of power. Indeed, he argues that this need not be the case:

> Counterpublics are often called "subaltern counterpublics," but it is not clear that all counterpublics are composed of people *otherwise* dominated as subalterns. Some youth-culture publics or artistic publics, for example, operate as counterpublics, even though many who participate in them are "subalterns" in no other sense. At any rate, even as a subaltern counterpublic, this subordinate status does not simply reflect identities formed elsewhere; participation in such a public is one of the ways by which its members' identities are formed and transformed. (57)

What is critical for my purposes here is understanding that participation in publics and counterpublics is neither completely voluntary nor completely proscribed and that counterpublics can be used to create the kind of solidarity that allows for challenging a problematic public. In short, there is room for agency, but that agency is always limited and constrained. Concerning the latter, an important tenet of alternative rhetoric is that not only are language, rhetoric, and discourse not neutral, but the dominant versions of these are systematically detrimental to some groups. For example, Jose Esteban Muñoz argues that the traditional notion of masculinity (and the many discursive practices that enforce it in our society) "is calibrated to shut down queer possibilities and energies" (1999, 58). Thus, at the age of thirteen, when I hear my father say to me, "You walk like a girl in those sandals," language is being used to call me to account for transgressing a male/female binary, and, in retrospect, I see my father as participating in a larger system of compulsory heteronormativity, the purpose of which is to socialize boys and girls not only into narrowly defined gender roles but to stigmatize behaviors and marginalize individuals who fall outside the supposed norms. A critical question for alternative rhetoric, then, is how does one resist such as system? Or, in the terms I have been using in this article, as individuals how do we learn to extend beyond the limits of our own lived experiences, and as a discipline how do we sort out our complicity in the discourses of power and transform the very discursive practices we teach?

The third challenge for enacting an understanding of identity as performative is understanding the need to continue to address the marginalization of groups within American and other societies without continuing to recreate the very terms that make that marginalization possible. The critical question here was posed more than twenty years ago by Chakaravorty Spivak in her now-famous question "Can the subaltern speak?" One of Spivak's concerns in raising this question is that speaking from a marginalized position (such as "woman") can serve to reinscribe the power relations of the very system of power the speaker intends to unseat. Another of her concerns is the lack of substantive attention to ideology in some of the best postmodern theory, particularly Foucault's and Deleuze's failures to address "their own implication in intellectual and economic history" (1988, 271). In our own field, Deepika Bahri argues that shallow appropriations of postcolonial concepts can underestimate the complexities of addressing underlying differences. For example, following Spivak, Bahri argues that the very act of invoking marginality can have an objectifying effect: "The naming of the margin in euphemistic terms is a way of reducing discomfort and diverting attention away from precisely those problems of marginality, otherness and of historical particulars that should be addressed" (1998, 37). She also warns against the co-optation of the notion of *hybridity* in a manner that "tends to avoid the question of location because it suggests a zone of nowhere-ness, and a people afloat in a weightless ether of ahistoricity" (39). On the other extreme, she warns that "anxiety in the Western academy over lost subaltern voices can turn into a frenzied quest for the genuine native, leading to fetishization of the extreme margin in terms of particularly abject otherness" (40). Bahri's concerns point to the need for a more substantive understanding of the discursive nature of language and rhetoric and the performative nature of identity, and, further, they suggest that alternative rhetoric must be defined as more than the use of hybrid language or other transgressive discourse practices.

Principle #6: Closeting is an Exercise of Unacknowledged Privilege

A third principle from queer theory that can help us break the cycle of oppressive discourse conventions that maintain marginalizing identity binaries is the notion that closets of various kinds are created largely through the operation of unacknowledged privilege. As Cushman's argument (2008), cited earlier, suggests, not all difference is immediately and visually apparent; indeed, LGBT people, mixed race people, those abled in other than the expected ways, and many others often have to choose to make their difference visible. Most relevant here is Sedgwick's claim (1990), cited earlier, that there is an epistemology of the closet operating in Western society that creates a fault line in that culture that is harmful to all because it is based on the false pairing of heterosexuality as normal and natural with homosexuality and other forms of sexual identity as abnormal and unnatural. Although Sedgwick's epistemology of the closet refers specifically to the issues surrounding sexual identity in our culture, her argument can usefully be read as suggesting that the places to start unseating oppression in its many forms are the fault lines of identity that have been stigmatized in our society, not only because society has defined these as critical identity issues but also because (as Foucault taught us) these are the places where the operation of cultural values becomes visible, where seemingly transparently good cultural values and neutral discourse practices can be deconstructed. For my purposes, Sedgwick's argument is important not only because it suggests that even those who enjoy heteronormative

(or other) privilege have a stake in efforts to unseat systemic marginalization but also because I read her argument as entailing a necessary
acknowledgement of the role that dominant culture plays in creating
the very closet from which lesbians, gay men, bisexuals, and transgendered or transsexual people must emerge to publicly claim a fundamental aspect of our identities. This position calls for a more active
understanding of how we all have participated in systemic marginalization, even though we may not have intended to do so. Much as I try to
get my students to understand that one can participate in racism without burning crosses on lawns, we all must set out to understand how
we have participated in the marginalization of others even if we had no
idea we were doing so.

Sedgwick's notion of the closet and its underlying epistemology is a
useful metaphor for understanding the nature of this process. First, it
suggests that the nonnormative is often invisible or otherwise shunted
off from the center of society, that it must be brought into the light.
This principle is not only relevant to LGBT people; indeed, those who
identify as mixed race are often not easily identifiable as such and must
make this status visible. Second, it calls us to think about how closets are
created, how they are built in our society. For example, J.K. Rowling created a stir at a 2007 event at Carnegie Hall when she announced that
one of the most beloved characters in her enormously popular *Harry
Potter* series, Headmaster Albus Dumbledore, is gay. As scholars who
had written on sexual identity and other difference issues in the Potter
series, my colleague Tison Pugh and I were called upon to comment
upon this revelation. In earlier work[6] we had noted that although there
is very little actual homophobia in the lengthy series of books, nonnormative sexual identities are conspicuous by their absence. Although
Rowling creates an entire alternative world in which she makes at least
token gestures on gender and race issues by including women in positions of power and interracial couples, Pugh and I observed that not a
single character is identified in the books themselves as a homosexual
and "among the approximately eighty students at Hogwarts [School
of Witchcraft and Wizardry] featured in the six books to date, not one
questions his or her sexual identity" (2006, 263). Thus, it seems unreasonable to give Rowling much credit for bringing a character out of the
closet she built for him.

---

6. See Pugh and Wallace (2006; 2008).

Rowling's failure to see that she herself created Dumbledore's closet mirrors the largely unacknowledged operation of heternormativity in Western societies. Given the debates over gay marriage and adoption, active homophobia has become easily identifiable. However, the more subtle forms of heteronormativity that operate in dominant discourse practices remain largely invisible, and those who use them, even without malice or awareness of them, substantively participate in the perpetuation of heteronormativity in our society. My point here is that engaging in alternative rhetoric that actively works to unseat systemic inequity requires more than shunning overt prejudice or challenging overt prejudice when it is expressed by others. Rather, we need a more fine-grained parsing of oppression, and we must be prepared to sort out our own often unwitting participation in the various kinds of closets that contain not only those who differ from the presumed norm but also limit our individual and collective responsibility for creating and maintaining the cultural values and discourse practices that create that oppression.

Principle #7: The Substantive Copresence of the Other is Necessary for the Oppressed to Have Rhetorical Agency (and it Often Must Be Claimed Rather than Granted)

At first blush, is seems almost too obvious to mention that the marginalized must come to have *copresence* in culture at large to engage in alternative rhetoric. However, being present as an other in society is often a tricky business: if we are not present as queer, as other, we risk reinventing the very closets that marginalized us, but, as Spivak warns us, it is important to be present without simply reaffirming the underlying marginalization that created the need to speak. Several scholars in queer theory have examined this seeming conundrum. The notion that one must be addressed to have identity is hardly new with queer theory. Indeed, Butler's notion of the basic discursive reciprocity necessary for both rhetorical agency and articulating one's identity is based in the Hegelian sense of the other: "The Hegelian other is always found outside; at least, it is *first* found outside and only later recognized to be constitutive of the subject" (2005, 27). Similarly, Warner's definition of a *public* as "a space of discourse organized by nothing other than discourse itself" is caught up in the classic semiotic problem that discourse conventions both presume the existence of a shared understanding of their meaning and depend upon continued use for their very existence: "A kind of chicken-and-egg circularity confronts us in the idea of a public.

Could anyone speak publicly without addressing a public? But how can this public exist before being addressed?" (2002, 67).

Queer theory adds two important concepts to this basic understanding of what it means for those who are marginalized to gain presence in this basic meaning-making process. First, as Warner argues, the presence of the queer, the other challenges basic bourgeois notions of self and society:

> The bourgeois public sphere consists of private persons whose identity is formed in the privacy of the conjugal domestic family and who enter into rational-critical debate around matters common to all by bracketing their embodiment and status. Counterpublics of sexuality and gender, on the other hand, are scenes of association and identity that transform the private lives they mediate. Homosexuals can exist in isolation; but gay people or queers exist by virtue of the world they elaborate together, and gay or queer identity is always fundamentally inflected by the nature of that world. (2002, 57–58)

As is abundantly clear in the discourse surrounding gay rights, the very existence of queers as people claiming equal rights before the law challenges the usual notions of such basic American institutions as family, marriage, parenthood, and what constitutes socially responsible action. Thus, the copresence of the queer requires a fundamental redefinition of fundamental notions of morality and rhetorical agency.

Butler's version of the complex relationship between the need for the queer to be addressed to have identity and the need to renegotiate the terms of that address presses even further than does Warner's. Butler argues that not only do such encounters require the renegotiation of basic cultural values but they also require reexamination of the self, of one's own identity. In some sense then, the copresence of the queer requires the reversal of the usual power relationship in the homo/hetero binary because homosexuality and other forms of sexual identity become the occasion for those who identify as heterosexual to examine both their own heteronormative privilege and their participation in heterosexist cultural values and discourse practices. Further, breaking this binary requires a fundamental redefinition of the presumed relationship, with risk to both parties. Butler explains that this process of definition is painful but also that it provides for the possibility of real change:

> To be undone by another is a primary necessity, an anguish, to be sure, but also a chance—to be addressed, claimed, bound to what is not me, but also

to be moved, to be prompted to act, to address myself elsewhere, and so to vacate the self-sufficient "I" as a kind of possession. If we speak and try to give an account from this place, we will not be irresponsible, or, if we are, we will surely be forgiven. (2005, 136)

Generally speaking, queer people and others who are marginalized by dominant cultural values and discourse practices are used to the potential pain involved in the constant monitoring and negotiation of identity; further, we have something real to gain from changing the values and discourse practices that marginalize us. However, those who enjoy positions of privilege in dominant culture often find such work both unusual and unpleasant, and they may see little immediate benefit in engaging in such work. For this reason, I am less sanguine than is Butler that those in positions of power will see the need to engage in this process and to be forgiven, even though I believe she is right that this larger process is sorely needed. Although I would like to believe such a utopian future is possible, I suspect that those in power will have to be called to account, that the burden of developing an alternative rhetoric will lie mostly with those who need it most urgently. In short, queers and others who are marginalized in our society will likely have to continue to actively make ourselves copresent in the varied cultural institutions that comprise our society. Yet, we must also understand that an alternative rhetoric cannot solely be the responsibility of those who have been oppressed, as it is fundamentally unfair to require the oppressed to find the means to educate their oppressors.

Principle #8: Disidentification Strategies Contest the Terms by Which the Self is Articulated

The final principle I draw from queer theory builds on the need for copresense of the queer/other in society by suggesting that one powerful means of creating presence without recreating the problematic underlying binary is simply to contest the usual terms for articulation of self. For example, one important means for creating the *copresence* of the marginalized within a discourse is the act of those of us who have been marginalized claiming the right to redefine the discourse practices—even terms like *queer* and *bitch* that have been used to mark us—in ways that claim not only a place at the table but call others to question how that table has been constructed and for what purposes it is used. Of course such resistance is hardly a new strategy, but Muñoz sees such resistance as part of a larger strategy of *disidentification*. He sees disidentification as a critical tool for moving beyond shallow multicultural inclusion toward a "more progressive identity discourse" (1999, 10) because it begins at points of conflict within the culture and "does not dispel those ideological contradictory elements; rather, like a melancholic subject holding on to a lost object, a disidentifying subject works to hold on to this object and invest it with new life" (12). In the terms I have been using, *disidentification* is critical for an alternative conception of rhetorical agency because it allows a marginalized person to act without the need to, in Muñoz's terms, "evacuate the politically dubious or shameful components within an identificatory locus" (12).

As I have already argued, no rhetorical agent or group of agents is free to simply redefine the terms of its address at will, yet the very discursive nature of language, rhetoric, and culture means that change is possible. Disidentification then can be a powerful means of creating the copresence of the other if one is willing and able to bear the potential consequences of claiming a stigmatized identity or refusing to engage dominant culture in the terms it expects. French feminist Hèléne Cixous's *éciture féminine* illustrates the latter. Cixous counsels women to engage in embodied writing not just as a means of self-discovery and self-expression but as a means to power: "Write your self. Your body must be heard. Only then will the immense resources of the unconscious spring forth" (1976, 880).

In one sense, Cixous's call to women is similar to calls for those who are marginalized due to race to make themselves visible; Powell explains, "My writing has always been an attempt to live in the shadows of presence. To insist upon an existence, a voice. To write myself and my body into comprehensible space" (2002, 12). However, I read Cixous's *éciture féminine* as calling for more than just existence as other; I read her as calling for active disidentification, although she does not use that term. I recognize that my reading of Cixous's *éciture féminine* as calling for disidentification runs counter to other readings in our field that are rightfully suspicious of the extent to which disidentification can be practiced in rhetoric and composition. For example, in her article about *écriture féminine* and composition, Lynn Worsham argues that this call for women (and others) to engage in embodied writing cannot easily be integrated into composition because *éciture féminine* depends on disruption: "Violations of the accepted codes through which the social word is organized and experienced have the power to disorient and disturb." *Ériciture féminine* works through such things a parody and pastiche (1991, 86) and mimicry (87), and resists any theorizing of itself" (89). She concludes, "If it [*écriture féminine*] refuses to be objectified, if it exceeds any system's power of recuperation, then it cannot be brought within the university as we know it. It cannot be" (92).

Worsham's reading of the dangers of applying Cixous's calls for embodied writing in rhetoric and composition is understandable given the slow progress of cultural and linguistic change. However, I read in Cixous a clear call to disidentification, and I contend that, as difficult as it may be, we need to conceive of our field and its mission differently if we hope to follow Cixous's (1976) calls for women to speak/write their bodies despite very real power structures that will not welcome such efforts:

> Write, let no one hold you back, let nothing stop you: not man; not the imbecilic capitalist machinery, in which publishing houses are the crafty, obsequious relayers of imperatives handed down by an economy that works against us and off our backs; and not *yourself*. (877)

> But we are in no way obliged to deposit our lives in the banks of lack . . . (884).

> Wouldn't the worst be, isn't the worst, in truth, that women aren't castrated, that they have only to stop listening to the Sirens (for the Sirens were men) for history to change its meaning? You only have to look at the Medusa straight on to see her. And she's not deadly. She's beautiful and she's laughing. (885)

> Beware, my friend, of the signifier that would take you back to the authority of a signified! Beware of diagnoses that would reduce your generative powers. (892)

My reading of these calls to voice from Cixous leads me to wonder why Worsham doesn't see the indentured nature of composition as a place that can be generative—a place for laughing, for a kind of resistance that might not set as its goal the overthrow of the system per se but instead finding places for resistance. Worsham is right, though, that enacting this call to a different kind of voice is a complicated business and that we cannot assume open resistance will always be an appropriate or effective strategy. The most basic point driving the concept of alternative rhetoric that I develop in this book is that we must take such disruption as a central goal for our discipline; however, I would not argue that disruption is our only goal or that disidentification should be our only strategy. Rather, I imagine that all of the principles I have outlined in this chapter are important for the practice of alternative rhetoric and for writing pedagogy. For example, the genres and conventions that comprise the discourses of power cannot be ignored, and there is much of value that we can help our students gain as they interact with privileged genres and discourse practices. However, to embrace alternative rhetoric we must do so in ways that presume some of our students will choose to resist the discourses of power, and we must be prepared to help them do so in substantive ways.

COMPELLED TO WRITE: GRIMKÉ, DOUGLASS, ANZALDÚA AND SEDARIS

I conclude this chapter with a brief argument that one important way to identify strategies for engaging in alternative rhetoric is to look at the work of American rhetors who were compelled to write from the margins of our society. To that end, I spend a chapter each examining the work of abolitionist Sarah Grimké, who wrote what is now seen as the first feminist treatise in the United States; Frederick Douglass, whose autobiographies have been widely examined for their literary value but not often read as rhetorical texts; Gloria Anzaldúa, whose *Borderlands/La Frontera* can be read as the first feminist/chicana treatise in the United States; and popular memoirist and National Public Radio figure David Sedaris, whose books provide an irreverent counterpoint to the other work I examine.

Of course my choice of these figures limits what I see, and certainly other choices were possible. To be blunt, I chose these writers because they have interested me for some time to the point that I have used their work in teaching courses that range from entry-level first-year composition courses to graduate courses in rhetorical history and theory. I see in each a slightly different understanding of what it means for a writer to feel compelled to write in response to systemic injustices in our society. Further, the work of each is intersectional in some significant way: Grimké is a privileged white woman advocating for abolition who is forced to defend her right to speak as a woman; Douglass begins his public career almost as a side-show oddity—the articulate ex-slave—and ends his career as one of the most important advocates for abolition and women's rights in American history; Anzaldúa writes not only in multiple languages and dialects but from marginalized positions due to gender,

race, class, sexual identity, and dominant conceptions of physical abledness; and Sedaris uses his privileged position as a middle- to upper-class
white male humorist to speak unabashedly of his homosexuality, his
struggle with various addictions, and his obsessive/compulsive nature.

Further, for each author, a body of critical work exists that informs
my readings of them as alternative rhetors, although little of that work
has taken up the kind of analysis I see as necessary for understanding
what these authors have to offer the theory and practice of alternative rhetoric as I have defined it. I recognize, of course, that another
important way to examine what constitutes alternative rhetoric in practice would be to bring to light the work of rhetors whose work has not
received much attention. For good or ill, that is not my project in this
book; instead, I chose these four authors because their work provides
glimpses into two important periods in American history and because
their work speaks from a variety of marginalized positions. For Grimké
and Douglass, the bodies of critical work are largely historical and literary, and the two writers engage in two of the most important diversity
issues in nineteenth-century American society: the abolition of slavery,
with its attendant race issues, and women's suffrage. Although the two
are not quite contemporaries, the difference in their positioning in
society on these issues makes them an important pair for understanding the complexities of engaging in discourse that seeks the redress of
societal inequities.

Anzaldúa and Sedaris are not quite contemporaries either, but the
pair provide glimpses into what it means to address equity issues in
American society in late twentieth century and, in Sedaris's case, early
twenty-first-century America. As I have already noted, Anazalúa's work
addresses the widest range of difference issues, yet our field has paid little attention to the ways her work, and the critical body of work about it,
extend beyond feminism and critical race theory. For Sedaris, the body
of critical work is just now emerging, and as the only living writer of the
four, his corpus of work is not yet complete. However, examining his
work is particularly important as he is the only economically privileged
white male amongst the four and because his differences from dominant society both intersect with and diverge from those of Anzaldúa.

Finally, I chose this set of four writers because of the range of
genres they write in. From the standpoint of neo-Aristotelian rhetoric, Grimké is the most traditional, writing mostly expository text in
which she uses traditional forms of argument and support. What makes

her work interesting for my purposes is the ethos battle she faced; in her day, women who spoke and wrote in public were considered immoral. Although Grimké rarely speaks of her own experience, one of Douglass's primary contributions to public discourse was his own story; thus, I focus on Douglass's autobiographies rather than his writing for newspapers because I want to read him as an early example of using personal experience as a primary means of persuasion and because I believe his case provides an important example of how embodied writing can be used to great effect. I am well aware, however, that in doing so I run the risk of engaging in a version of limiting his voice similar to that of his early white abolitionist handlers, who advised him just to tell his slave story and leave the larger argument to them. To address this concern, I have made a conscious effort to look beyond Douglass's original account of his slave story and have included also his accounts of his struggles to gain a full voice within the abolitionist movement and to manage conflicts with women's suffrage advocates. Like Douglass, both Anzaldúa and Sedaris can be seen as using personal experience in their writing. However, in *Borderlands/La Frontera* and her other writing, Anzaldúa's use of her own story usually occurs in the service of some larger point she explicitly argues. Thus, her writing mixes narrative and expository forms actively, and she also uses code-switching in ways that move beyond its usual function to add color to a predominately traditional piece. Of the four, Sedaris relies most directly on personal narrative and is the least interested in making direct arguments about injustice in American society. Yet, when my students and I stop laughing and examine his stories more closely, we find a surprising amount of critical analysis, and we marvel at his skill in making telling points without seeming to do so.

Taken together, these four authors provide an interesting set of texts from which to explore alternative rhetoric in practice because they wrote at different and interesting moments in American cultural history, because they wrote from different positions within American society, and because their work represents a range of mixing of traditional expository and narrative genres. I offer my readings of their work in the next four chapters not as definitive examples of what it means to engage in alternative rhetoric but as cases to help us consider the range of strategies that may comprise such practice and how such practice will be affected both by how society seeks to constrain the rhetorical agency of those it marginalizes and how those marginalized resist such constraints.

PIANO LESSONS

Mr. Elkin always wore a coat and tie as he sat on a chair turned away from the dining room table and toward the piano where I sat, banging out C-D-E, "bone sweet bone," E-D-C, "bone sweet bone," C-D-E-D-E, "it's my favorite song," using only my thumb firmly planted on middle C and my forefinger and middle finger anchored to the D and E keys right above middle C. Mr. Elkin seemed overdressed for a Tuesday afternoon in our dining room with its worn green linoleum floor, and he must have been bored out of his mind as I stumbled on C-D-D, no E, E-D-C, C-D-E-D-E.

At the time, it did not occur to me to wonder why Mr. Elkin wore those bold plaid sport coats and loud ties. It might have been because he was short and his semiformal attire made him feel like a more significant man, or maybe he thought he'd be more authoritative as a music teacher if he looked the part. But as soon as he opened his mouth, his authority was gone: "Oh Mrs. Wallace, you look soooo lovely today," cackle, cackle, waving his hands around. You see, Mr. Elkin was a sissy, and the brightly colored coats and ties just made that more apparent.

We found Mr. Elkin through the Barber family down the street, whose two daughters took lessons from him. He became our piano teacher on Mrs. Barber's recommendation because he would come to our house for the lessons and because he was cheap. Mom always paid Mr. Elkin in cash—mostly singles, I think. Dad thought Mr. Elkin must have money because he was always talking about his father, Burt Elkin, Sr., the doctor, because he could hardly make a living giving piano lessons, because he dressed so well, and because he regularly ate at the cafeteria next to Penn Traffic—a place we couldn't afford to eat, Dad said, because it would cost us "Mom's whole grocery budget for the week just to have one meal!"

Mr. Elkin taught all the musically inclined (and, in my case, the not so musically inclined) kids on Juniper Street, picking up new students from younger families as the older kids (and their parents) lost interest. Although I didn't pay much attention to Mr. Elkin, my impression was that he wasn't respected among the adults on Juniper Street despite his sport coats and his obvious talent when he demonstrated how a piece should be played. In fact, the Juniper Street neighbors collectively rolled their eyes at Mr. Elkin's flamboyant clothes and his high, girlish laugh, but I never heard anyone say what is dreadfully obvious to me thirty years later: Mr. Elkin was a flaming queen.

The tacit don't-ask-don't-tell policy had its uses. As far as I know, no one ever called out "Faggot!" as Mr. Elkin walked up the stairs of the houses that had pianos on Juniper Street. And everyone knew—even without checking to see if one of his many rings looked like a wedding band—not to ask after his wife. When Mr. Elkin spoke of his many lady friends he ate with at the cafeteria next to Penn Traffic, we knew there was no hanky-panky going on.

Eventually, I learned to put basic chords together well enough to stumble my way through "The Old Rugged Cross," "Just as I Am," and other hymns Dad hoped my sisters and I would learn to play beautifully, but my mediocre piano skills are not the only thing I learned from Mr. Elkin, or more specifically from the way the residents of Juniper Street treated him. I learned that homosexuality was unspeakable, that it might be tolerated in a quirky little man who gave cheap piano lessons, but it wouldn't be named. And I learned that I needed to hide any nelly, nancy-boy mannerisms that might make me appear too much like him. I learned that only queer, feminine men were gay.

Despite the provincialism of our little street in our little western Pennsylvania town, I suspect Juniper Street was a special place for Mr. Elkin because when he died suddenly (ten years after I quit my lessons), we discovered he had made his funeral arrangements with the funeral home in the big house at the end of the street. This was odd because Mr. Elkin didn't live in our little town of 3,000 people; he lived in the more sophisticated town of 20,000 just six miles away.

"Burt was quite a character" was the theme of his wake. Fred Bowser, the funeral director, told of the day Mr. Elkin came in to make his funeral arrangements, breaking into an uncanny impression of Mr. Elkin's voice. "Oh now, Bowser," punctuating his impression with that limp-wristed gesture that means "gay" without saying it. I barely looked at Mr. Elkin, wearing one of his bright jackets and lying in a cheap casket—there was no money. Fred Bowser found out when Mr. Elkin made his arrangements that Burt Sr. had lost all the family money during the depression. It turns out that Mr. Elkin was just a struggling piano teacher and the only gay person I knew until I took typing in tenth grade from high-toned Mr. Liggett, whom the nasty kids who did not live on Juniper Street called "Suzy" behind his back.

I'm glad young gay and lesbian kids have more visible role models than I did in the late sixties and early seventies in the coal-mining hills of Pennsylvania. Even flamboyant, stereotypical Jack on *Will and Grace* strikes me as better than the code of silence I grew up with. In retrospect, I'm of two minds about how my parents and the other adults on Juniper Street treated Mr. Elkin. I'm glad he received a modicum of respect and that I never heard any of them speak of him in openly disparaging terms. However, the silence and innuendo may have ultimately been worse for me (and for him) because homosexuality could never be discussed; no one needed to learn that Mr. Elkin's version of gayness was just one expression of homosexual masculinity.

2

SARAH GRIMKÉ
Breaking the Bonds of Womanhood

*Nothing, I believe, has tended more to destroy the true dignity of
woman, than the fact that she is approached by man in the character of
a female.*

Grimké, 1838

*Prior to judging an other, we must be in some relation to him or her.
This relation will ground and inform the ethical judgments we finally do
make. We will, in some way, have to ask the question, "Who are you?"*

Butler, 2005

Sarah Grimké's *Letters on the Equality of the Sexes and the Condition of
Women,* published in 1838, is widely recognized as the first systematic
treatment of women's rights to be published by an American woman.[1]
Indeed, feminist scholar and Grimké biographer Gerda Lerner argues
that Grimké's *Letters* "anticipated by dozens of years the main points
advocates of woman's rights would make for the next century" (1998,
26). The story of how this text came to be written and how it has come
to the attention of feminist scholars only in the last forty years, and even
more recently to feminist rhetoricians, illustrates how examining the
cultural constraints Grimké faced, as well as the rhetorical strategies she
used in response to them, complicates what should not be read as a simple coming-to-voice story. As the opening epigraphs illustrates, Grimké
understood more than 150 years before the advent of postmodern theory that identity is both constrained and constructed, and I believe there
is much to gain from reading her as, in Butler's terms, bringing herself,
as a woman, into a different relationship with men and with her society
at large. In a very real sense, Grimké is compelled to write to break the
bonds of womanhood that sought to limit the public role she and her
sister Angelina took in the abolitionist cause; in assuming this role, the
two sisters became in some sense others—women who stepped out of

---

1. For more on this, see Bartlett (1994), Kohrs Campbell (1989), and Nies (1977).

the conventional bounds of modesty and morality yet claimed the moral right, indeed the moral obligation, to do so.

More specifically, I sketch Grimké's journey to voice and her contributions in her *Letters* in a new light that casts her as a queer figure in her culture, despite the fact that sexual identity issues are never raised in her work. Any account of Grimké's life must be read from the complex and, at times, contradictory interactions of gender and race, and her *Letters* can be usefully read as growing out of the abolitionist counterpublic, which centered on race, and attempting to aid in the creation of a counterpublic based on gender. In her efforts to contribute to the creation of a counterpublic based on gender, Grimké's *Letters* are particularly interesting because they energetically sought to create a copresence for women in society.

Grimké's struggle for voice is an interesting case for reconsidering the three principles I introduced in chapter one, by which the field of rhetoric and composition has sought to deal with the problem of the social identity of the author. She was denied access to the discourses of power not because her sociocultural background could not have prepared her well for such interactions but solely because of her gender. In claiming a voice, she used rather traditional genres and patterns of argument, so she should not be seen as a figure whose rhetorical practice explicitly sought to expand the canon of acceptable practice; rather she used mostly traditional methods to unsettle problematic dominant cultural values about women and slaves.

From the standpoint of the queer theory principles I introduced in chapter one, Grimké can usefully be read as working to make women copresent as a force in public discourse and as using disidentification strategies to challenge the prevailing notion that women were biologically unsuited to public discourse and thus could only persuade based on seduction. In this sense, Grimké's *Letters* are a dramatic example of identity as performative, of a marginalized person claiming a voice and attempting to change an important aspect of her own and all women's identities. As the discussion that follows illustrates, the remaining two queer identity principles operate in more complex ways in Grimké's text and life. For example, her bold steps into public discourse with her sister in their speaking tour and the publications of her *Letters* might be read as a kind of coming out of the closet. However, Grimké's audacity was met with various forms of resistance that essentially pushed her back into her discursive closet.

At first blush, Grimké's *Letters* might be read as failing to engage in an intersectional perspective as they are most certainly an instance of a scholar doing important work based on a single axis of difference—gender. However, such a reading of her *Letters* would be reductive without an understanding of the cultural context and personal circumstances that led Grimké to write her *Letters*. Although I rely on a body of excellent scholarship in my analysis of Grimké's work, my purpose is somewhat different from previous work in that I focus not only on her struggle to gain voice from a marginalized position but more specifically on the techniques she uses to do so and how her embattled position as a woman worked in concert and conflict with other aspects of her identity. In short, I take an explicitly intersectional perspective in my version of understanding what it meant for Grimké to grapple with one of the most restrictive bonds of womanhood in the nineteenth century—the belief that it was immoral for women to speak in public. The tension between Grimké's all-too-clear understanding of how women's identities and roles in the society of her day were limited and her determination to challenge those limits is neatly captured in the complementary closing of each of the letters that comprise her treatise: "Thine in the bonds of womanhood." Although an intersectional perspective helps provide a broader context for reading Grimké's *Letters,* it cannot be missed that they are largely about one difference issue, and thus they are an important instance of alternative rhetoric because they illustrate in some detail the real need for arguments that focus primarily on a binary relationship of inequity but also the potential dangers of doing so.

As the discussion that follows illustrates, the extant literature about Grimké and her work provides ample evidence that she understood and was even embarrassed by her economic privilege. Indeed, she and her sister Angelina took clear steps to avoid the fruits of slave labor, to financially support former family slaves, and to challenge racial discrimination within the Quaker community they joined as adults. Ironically, the most useful place to begin to understand the extent to which she understands her own opacity is in her religious beliefs. One of her chief tools in challenging the moral injunctions against women speaking in public was her steadfast belief that men had misinterpreted the Bible, twisting it to their advantage and to the detriment of women and society more generally. Early in her treatise, she argues, "I believe the world will be materially advanced by every new discovery of the designs of Jehovah in the creation of women" (1838, 3).

As the opening epigraphs suggest, Grimké's arguments for the right of women to have public voices is both firmly rooted in debunking the traditional biblical arguments used to limit women's roles and in a vision that extends beyond the scope of those arguments. Grimké's work illustrates that in her circumstances, attempting to create a substantive copresence for women to speak in her society required her to set some kind of moral base. Indeed, the pastoral letter that, in part, motivated Grimké to write her own letters contained thinly veiled arguments labeling Grimké and her sister Angelina as "promiscuous" and immodest for daring to speak about "things which ought not to be named" [slavery] and fall outside of the purview of "the charm of domestic life" (1838, 24). Her work also illustrates the discursive nature of such dialogues, particularly the kinds of disidentification that Grimké used in her attempts to unseat fundamental assumptions about gender. Nineteenth-century Christian views of womanhood were the elephant in the room which Grimké simply could not ignore. Thus, her *Letters* can be read as a classic case of stasis, of finding the points of agreement and disagreement and using widely accepted techniques—for example, biblical exegesis—to try and move her audience to a new position—that women have a larger god-ordained role in society than men have allowed them. In this regard, her arguments are much like those used more than fifty years earlier by Margaret Fell, who attempted to carve out a larger role for women in the Quaker faith and in seventeenth-century British society.[2]

In the body of this chapter, I take up two complementary tasks. First, I describe Grimké's struggle to maintain propriety as she developed a new sense of self and of rhetorical agency that drove her to challenge the widely held belief in nineteenth-century America that women were not able or fit to participate in public discourse unless their audiences were composed solely of other women. Understanding her exercise of alternative rhetoric requires attention not only to the genre and rhetorical practices she engaged in but also to the personal and cultural forces that shaped the kairotic moment she embraced. Second, I explore the particular transgressive techniques she used in her *Letters*, both as a means of better understanding how the relatively voiceless can challenge the very dominant cultural values that seek to marginalize them, and as a cautionary tale about the dangers of focusing on a single difference issue in doing so.

---

2. Lerner reasons that it is unlikely that Grimké was familiar with Fell's work because Fell's pamphlet was printed only once and was not printed at all in the United Status until the twentieth century (1998, 21).

MAINTAINING PROPRIETY WHILE CREATING A
GENDER-BASED COUNTERPUBLIC

Sarah Grimké was born November 26, 1792, into a wealthy, slave-owning Charleston family. Because of moral objections to slavery and frustrations with the limited opportunities offered to women in Southern society, Sarah and her younger sister Angelina rejected the privileged society to which they were born and became, for a few years, "the acknowledged leaders of the female antislavery movement" (Bartlett 1988, 3); they are now seen as "comets that soared briefly to signal the beginnings of the women's rights movement" (Kohrs Campbell 1989, 25). The story of this journey to voice is told in detail in Gerda Lerner's (1967) comprehensive biography: *The Grimké Sisters from South Carolina: Pioneers for Women's Rights*.[3] The brief version of that story I trace here focuses on the major events and cultural forces that lead to their emergence as embattled public figures.

Sarah Grimké's coming-to-voice story is intimately intertwined with that of Angelina, who was, until recent feminist scholarship on Sarah's *Letters*, seen as the more interesting figure because of her greater acumen as a speaker (Nies 1977, xii). Indeed, the sisters' public career was launched when noted abolitionist leader, William Lloyd Garrison, published a letter from Angelina supporting abolition in *The Liberator*. The furor over the letter embarrassed Sarah but also began a series of events that lead to the invitation to Angelina (and Sarah with her) to become "the first female abolitionist agents in the United States" (Lerner 1967, 145). Although the sisters were hired and trained to speak to small groups of women, their tour of New England was so successful that larger halls and churches were required and men began to attend.

As I discuss later in this chapter, women speaking to mixed or "promiscuous" audiences raised questions about the public roles of women and fueled the sisters' notoriety to the point that they were forced to advocate not only for the abolition of slavery but also for the rights of women to participate in public discourse. At the height of their popularity, the sisters were invited to present abolition petitions and address the legislative committee of the Massachusetts House of Representatives, and, when Sarah fell ill, Angelina became the first woman to address a

---

3. A brief chronology of Grimké's life can also be found in Bartlett's *Liberty, Equality, Sorority: The Origins and Interpretation of American Feminist Thought: Frances Wright, Sarah Grimké, and Margaret Fuller* (1994). Unless otherwise noted, the chronology of Grimké's life I trace in this chapter is largely based on these two important sources.

legislative body in the United States on Wednesday, February 21, 1838 (Lerner 1967, 1–2). The success of their speaking tour and the attention it brought to women's rights (in addition to abolition) has been heralded as either the beginning of the split in the abolitionist movement over women's rights or the addition "of the cause of woman's rights to the cause of abolition, to mutual benefit" (164).

Backlash against the sisters' dramatic emergence on the public scene came both from within the abolitionist movement itself and from the New England clergy. I take up the former (particularly Theodore Weld's opposition to their advocacy on behalf of women's rights) later in this chapter. The resistance of the clergy to their efforts was crystallized in the publication of a *Pastoral Letter of the General Association of Massachusetts to the Congregation Churches Under Their Care* on July 28, 1837, which was written by Nehemiah Adams, "a Congregational minister with strong pro-South sentiments" (Nies 1977, 5–6). This letter was read from the pulpits of churches and it effectively barred the sisters from conducting meetings in churches. Ironically, rather than silencing the sisters, the *Pastoral Letter* galvanized the support of groups of Boston women for the sisters' tour and increased the interest in Sarah's *Letters*. Before the *Pastoral Letter* appeared, Sarah had begun publishing her *Letters* at the request of Mary Parker, the President of the Boston Female Anti-Slavery Society, in *The Spectator*, a religious newspaper based in Boston (Lerner 1967, 187; Nies 1977, 6), but the thinly veiled attack on the Grimkés' public role and on the version of Garrisonian abolitionism they espoused gave Sarah's *Letters* increased urgency.

Grimké's *Letters* were also published in Garrison's *The Liberator*, but after the splash of their initial publication, they were largely lost until the twentieth century as they were never collected and reprinted as many other abolitionist works were. Indeed, the Grimké sisters disappeared even from abolitionist history until 1961 "when Dwight L. Dumond, the historian who discovered the Weld papers, dedicated a chapter in his book to them" (Lerner 1998, 41). Publication of Lerner's biography of the sisters brought them to the attention of feminists, and subsequent work by Lerner and by Elizabeth Ann Barlett to recover and publish the sisters' writings has made their work available for scholarship by rhetoricians. This work began first in speech communications,[4] and the inclusion of excerpts of Grimké's *Letters* in the second edition

4. For more on this, see Japp (1993), Kohrs Campbell (1989), Vonnegut (1993), and Zaeske (1995).

of Patricia Bizzell and Bruce Herzberg's *The Rhetorical Tradition* (2001) has helped bring this work to the attention of scholars in rhetoric and composition. In short, the recovery work for the Grimké sisters and for Sarah's *Letters* is largely done.

For my purposes, the need that remains in understanding how Grimké functions as an alternative rhetor is a better understanding of how she struggled to simultaneously maintain propriety in the eyes of others and smash some of the fundamental values of her culture. I see four distinctive phases in this process, in which Grimké struggled with the bounds of propriety: escaping a bourgeois and somewhat provincial notion of family and her role within it, joining a religious community that provided some intellectual and social means for defining new roles but ultimately limited those roles, being recruited and trained in a progressive movement that provided critical but problematic sponsorship for her public role, and retreating into a revised version of the bourgeois family institution when the costs of continuing to challenge propriety became too great.

Escaping the Trap of Bourgeois Privilege

Sarah and Angelina Grimké were likely as surprised as anyone that they briefly became leaders of their generation's women's movement. Indeed, Lerner's and Bartlett's accounts of the events that led them to leave their positions as privileged southern ladies and, eventually, to become the first female abolition agents in the United States, detail the struggles the sisters faced in redefining their own understandings of themselves. Both sisters were deeply disturbed by the role of slavery in their home lives, and both sisters were frustrated by the limits their womanhood placed on their ability to participate not only in the public policy debate over slavery but also in society in general. While the sisters shared many frustrations and successes, for my purposes, Sarah Grimké's story is the more important of the two, first because she is now recognized as being more committed to "the woman question" than Angelina and as having the more well-developed feminist agenda (Bartlett 1988, 19). Second, Sarah's case is the more interesting because her struggles to define herself as a speaking/writing woman illustrate many kinds of obstacles the disenfranchised may face in coming to voice as well as the means she used to redefine her own understanding of herself several times to attain a public voice.

Sarah Grimké is probably best seen as an intelligent and talented woman who was driven by the limitations on women in her age to seek out a more meaningful purpose for her life than what was envisioned for women by the men in her day. In the third of her *Letters*, she writes of the culpability of men in creating the conditions that subjugate women: "He [man] has done all he could to debase and enslave her mind; and he now looks triumphantly on the ruin he has wrought, and says, the being he has thus deeply injured is his inferior" (1838, 11).

For Grimké, the first step in throwing off the limits created by these conditions and in finding a new identity and a new voice, was escaping her home life in Charleston; doing so required escaping from the sense of self her family and community attempted to impose on her. One of her chief complaints about her life in Charleston was that she had been denied the kind education her brothers received. Although her father is said to have admitted she "would have made the greatest jurist in the land—had she not been a woman," he refused to allow her to study with her brothers "and her schooling was changed to the more typical fare for a young woman of her day—French, watercolors, harpsichord, and embroidery" (Bartlett 1994, 57). Bartlett argues that this denial was formative for Grimké: "She learned very early what it meant to be denied something because of her gender, a lesson that shaped the course of her life both in what she did not become and in her life's testimony to the liberty and equality of women" (57–58).

Taking Up New but Limited Roles in a Religious Community

After a brief flirtation with privileged Charleston social life, Grimké turned her back on this role, looking to austere forms of Christianity to provide a meaningful context for her life. In 1819, she traveled with her father to Philadelphia and attended him until his death. Soon thereafter, Grimké became a Quaker and, for a time, both she and Angelina (who joined her in Philadelphia) found the community of Quakers they lived among to be a more hospitable context, both because it opposed slavery and because it encouraged all of its members, including women, to interpret the scriptures for themselves and seek their own inner light. During this period, Sarah also twice rejected marriage proposals from Israel Morris, a Quaker widower (Lerner 1967, 64), perhaps because she was not enamored with the prospect of raising Morris's eight children "in the austere Quaker life of Philadelphia" (Nies 1977, 16).

Bartlett sees Quakerism as most significant for Sarah because it was her "first introduction to the more general Puritan idea that each person must read and interpret the Bible for him- or herself and take responsibility for his or her own soul" (1988, 17). Indeed, Sarah's sense of spirituality is a critical component of her journey to voice. Although race and gender get the most attention in scholarship about Grimké and her writing, a truly intersectional perspective must also account for the sense in which she saw herself on a spiritual journey, and her experiences with Quakerism illustrate the important but problematic role organized religion played in that spiritual journal. In a very real sense, participating in the Quaker community gave the Grimké sisters both a sociocultural and an intellectual space in which to develop understandings of themselves beyond those available to them in their privileged Southern family; however, the Quaker community also limited the very sense of agency it fostered in the sisters. As Lerner details in her extensive biography of the sisters, it would be a mistake to read their Philadelphia Quaker years as wholly positive. Although the sisters escaped daily contact with slavery and found new opportunities for study, they did not completely escape the limits of their society placed upon them because of their gender. Indeed, the orthodox Quaker community they belonged to and lived among denied Angelina the opportunity to attend a new women's seminary, and the powerful Quaker elder, Jonathan Edwards, thwarted Sarah's longstanding attempts to become a Quaker minister in a public rebuke that Lerner describes as "an unprecedented act . . . intended as a personal rebuke" of Sarah for which "there was no sanction in the Discipline for cutting short the utterance of any member in meeting" (1967, 142; Nies 1977, 28).[5]

For the sisters, their increasing estrangement from their Quaker community placed them in some jeopardy of a kind of homelessness (despite the fact that they had some independent means at their disposal), but it also prepared them for the next stage in their move away from dependence upon a community for their identity and toward the emergence of their own voices. From a twenty-first century perspective, it can be difficult to imagine that to maintain any sense of propriety, the sisters needed to marry, to remain in residence with their family, or to have the protection of a community such as the Quakers to sponsor them. For Sarah and Angelina Grimké, identity and voice were critically connected—to lose the sociocultural umbrella that provided the imprimatur of propriety was to lose the very credibility necessary for them

---

5. Nies argues that the Grimké sisters would have likely been more at home in the more liberal Hicksite Quaker faction but that they remained orthodox Quakers in part because their friends and hosts were part of that community (16).

to have any effective voice in the society they wished to change. Judith Nies explains that part of Sarah's concern about Angelina's determination to accept a role as a public speaker was based on the possible loss of their Quaker community: "Sarah also knew that involvement in a worldly political cause was likely to bring expulsion from the Society of Friends, not a consideration to be taken lightly. There were few social circles open to an unmarried woman barred from her homeland" (1977, 19). Further, Lerner reasons that because they had no friends outside the Quaker community, where they would live if they left the community was a critical issue: "As unattached females they could not, respectably, live alone" (1967, 134). However, the break with the Quakers was also necessary for the sisters, and particularly so for Sarah—who felt a real calling to ministry—so they could give up the hope of having fulfilling roles within that community and prepare to take the next step. Indeed, Lerner explains the complicated role the break with the Quakers played for the sisters:

> They had reached the limit of freedom their age permitted to women. They were spinsters, aged forty-three and thirty, alone, without training and occupation and purpose—by the standard of their day, their lives were over. Instead, it was like the long incubation of the butterfly in the cocoon—all that had come before was merely preparation. Their real life, their role as pioneers of a future freedom, was only just beginning. (111)

The Grimké sisters' experiences with Quakerism remind me of the many talented women I knew in the Bible college I attended who were given intellectual tools and opportunities to develop communication skills and then were subtly and not-so-subtly channeled into support roles. I remember sitting with pride in the college chapel as my younger sister took the platform and delivered a sermon she'd honed in her preaching class, but then being shocked to learn that on her summer mission trip to India, she had had to sit by while a younger, less-gifted male member of the team gave the sermons. Because of experiences like this, my sister soon abandoned her long-standing calling to be a missionary, much as Sarah Grimké was forced to give up her goal to become a Quaker minister and leave her religious community.

Sponsored Voices in a Progressive Cause

The sponsorship of a politically liberal group was ultimately the vehicle for Sarah and her sister to find dramatic public voices that not only participated in the counterpublic surrounding abolitionism but also helped form the emerging counterpublic surrounding women's rights. Ironically, Sarah's initial reluctance to participate in the next step in the process she and Angelina followed to finding their public voices is reflected in her consternation about the publication of Angelina's signed letter in support of abolitionism. As Nies notes, Sarah's reaction reflects the widely held belief that "a woman's name was supposed to appear in print only three times in life—at birth, marriage, and death—a signed letter in support of a controversial cause and a notorious figure like Garrison was a radical act" (1977, 18). Indeed, as Lerner reports, Angelina herself wrote that she could not have taken this public action on her own, but once committed she said "nor would I have recalled it if I could" (1967, 125). Eventually Sarah reluctantly agreed to join Angelina on the speaking tour to which Angelina had been invited because their mother urged Sarah to do so (Lerner 1967, 142).

Despite these concerns about taking up public roles, the sisters quickly came to see they were "ushering in a new era" (Lerner 1967, 12). Nies argues that as invitations for speaking engagements from the women of Massachusetts "poured in,"

> Sarah began to realize for the first time that she and Angelina were com-
> municating much more than information about slavery when they stood up
> to speak. They represented the possibility of a new reality, a reality in which
> women might travel and speak and learn about the larger world. (1977, 20).

Understanding what "pioneering" meant to Sarah and Angelina is criti-cal: although it was a generative place, it was not a comfortable one: Sarah felt compelled to speak and write, but these public roles brought her little acceptance in her own time. Indeed, the struggles the sisters faced illustrate both how their identities were inextricably caught up in the agency they were able to take and how the sponsorship that led to these voices was itself complex and ultimately had a silencing effect.

The sponsorship of abolitionist groups provided the Grimké sisters with training and experiences in engaging in public policy debates as well as a broader context for social action than they had found in the limited context of speaking in Quaker meetings and advocating against the continuing racism within the Quaker community in which they lived. They received training from notable abolitionist activist Theodore Weld, who played a complicated role in their lives, first as enthusiastic mentor, later as a critic of their attempt to speak publicly on women's rights, and finally as Angelina's husband. Initially, abolitionist leaders such as Weld and Garrison had a limited role in mind for the Grimké sisters: speaking to small meetings of women in support of the larger abolitionist cause. However, as savvy activists, they did not shy away from using the notoriety gained with the sisters' growing popularity in the service of furthering the abolitionist cause; in a sense, they capitalized on the sisters' "freak value" but then opposed the sisters' efforts to develop their own agenda. The problem, at least for Weld, began when the sisters eagerly engaged in the questions raised about the propriety of women speaking in public. As Sarah Grimké's case illustrates clearly, male abolitionists played an important but problematic role in the launching of the women's movement of their day. Indeed, Bartlett reports, "Many women's rights advocates started in the abolition movement. For one thing, the movement taught them the political tactics of speaking." However, Bartlett further argues that this training led these women to an increased "awareness of their own subordinate status. Many, including Grimké, came to see parallels between their own position and that of slaves" (1988, 14).

I should note here that there is no evidence that Grimké began abolition work as a means to the end of becoming a spokesperson for what was called "the woman question." As I have already noted, she joined Angelina only reluctantly, and the abolition of slavery was certainly a lifelong passion for her, beginning at age four when she saw a slave being whipped and "rushed out of the house, sobbing. A half hour later her nurse found her on one of the wharves, trying to convince a captain to take her away to someplace where such things did not happen" (Lerner 1967, 19). Further evidence of Grimké's commitment to the abolition and eradication of slavery can be seen in her support of the Free Produce Movement in which the fruits of slave labor were eschewed, in the actions she and Anglina took to break color barriers within the supposedly liberal Quaker meetings in Philadelphia, and in their efforts to free family slaves and to support the mulatto sons of their brother. However, abolition is probably best read as an important cause which brought Grimké and her sister to the public eye and which occasioned her more original work on women's rights.

The Grimké sisters' speaking tour brought the nineteenth-century limits on women's roles into relief largely through the issue of women speaking to promiscuous audiences. Speech communication scholar Susan Zaeske explains that the prohibition of women speaking to promiscuous audiences (in this case, audiences composed of men and women) "drew upon and reinforced deeply-rooted myths about women and their proper role in politics," most notably "that woman by nature was irrational and could persuade only through seduction" (1995, 197). Karlyn Kohrs Campbell explains that this perception of women's unsuitability for participation was rooted, in part, in "[b]iology, or rather ignorance of biology" (1989, 11). She explains further:

> Harvard medical professor Dr. Edward Clarke (1873) argued against higher education for women on the grounds that the blood needed to sustain development of the ovaries and womb would be diverted to the brain, which he believed was a major cause of illness. (12)

Nies argues that these beliefs had a biblical basis, linking a lack of capacity for higher education to physical weakness and the very nature of women: "It was generally believed, and buttressed by appropriate Biblical quotes, that women had smaller brains and inferior intelligence and that to educate them would destroy their essential nature" (1977, 21–22). Given the widespread nature of these beliefs, Angelina herself was surprised that nothing untoward happened the first time she spoke to an audience of men and women: "For the first time in my life I spoke to a promiscuous assembly . . . and found the men were no more to me than the women" (Zaeske 1995, 201). In a very real sense, the Grimké sisters put themselves forward to challenge and change a fundamental value that grounded and informed dominant society's understanding of them and their moral character. Their speaking and writing risked the very sense of propriety that was essential to their ability to speak and forced others to ask "Who are you?" in a way that brought the usual underlying moral basis for that judgment into question.

The sisters, their supporters, and their detractors all understood that the limitations on the roles of women in public life were challenged by the sisters' speaking tour. Lerner reports that soon after men began coming to the sisters' speaking engagements, Sarah and Angelina began to argue openly for women's right and obligation to speak: "Women must cast off their embarrassment and restraint in the company of men and begin to look on themselves as moral responsible beings" (1967, 166). It is no accident that the most public resistance to the sisters' speaking to men came from the clergy because in some sense the stakes were highest for them, as the church was the one social context outside the home in which women could actively participate, and women's financial and other support of churches was critical (Bartlett 1988, 13;

Vonnegut 1993, 220). For this reason, Zaeske explains, it was critical for the clergy to oppose the Grimké sisters' public roles because they "were threatened by women gaining power," yet Zaeske also claims that abolitionist women largely laid to rest the promiscuous audience argument against public roles for women (1995,198). As I have already noted, the public rebuke of the Grimké sisters in the *Pastoral Letter* largely backfired because it fueled interest in the controversy. Indeed, Zaeske notes that by the 1850s the promiscuous audience argument seldom appeared in the North, largely due to the "rhetorical efforts of women such as Angelina and Sarah Grimké, Lucretia Mott, and Abby Kelley increasingly rendered the 'promiscuous audience' threat an anachronism. Doing so was a critical early step in the woman's rights movement" (204).

Retreating to Private Life

With twenty-first century hindsight, it is tempting to read Sarah and Angelina Grimké in romantic terms, as larger-than-life crusaders who successfully battled back gender and race prejudice and made an important stride forward for women's rights. While there is some truth in such a reading, it is also an oversimplification because even though they successfully fended off the public attack of the clergy, the women were eventually silenced through the efforts of their supposed allies and because of the difficulties they encountered in defining public identities that were consistent with their own understandings of womanhood.

Leading male abolitionists were mixed in their response to the sisters' defense of women's right to speak about abolition. Garrison supported them, most notably evidenced by his simultaneous publishing of Sarah's *Letters* in *The Liberator*. Other abolitionist leaders such as Weld and John Greenleaf Whittier opposed dilution of the abolitionist cause with the cause of women's rights. Kristen S. Vonnegut sees the letter Whittier wrote to the sisters as revealing

> the depth of hostility engendered when women stepped out of their sphere. As an abolitionist, he saw the need to recruit women for the public struggle against slavery; but as a man, he resisted the idea that women might have their own grievances. Not only did he subsume women's oppression under the heading of white people's grievances, but he also ignored the African-American females who constituted a large percentage of the slave population he wanted to save. (1993, 219)

The problematic role of the Grimké sisters' abolitionist sponsors should give us pause to consider the implications of offering rhetorical training to those struggling to find voice but also of setting limits on the extent and purposes for which they can use that training. Even in as worthy a cause as the abolition of slavery, the line between altruism and paternalism was confused at best, and those of us who make it our business to teach rhetoric would do well to sort out how our sponsorship of fledgling voices also seeks to limit those voices.

The paternalism of male abolitionist sponsorship was most chilling when it became personal. Because of his personal ties with the sisters, Weld's disapproval is more complicated and ultimately more devastating. His initial response shared Whittier's insistence that the cause of abolition should not be supplanted by the woman question. His interactions with the sisters after the appearance of the *Pastoral Letter* have been described as a "harsh letter to both Grimkés, announcing that the American Anti-Slavery Society was disassociating itself from the sisters' 'public holdings-forth to promiscuous audiences'" (Zaeske 1995, 195) and the more indirect (but ultimately more demeaning) argument that he regretted Sarah's *Letters* because it was something "any woman could do" while their function as female antislavery agents was "unique"; he urged them to "let others do the lesser work, let *them* do the work they were best qualified to do" (Lerner 1967, 200). Both of the sisters resisted Weld's attempts to limit their roles, Angelina "with some heat" (200); however, Weld's attacks eventually silenced them. Angelina gave up her plans to lecture on women's rights in Boston, and Weld's critiques of Sarah's less-engaging speaking style lead her to retire from public speaking in the spring of 1838 (Vonnegut 1993, 217). Bartlett reasons that Weld's lack of support for the sisters' feminist agenda and his specific attacks upon Sarah's speaking abilities were the primary reasons her written arguments fell out of print or remained unfinished:

> One can speculate as to why Sarah Grimké did not republish and widely circulate her *Letters on the Equality of the Sexes* during her lifetime, and why she did not finish and then publish the fragments of manuscripts contained in this volume. Theodore Weld had been able to accomplish what none of the New England clergy had—convince Sarah to remove herself from the abolitionist lectern. He did so not by questioning her rights or her propriety but her capabilities and her effectiveness as a speaker. (1988, 20)

Garrison himself hints at the possible treachery of friends in his warn-
ings to Sarah about "those who posed as friends but who might be ene-
mies to her most closely held ideas" (quoted in Nies 1977, 26). Indeed,
Nies argues that although Weld was "considered a saint in the abolitionist cause . . . his performance toward woman's rights is somewhat
shabby" (27). She reads Weld's attempts to keep Sarah from speaking at
the Odeon lectures as ruthless:

> He knew what the effect of such a tactic would be. Sarah had told him of
> her long futile efforts to speak out in Quaker Meeting, of the rudeness of
> the elders of the meeting, of the unprecedented action of Elder Jonathan
> Edwards' asking her to be silent in the middle of her being moved to
> speak. . . . After receiving Weld's letter, Sarah never spoke again in public. (28)

Thus, the sponsorship of the male abolitionist establishment not only
served as a critical means for Sarah and Angelina to find voice but
also a powerful means of limiting their voices as they developed their
own agenda. In Weld's case those actions were further complicated by
his personal relationship with Angelina that blossomed into marriage
after the sisters gave up their public role. Although both sisters made
some attempts to continue writing and participating in the women's
suffrage movement after Angelina's marriage, they were never again to
regain their celebrated leadership role. Indeed, Nies reports that when
Elizabeth Cady Stanton tried to recruit the Grimké sisters into the suffrage movement, she was advised by Lucretia Mott to "have little hope of
them, after such a flash and such an effectual extinguishment—We must
not depend on them" (1977, 77).

Ironically, the reason for the sisters' "flash" is largely the same as for
their "extinguishment." That is, as pioneers for women's rights to participate in public discourse, the sisters illustrate the potential discursive
power of breaking gender expectations but also the resilience of dominant notions of gender to restrain and punish those who dare challenge
the expectations of dominant culture. Lerner explains, "During the
months of work as 'female agents' they had been alternately idolized
and treated as freaks by their audiences, while male reformers were ever
conscious of the need to patronize and protect them" (1967, 177–78).
The shock value of women speaking in public to mixed audiences about
the abolition of slavery created a kairotic moment for the examination
and renegotiation of women's public roles in American society, but it
also occasioned backlash from various quarters. In one sense, Sarah

and Angelina Grimké can be seen successfully challenging dominant gender roles and contributing much to the development of the women's rights counterpublic because they were a critical part, perhaps the critical component, of challenging the beliefs about gender that supported the "promiscuous audience" prohibition. However, theirs is not a simple and happy coming-to-voice story; rather it involved a series of painful departures from the support of family and other social institutions, and ultimately ended in a betrayal of sorts. Furthermore, the flash of their public role, particularly the vicious and unwarranted attacks on their modesty and respectability, heightened their own sense of propriety about other aspects of their gender. Indeed, Phyllis M. Japp reports that Angelina "viewed Weld's proposal of marriage as a sign to the world that she had not been contaminated by her public activities and was still desirable as a woman" (1993, 210).

When Sarah joined the Weld household, both women were determined to live without domestic help because of their personal beliefs and public stances against slavery and other forms of class-related subjugation of women. In retrospect, Japp sees Angelina's struggle to maintain some public life while refusing to hire help to raise and care for her family—trying to maintain the nineteenth-century notion of a woman— as a version of what is now known as superwoman syndrome (1993, 211), and Lerner details how both sisters came to understand the "woman question" in a much more concrete way:

> It was one thing to advance the slogan of women's equality and her equal rights in society, it was quite another to live that equality and make it come true. Angelina and Sarah, for the first time in their lives, began to understand what the "woman question" was all about. They were no longer sheltered by wealth, privilege or spinsterhood from the basic problem that was to haunt the average woman during the next century: how to have enough energy left over after a day of cooking, housework and childcare to concern herself with issues outside of the home or to do anything about them, even if she cared. (1967, 292–93)

This struggle occurred despite Weld's support of public roles for Angelina and Sarah after his marriage to Angelina (Lerner 1967, 291). Indeed, the three collaborated on *American Slavery As It Is: Testimony of a Thousand Witnesses*, published in 1839, "a searing indictment of slavery" and "the most important antislavery publication before *Uncle Tom's Cabin*" (Lerner 1998, 27). But, of course, this work was part of the shared concern that first brought the sisters into contact with Weld and not directly related to Sarah's passion for women's issues. Further, Lerner explains that working on this project was emotionally and physically exhausting, not only because the sisters had to recount their own painful experiences with slavery but also because they engaged in "six months of intense research and editing. It was the last sustained intellectual work they were able to do for a long time" (1998, 27–28).

In summary, after the promise of their speaking tour and the initial sensation created by Sarah's *Letters*, the sisters' ability to champion the very issues they had raised were limited by their lack of formal education, by the public censure of their role as women in public policy debates, by the betrayal of mentors who attempted to deny their right to develop their own agenda, by the roles they took up in the Weld household, and by their own understandings of what it meant to be women in their time and culture. Their experiences illustrate that those of us who speak against inequity and take it as our job to teach others to do so as well must consider carefully the implications of our efforts and also attend to the ways in which they may limit the agency of those we seek to help come to voice.

TRANSGRESSIVE TECHNIQUES IN GRIMKÉ'S *LETTERS*

The preceding discussion makes it clear that the intent to engage in rhetoric aiming to unseat inequity is not a guarantee that one's efforts will result in change to the underlying values that create inequity. Indeed, even a context in which the transgression of societal expectations is brought to the fore in a dramatic and engaging fashion resulting in an unprecedented and thorough explication of a systemic prejudice may have a limited effect, even for those directly involved. In this case, after the initial shock of the Grimkés' speaking tour and Sarah's *Letters* subsided, their work was largely lost or was otherwise unintelligible to the American public for more than a century. In attempting to reclaim that work now in the service of exploring alternative rhetoric, I am part of a larger feminist movement that seeks to repair the history of the abolitionist and women's rights movements. Particularly, I contend that Grimké's *Letters* deserves attention as an important text that engages in alternative rhetoric, and I turn now to describing more specifically Grimké's rhetorical approach and the specific strategies she used to transgress the moral values of her day and make an argument for a different understanding of gender roles.

Clearly, in writing her *Letters*, Grimké intended to transgress the social mores of her day, to challenge the status quo and unsettle problematic social values. However, as I have already discussed, Sarah and Angelina Grimké should probably be seen as seizing moments of uncertainly within their cultural context rather than as setting out to explicitly challenge the subjugation of women. When their meetings attracted mixed audiences, the Grimké sisters understood they were breaking new ground, and the title alone of Sarah's *Letters on the Equality of the Sexes and the Condition of Women* was "heresy" (Nies 1977, 17). Although Sarah and Angelina did not set out to become spokespersons for women's rights, they did not shy away from public positions they knew would be seen as challenging the mores of polite society in their day. Thus, although the religious grounding of the arguments in Grimké's *Letters* may seem anachronistic today, in 1838 it was highly radical: Nies says, "Sarah's proposing that women could deal with issues of sin and salvation was roughly the parallel to proposing a woman to head the Joint Chiefs of Staff today" (22).

Responding in Kind

Although the acts of speaking and writing were transgressive for Grimké, questions remain. How did she perform these transgressive acts? What did the practice of her alternative rhetoric look like? At the level of genre, Grimké is probably best seen as appropriating the existing genre of the public letter and claiming a stance within it not usually afforded to women. In one sense, she simply responds in kind to the *Pastoral* and other public letters used to criticize her and her sister Angelina's public abolitionist advocacy. Responding to these letters allows Grimké to maintain a veneer of polite civility from which she makes some of the most radical social arguments of her day—a tension best captured in the complementary closing she uses for each of the fifteen letters: "Thine in the bonds of womanhood." Within her *Letters*, Grimké takes an almost apostolic stance at times, arguing for sweeping changes to social structure based on her challenges to the accepted reading of biblical texts:

> As there is an assumption of superiority on the one part, which is not sanctioned by Jehovah, there is an incessant struggle on the other to rise to that degree of dignity, which God designed women to possess in common with men. (126).

Grimké's *Letters* are not the first instance in which she took this apostolic stance in print. Indeed, Jami Carlacio argues that Grimké's previous letter challenging Southern clergy to take a stand against slavery, "Ye Knew Your Duty, But Ye Did it Not," is an example of epistolary rhetoric in which Grimké claims moral superiority over Southern ministers "by offering them an opportunity for reconciliation" (2002, 257). As Carlacio argues, taking this apostolic stance within a seemingly innocuous genre is an act of defiance on Grimké's part, and in the terms I introduced in chapter one, this defiance amounts to the performance of a new gendered identity for Grimké in which she seizes the right to be copresent in the discussion through discourse.

A more subtle resistance to the dominant values of the day that presumed women should not be engaged in public policy debates emerges in Grimké's use of a series of letters to get a comprehensive argument for women's rights into the public milieu. In this sense, her fifteen letters are ostensibly merely responses to others' letters, but, taken together, they become a comprehensive treatise debunking the major arguments against public roles for women in nineteenth century American society. Thus, in some sense, Grimké can be read as using a stealth strategy; she does not set out to present a comprehensive treatise challenging gender discrimination, she merely responds to others, trying to correct inaccuracies in what others have said, but in doing so, she does not shy away from making sweeping moral arguments.

Setting the Record Straight

Throughout her letters, Grimké seeks to the set the record straight in a number of ways. One of her chief tactics is to challenge the presumed naturalness/god-given nature of gender roles and to expose these as man-made cultural constructions. For example, Grimké begins her argument by locating a correct understanding of the role of women in every "new discovery of the designs of Jehovah in the creation of women" (1838, 3)—a critical means for creating a basis for a different kind of argument. Like Margaret Fell before her, Grimké pits the "true" designs of a sovereign deity against the lesser and imperfect constructions of the female gender by men:

> He [man] has adorned the creature who God gave him as a companion, with baubles and geegaws, turned her attention to personal attractions, offered incense to her vanity, and made her the instrument of his selfish gratification, a play-thing to please his eye and amuse his hours of leisure. (17)

Taking this appeal to an absolute authority as a starting point for exploring alternative rhetoric is highly ironic in the sense that it runs contrary to postmodern understandings of truth and authority. However, in some sense, Grimké's arguments prefigure later postmodern and feminist theory in that they attempt to force a reexamination of the constructed nature of what were taken for obvious truths in her day and because they expose the privileged role of men (particularly white Christian men) in determining and enforcing these truths.[6] Further, such a strategy indirectly acknowledges a kind of opacity of her own knowledge: she does not claim to know all and imagines a process of further discovery based on a challenge to culturally constructed cultural values that have erroneously stood in for Truth.

Reinterpreting Pivotal Events

One of the means Grimké's uses to disidentify herself and other women from the assumption that they are unsuited to participate in public discourse is to reinterpret pivital events to challenge both the so-called truths and the means by which they are constructed and maintained. Most notably, she renames the "curse" of Eve in the Garden of Eden to be subject to her husband as a prophecy of the difficulties to come because of the fall from grace rather than as a condemnation of women to a permanent subservient role (1838, 7). This rereading is important because it makes it possible for Grimké to challenge the notion of the understanding of women's subservience prevalent in her day by running history through a protofeminist sieve to call out the heroism and leadership of many women.[7] Yet another of Grimké's strategies to challenge the presumed subservience of women is to expose the cultural means men have used to deny women the means to redefine their own position:

> I am inclined to think, when we [women] are admitted to the honor of studying Greek and Hebrew, we shall produce some various readings of the Bible a little different from those we now have. (16)

Sorting Out Complicities in Oppression

Two of the techniques Grimké uses are particularly relevant for understanding how she moves to create women as a collective group

6. Although Grimké's *Letters* is seen as her most original feminist work, her later writings display a more sophisticated feminist voice. Thus, her *Letters* provides an important snapshot of her public voice as it first emerges (Bartlett 1988, 29).

7. For more on this, see Letter IX.

that has copresence on equal terms with men. First, she attempts to move beyond the usual scriptural arguments to expose the privilege inherent in men's oppression of women. Grimké argues that women have been seen as a "profitable kind of property" (1838, 13) and that as men have placed women on a "lower platform than man, they of course wish to keep her there" (61). In addition, Grimké comes closest to an explicit examination of one aspect of her own privilege by showing she understands that although "man has inflicted an unspeakable injury upon women," women have been culpable in their own oppression "by submitting to be thus regarded" (24). Indeed, Grimké sees that substantive change will require women to relinquish the so-called privileges of their infantilization:

> Men and women are equally bound to cultivate a spirit of accommodation; but I exceedingly deprecate her being treated like a spoiled child, and sacrifices made to her selfishness and vanity. (127)

Grimké's arguments about the operation of gender privilege illustrate that unseating fundamental cultural values requires a renegotiation of the moral terms on which such values are based, specifically that both oppressors and oppressed must be willing to take responsibility for their participation in systems of oppression and in the cultural institutions that perpetuate them. In short, Grimké's arguments here illustrate the need for a discursive understanding of morality, and although she was largely unsuccessful in convincing her society at large to engage with her in that discussion, her work served as the basis for other feminists to continue that work (Kohrs Campbell 1989, 25; Nies 1977, 23, 24), and her *Letters* can now be read as the first systematic attempt to shift the moral grounds on which gender is understood in American culture.

Managing Gender Essentialism

Another aspect of Grimké's rhetorical strategies that is particularly relevant for my purposes is the means by which she challenges gender essentialism but also makes essentializing moves in her arguments for change. In her attempt to create women as a truly copresent force and to argue against gender essentialism, Grimké can be read as subtly reinforcing a kind of subalternity for women because she does not fully engage in the kinds of more nuanced understandings of gender as intertwined with other difference issues demanded in third-wave and transnational feminism. Much like Simon de Beauvior, who wrote a century

later, Grimké challenges the presumption that the roles women can take
in society are by nature different from those which men can take:

> Now to me it is perfectly clear, that WHATSOVER IT IS MORALLY RIGHT
> FOR A MAN TO DO, IT IS MORALLY RIGHT FOR A WOMAN TO DO; and
> that confusion must exist in the moral world, until woman takes her stand on
> the same platform with man, and feels that she is clothed by her Maker with the
> *same rights,* and of course, that upon her devolve the *same duties.* (1838, 122–3)

Here, Grimké seeks to unseat essentialist assumptions about gender/sex
roles but also makes an essentializing move in her presumption that all
women have been affected by patriarchy to some extent and thus action
is required on behalf of women (as well as society in general) to correct
the attendant problems. Grimké makes a typical first-wave feminist argument in which inequity is challenged but the underlying binary (and
presumably natural) difference on which is it based (sex as distinctly
male and female) is not explored. In effect, Grimké creates *women* as a
disenfranchised class using a single feature but ignores the many identity features that differentiate women's experiences with gender-based
oppression (e.g., race, class, religion, age, and geographical location).

I want to be careful here about reading Grimké as engaging in an
identity-based assumption about gender—one which many queer and
third-wave feminist theorists would likely find problematic because the
focus on a single, binary identity feature as a unifying basis for a creating a marginalized class does not attend carefully enough to the issues
that differentiate experiences with oppression within that class.[8] Of
course, it would be unfair to dismiss Grimké's arguments because they
did not anticipate theory developed more than 150 years after she wrote.
However, I think we need to do more than just give Grimké a pass here
based on the fact that she wrote in a different era. Rather, it is more useful to read Grimké's arguments as illustrating the difficulties of negotiating the challenges of representing the very real oppression that groups
face without glossing over important differences within those groups. In
this regard, Grimké provides both a model of restraint in not proposing
a single course of action presumed to be viable and useful for all women
and a cautionary tale.

In regard to the former, Grimke's essentializing move casting all
women as negatively affected by patriarchy does not extend to a new

---

8. For more on this, see Kopelson (2002).

version of essentialism when she turns to the roles she hopes women will take up in society once they have been unshackled from the chains of patriarchy. Rather than proposing that all women are naturally fitted to be earth mothers or are by nature better mediators, Grimké declines to define any specific roles for women to play:

> It is not my intention, nor indeed do I think it is in my power, to point out the precise duties of women. To him who still teacheth by his Holy Spirit as never man taught, I refer my beloved sisters. There is a vast field of usefulness before them. (1838, 123)

The Quaker belief that each individual, regardless of gender, should receive enlightenment and guidance from the divine is likely at work in the self-determinism Grimké proposes for women. However, I think her position here can also be read as an interesting instance of the possible tension between one's individual identity and one's participation in a collective identity based on a widely acknowledged difference issue. In this case, Grimké deftly maneuvers between the need to make an essentializing argument about how women have been collectively assigned to a marginalized position and the need to allow individual women the right of self-determination for their own roles, and her argument serves as a model for sorting out the complicated issues involved in arguing for collective identity without invoking problematic stereotypes.

There is also a cautionary tale in Grimké's arguments about women's roles that relates to the difficulties of attending to differences beyond those that one has experienced firsthand. In her fifth letter, which examines the condition of women in Asia and Africa, Grimké argues that men have invariably "either made slaves of the creatures whom God designed to be their companions and their coadjutors in very moral and intellectual improvement, or they have dressed them like dolls, and used them as toys to amuse their hours of recreation" (1838, 27). The series of examples Grimké uses to substantiate this universalizing claim invokes a kind of colonialist exoticizing of the other that rankles against postcolonialist and third-wave feminist sensibilities in that she seems to be inviting Americans of her day to distance themselves from these obviously retrograde foreign practices. Thus, Grimké's arguments illustrate not only how a rhetor can use rather traditional rhetorical devices for alternative purposes to deconstruct one of the most commonly held concepts of her day (the subservience and dependency of women on men) but also the danger of attending to only one aspect of identity (gender) without examining the kinds of privilege and marginalization that can be inherent in one's arguments for change.

Interchapter

JUMPER CABLES AND DOUBLE CONSCIOUSNESS AS A HABIT OF MIND

"Um, I think it's mostly a matter of confidence." By this my brother meant that I lacked confidence.

It was one of the first serious talks Dan and I ever had. I was living at home again after college and nine harrowing months at seminary; he was just eighteen. We were talking about the conversation I had with the man I rescued in the snowy parking lot of the mall by giving his car a jump start. I knew it was better to attach the ground cable to my engine block, but the man had insisted that connecting it to the negative terminal was better, black to black and red to red. If he had been helping me, I would have hooked up the cables any way he wanted, but since I was helping him, it seemed like he should have listened to me. But he insisted; I folded, and I was telling Dan this story because this kind of interaction was not uncommon for me.

The explanation I pitched to my brother was an immodest one—an attempt to both understand and to cover the embarrassment I felt because I seemed unable to impose my will even when I was sure I was right.

"This sounds odd to say, but I think it's because I'm smart."

"Huh?"

"Well," I couldn't quite meet my brother's eyes as I propounded my theory, "I wonder if it's because I think so much faster than most people, so that in the time they have to figure out one scenario, I can think of several, and then I'm unsure." It was at this point that my brother suggested that a lack of confidence was closer to the mark. I tried to press my point. "But if I'm right, and I really do think faster, how would you even know?" He grudgingly admitted I had a point, but I could tell he wasn't convinced, and to be honest, I wasn't convinced myself.

More than twenty years later, I think I finally see what I was trying to puzzle out that night: why was it that second-guessing myself had become a habit of mind for me, and why wasn't my brother afflicted with the same kind of doubts? This little comparison/contrast exercise helps me identify three different ways my brother and I were socialized and thus the three causes of my second-guessing habit. First, I was the second child and oldest son in very traditional evangelical Christian family, and Dan was the baby of the family. My sisters—who were just one grade ahead of me and one grade behind me in school—and I were expected to live up to a strict code of conduct, which was not applied nearly as carefully to my brother, who was significantly younger than the rest of us. Second, while my sisters and I were model "preacher's kids" to the extent that each of us graduated from the Bible college at which our parents met, Dan was a bit more rebellious and had a cool relationship to our brand of Christianity, which led my mother to wonder several times whether or not her Danny was "saved." Finally, Dan is straight, and I was deeply in the closet at the time in a rural community in which there were no visible gay people who were not treated as aberrations to be ridiculed, dismissed, or pitied.

Now I find myself wondering what it was like for my brother to grow up without developing the overly critical voice I cannot escape—to be rewarded for naturally taking to the kinds of manly tasks Dad also excelled at, and to have his life follow the heteronormative pattern so that one day he would stand in front of our minister father, who beamed with pride as he pronounced Dan husband to his pretty blonde wife. Dan was right that it "was mostly a matter of confidence," but even that assessment made me feel less manly because it implied that this failing was a lack of character on my part.

* * *

The big pipe organ in the balcony at the back of the church sits silent while the worship team members, microphones in their hands, sing and sway, leading the congregation in the worship chorus displayed on the big screen on the platform. The aesthetic feels wrong to me. I long to feel the vibrations of the pipe organ filling the bright Sunday morning air of the spacious church. I try to follow along; I can read the words, but I don't know the tune, and I wish we could sing one of the hymns of my youth, a rousing one that would allow me to lose myself, to sing as loudly as I want—but this is not my church, not my service. I am here with most of my immediate family to see water poured over my brother's and his daughters' heads, but when the other family members move forward to stand in witness for the new Christians, I sit alone in our pew, clutching my camera as an excuse for staying behind. Avery, who is not quite three, cries out as the water hits her head, and I lean forward, trying to frame a shot in the low light, refusing to spoil the moment with a flash.

It was harder than I'd thought it would be to watch the rest of the family go forward, to sit in my pew with my camera—to feel alone and separated, yet honorable in that I wouldn't stand and say I'd do things I don't believe. The symbolism of sitting alone was hard—hard not to have someone special to sit with me, not to have a family of my own within this larger family, hard that on this day of celebration of the values they hold, no one seemed to notice that these values are difficult for me. Later in the service, the minister said "[p]ick up your pallet and walk" and invited us to accept grace. Should I have done so? Should I have knelt at the altar and accepted the bread and wine offered by the white-bred, gray-haired Eucharist team? No, I refuse to see my sexual identity—the major issue that separated me from the people at that service—as something for which I need to be healed. But my brother and sister-in-law could not have asked me to be godfather for my nieces because I could not have stood and made those promises to those people.

* * *

I climb the stairs to the third floor of the big house on the beach that will belong to my extended family for the next week. I am tired from a long day of travel, but my spirits immediately lift at the top when Avery spots me and comes running, smiling widely, crying out, "UNCLE DAVIE!" All eyes turns as Avery heralds my arrival, and my brother-in-law Steve makes that funny scowl I have learned over the years means he finds something puzzling or ironic. As Avery hurtles toward me, I brace myself to sweep her up in my arms, realizing that Steve's scowl is one of surprise that Avery, who is normally a bit shy at first even around family, is running immediately toward me to throw herself into my arms. I hear Steve say quietly "Well, I guess she sees you more," before the world stops for an instant as I take the last step and gather Avery in my arms, lifting her so she can wrap her arms tightly around my chest and press her head into my shoulder.

On this version of my extended family's every-other-year visit to the Outer Banks of North Carolina, Avery is my special buddy. She is the youngest of the children, four years younger than her sister and her next-in-age cousin, and she likes to be in charge, so there are tears when she cannot get the older kids to play the way she wants them to, and lots of chances for us to invent private games. We tumble together on the living floor aping the gymnasts in the first Olympics she will remember seeing, or she chases me around the beds in the room she shares with her sister for the week, squealing in delight when I let her catch me and the chase game morphs into the tickle-monster game.

I can only stay four of the seven days because I have to fly back to Orlando to start my duties as chair of my department. I get two hugs from Avery before I go and a long one from her mother, who says quietly in my ear, "I'll miss you for the rest of the week," and "You have a special bond with the girls." "Yes," I reply, "particularly with Avery this time."

Seven hours later, I'm walking briskly through the Orlando airport, rushing to catch the shuttle that will take me to baggage claim, and I call my dad's cell phone to let the family know I made it back to Orlando safely. Lil, my stepmother, answers: "Glad to know you made it back." "Did the weather break? Did you get to go to the beach after I left?" I start to ask, needing to feel a part of my family yet, but there is laughter on the line. "We're playing Shanghai [the latest favorite card game of the family]; just wanted to know you made it home, bye." "Oh, okay, good bye." The shuttle stops and the doors open, but suddenly I am not in a hurry anymore. I shuffle forward clutching my carry-on, letting the familiar sense of separation settle in—one part physical distance and one part solitariness—having no one with me to tell that I already missed my family and no one waiting to meet me outside the security gate.

* * *

Despite the fact that we grew up in the same town, the same church, the same house, and the same family, I was not socialized in the way Dan was. From my perspective, it took me nearly forty years to develop the sense of self that he seems to have found much earlier in life, and although I have found it now, I still feel a sense of distance on the occasions in which the family comes together, and most often when I look at my younger brother who has become a wonderful husband and father. Although I have long since accepted that I will never be a parent and take considerable pleasure in my uncle status, I can never seem to find a way to explain to my family that it is difficult to be the only single one, to be the one who sits in the pew taking pictures, to watch each of my siblings wed their life partners, and to sit on the outskirts my siblings' *Leave-It-to-Beaver*-for-the-new-millennium families and be reminded that even if I find a life-partner, there would likely be tension about whether or not I could bring him to the big house on the beach every other year.

For the most part, I choose not to speak of these things because I don't want to spoil baptismal celebrations and family vacations or perhaps because all those years of homophobia, heteronormativity, and closeting leave me still too timid for such risks. Whatever the reason, I don't make a fuss about being the only adult at the beach house who has to sleep in a kid's bed and share a bathroom with my nieces and nephew. But I leave early, not only because I have to get back to work but also because I fear a return of "date night" from the beach trip four years ago on which Gram and Pap babysat the kids, all the couples had dates, and I ate alone at the bar of a restaurant, glad that my siblings got a much-deserved night off from parenting but vowing not to put myself in a situation in which heteronormativity could so dramatically marginalize me within my own family again.

The point I have been wandering toward is that I cannot escape heteronormativity and the double consciousness it spawns even amongst the people I love most dearly, and I wish my family (and my society) understood that a bit better. Perhaps I underestimate my family; perhaps they want to understand why the physical layout of a rental house at the beach with its master bedrooms on the upper level designed for couples and kids'/teens' rooms on the lower level is a physical manifestation of heteronormativity, and that as much as I love them, I can only stay in such a place for a few days. But there would be costs to such conversations. In choosing not to speak of these kinds of things, I recreate a closet of sorts for myself: I show up for baptisms and celebrations and participate to whatever extent I can, but I don't raise the issues that are glaringly obvious to me but apparently invisible those who I love most dearly. I worry that if members of my family read these words, they will be hurt or will not understand. But I choose to make this public because I want other queer family members to know someone else has experienced some version of the marginalization and isolation you feel. I also write for straight people, hoping to help you understand how pervasive heteronormativity is and to invite you to pause to think about the queer family members and friends in your life and about how the continued physical and cultural construction of heteronormativity may be causing them either to cry out in frustration or to be silent, as it does me.

3

FREDERICK DOUGLASS
Taking an Ell to Claim Humanity

*The first step had been taken. Mistress, in teaching me the alphabet,
had given me an inch, and no precaution could prevent me from taking
the ell.*

Douglass, 1960

Persecution is precisely what happens without the warrant of any
deed of my own.

Butler, 2005

Some of the most frightening kinds of arguments outsiders have been
forced to make in American history and culture are claims in which
they seek status as humans. Many groups have had to argue for the
recognition of their full personhood: American Indians calling for
the recognition of their very existence in what were seen as unsettled
lands; American slaves seeking the right to literally own their own bodies, share in the fruits of their labors, and maintain their family relationships; American women seeking the right to vote, own property,
and control their ability to reproduce the species; and American lesbian, gay, bisexual, transgendered, and transsexual people arguing for
the right to marry, to adopt children, and to have control of their partners' medical treatment when necessary. At the heart of this oppression are various kinds of dehumanization, of defining some classes of
people as less worthy of education, of legal access to basic institutions
such as citizenship, marriage, and parenthood, and of fair treatment
under the law. The opening epigraph—from Frederick Douglass's
Narrative of the Life of Frederick Douglass: An American Slave[1]—illustrates
one of the myriad ways that Douglass and other African Americans
were dehumanized: the denial of basic literacy and the opportunities
literacy creates.

---

1. For the sake of simplicity after the first full reference in the text, I refer to Douglass's
   Narrative and *My Bondage* by these shortened titles.

In telling the story of how he became literate, escaped slavery, and came to have a powerful public voice, Douglass was keenly aware that he was "taking an ell," that he was fulfilling the prophecy of his new master, Hugh Auld, who remonstrated his wife for teaching Douglass the alphabet: "If you give a nigger an inch, he will take an ell . . . if you teach that nigger (speaking of myself) how to read, there would be no keeping him. It would forever unfit him to be a slave" (1960, 58). Douglass's story of "taking an ell" is interesting from the standpoint of alternative rhetoric because it dramatically demonstrates that for those who have been dehumanized by systemic oppression, basic humanity must often be claimed, and Douglass's account of this process in his *Narrative* illustrates not only the many forms that dehumanizing oppression can take, but it also suggests the many things "taking an ell" may entail. In addition, Douglass's story is important for my exploration of alternative rhetoric because it is arguably the most wildly successful literacy story in American history: an illiterate and unschooled slave becomes a leading figure in American policy debates over slavery and, to a lesser extent, women's rights in the latter half of the nineteenth century. His three autobiographies can be read as important examples of embodied writing, of the sorts of literacy narratives for which Morris Young and other compositions have called. In one sense, then, it is important simply to read Douglass's telling of his journey to voice as a case of someone who responded successfully to what Butler calls "persecution," someone who was forced to respond to discriminatory restrictions placed upon him solely because of his race and class status as a slave. However, my purpose is to use Douglass's case to press further into Butler's more complicated understanding of individual agency and collective responsibility that I sketched in chapter 1. In this sense, Douglass's case illustrates how, in Butler's terms, "To be human seems to mean being in a predicament that one cannot solve" (2005, 103). By this, Butler means that as much as we might yearn to be "wholly perspicacious beings" capable of absolute independent agency, doing so would mean eliminating the very means of doing so: "to eradicate all the active and structuring traces of our psychological formations and to dwell in the pretense of fully knowing, self-possessed adults" (2005, 102). As I have already discussed, what Butler adds to the usual discussions of the postmodern conundrum of agency is the explicit call for addressing one's own inability to find anything other than a contingent basis for agency that must admit the limits of its own knowledge in substantive ways.

Douglass's case adds to our understanding of this problem and offers three ways to take action in response to it. First, his case illustrates how oppression can serve as a means for a person to see the constructed nature of culture and the performative nature of identity. In this regard, Douglass shows us in great detail how persecution itself can lead to consciousness of both the cultural construction of culture and the limits of self-knowledge and what it means to transgress the sociocultural values and discourse practices that create and maintain persecution.[2] Second, Douglass's journey to voice provides a unique opportunity to examine the operation of oppression in broad terms because his story begins in complete illiteracy and socioeconomic disenfranchisement and ends with international prominence and relative economic comfort. Although Douglass's story is certainly not representative of all the struggles faced by those who have experienced systemic marginalization in American society, accounts of few, if any, other American figures provide such a rich opportunity for teasing out the many faces of dehumanization and the many ways Douglass sought to create the copresense of the other throughout his long public career. Third, like Grimké, Douglass engaged in an internal struggle to come to a new understanding of himself that lead to voice, experienced helpful but problematic sponsorship from those in positions of unexamined privilege, and struggled with the implications of managing the interactions between race and gender in public policy debates. In Douglass's case, powerful abolitionists such a William Lloyd Garrison and Wendell Phillips (both of whom wrote introductions to his *Narrative*) served as sponsors for his larger public voice, but also sought to limit Douglass's rhetorical agency, counseling him to present the simple narrative of a fugitive slave: "It was said to me, 'Better have a *little* of the plantation manner of speech than not; 'tis not best that you seem too learned.'" (Douglass, 2003, 226). Indeed, Wilson T. Moses argues that the very things that made Douglass an engaging public figure (tying into the slave narrative genre and the stereotyped roles of slave/victim and exemplifying a Horatio Alger success story) also invoked limits that Douglass would struggle to overcome in developing his own independent public voice/role (1991, 69). Thus, in a very real sense, "taking an ell" for Douglass meant finding a voice that not only allowed him to challenge the obvious prejudices and injustices of slavery but also to challenge the relatively more subtle forms of racism practiced by his liberal, white, abolitionist sponsors.

---

2. See Butler (2005, 10–11) for more on the role of persecution in consciousness raising.

In the body of this chapter, I explore Douglass's more specific contributions to alternative rhetoric first in terms of genre and immediate context to provide background for a more detailed analysis of the portions of his work I see as most relevant to alternative rhetoric. Then, in more detail, I explore what that body of work exposes about the operation of systemic oppression because, as I have already argued, Douglass's work provides a unique opportunity for probing the range of problems faced by those who seek to use alternative rhetoric to address inequity. Finally, I turn to teasing out actual techniques Douglass used in his work in the service of further describing the possible range of devices useful in alternative rhetoric.

TAKING AN ELL, NOT WRITING FREELY

In his speeches and writing, Douglass took up moral issues that had broad implications for American society—particularly how systematic oppression undermined the values that supposedly defined our country as a place of fairness and opportunity. Indeed, Benjamin Quarles, who edited the version of Douglass's *Narrative* I use here, argues that Douglass's "championing of the cause of the downtrodden points toward Douglass' major contribution to American democracy—that of holding a mirror to it" (1960, xii). Douglass's biographer Waldo E. Martin Jr. goes so far as to see Douglass as exposing America's "sham democracy" in which the holding of black people as "chattel" blatantly contradicted white America's claim of an "advanced civilization" (1984, 52). Gerald Fulkerson sees this move to expose the inconsistencies between the ideals of democracy and its actual practice in the United States as "the rhetorical stock-in-trade of virtually all social reforms" (1996, 85). However, even more than Grimké, who made much of how the oppression of women benefited men in very concrete ways, Douglass's calls for a more inclusive notion of American democracy highlighted the convoluted arguments some white Americans made to retain their privilege at the expense of others. Thus, Douglass can be read not only as speaking *against* slavery but also *for* a better version of America that refuses to condone unfair privilege. As Anita Patterson argues,

> Douglass provided the American public with a fresh and much-needed reassessment of the meaning of democracy at a time when rights rhetoric had already been put to notoriously bad use by Southern planters interested in holding onto their "freedom" to own slaves. (1999, 117)

For my purposes, one of the most important aspects of Douglass's efforts to change his society is the challenge he provides to the commonsense notion of unfettered agency—that any person in American society who masters the conventions of the dominant discourse is automatically enabled to speak or write freely. Indeed, Douglass's practice of rhetoric is important because it illustrates in some detail what it means to embody what Foucault calls a counter discourse. As Shelly Fisher Fishkin and Carla L. Peterson argue, Douglass essentially transforms himself from "a piece of property" into "a speaking subject" (1991, 189), largely by challenging the existing categories that had been used to define him as less than human and "reversing these categories" (191). It is remarkable that Douglass was able to move from his utterly disenfranchised position in slavery to become one of the most important voices of his era, as witnessed not only by his autobiographies and newspapers but also his public speeches in such historic venues as Boston's Faneuil Hall (McFeely 1991, 100), his lobbying of President Lincoln on a variety of issues (Martin 1984, 63), and his appointment as consul general to the Republic of Haiti. Indeed, Douglass is seen as one of the most important men of the nineteenth century (Fulkerson 1996, 82; Martin 1984, ix) and as "the figure to whom the mass of Negroes chiefly looked for leadership" (Quarles 1960, xii). However, it is perhaps even more remarkable that in this transformation Douglass also exhibits the ability to think about difference issues beyond the needs of the group he represented most directly. For example, Douglass was one of the most, if not the most, ardent male supporter of women's rights/suffrage in his era,[3] and, even though, as Martin notes, his primary concern was "about the impact of white supremacy on blacks, he also pondered its impact on others, especially whites" (109).

Not surprisingly, Douglass's work has been widely studied in speech communications as rhetorical texts, and, like Grimké, he has also recently been reclaimed by writing scholars as a rhetorician; excerpts from his autobiographies are included in the second edition of Bizzell and Herzberg's *The Rhetorical Tradition* (2001). As with Grimké, the identity issues in Douglass's *Narrative* are unmistakable; in this case, Douglass uses his own experiences to deconstruct dominant notions of *slavery* and *race* (mostly notably that African Americans are subhuman and thus fit only to be slaves). However, unlike Grimké, Douglass's primary means

---

3. For more on this, see Foner (1976).

of making his case is to narrate his own experiences. From the standpoint of considering the interplay of genre and personal involvement in alternative rhetoric, Grimké and Douglass make an interesting pair. The writings of both make it clear that they have a personal stake in arguing against forms of systemic oppression. However, Grimké does so without invoking her own experiences, while Douglass, at least in his autobiographies, embodies injustices in his own experiences as a primary means of persuasion. In the terms of neo-Aristotelian rhetoric, Douglass might be read as simply merging logos, pathos, and ethos because he recognizes, as did Sir Francis Bacon, that rhetoric involves not only swaying the mind but also moving the will to action. Indeed, in his introduction to Douglass's *Narrative*, Garrison describes Douglass's particular appeal: "There is in him that union of head and heart, which is indispensable to an enlightenment of the heads and the winning of the hearts of others" (1960, 7). However, I argue that more is operating in Douglass's case than a savvy use of the available means of persuasion; as will become clear later in this chapter, Douglass's very right to speak is constantly called into question. Thus, like Grimké, Douglass's practice of rhetoric is alternative because it involves questions of a fundamental right to speak—questions that must be addressed only necessary because of persecution, as Butler uses the term.

In terms of genre, what Douglass's struggle with this process adds to understanding the means and operation of alternative rhetoric is not the invention of a new genre, but the use of an existing genre for a new purpose. As an autobiography bearing witness to oppression, Douglass's *Narrative* participates in what Frances Smith Foster calls "the most democratic genre in American literature"; Foster notes that autobiography is not only one of the oldest American genres but is also important because it "offers the best opportunity for examining a variety of particular confrontations of culture by particular people in particular settings" (1985, 26). Douglass's *Narrative* was written the fall of 1844 and the winter of 1845 in response to claims that he was never a slave (Fulkerson 1996, 83), and it was a "smash," selling 11,000 copies in the United States before 1848 (Martin 1984, 25). *Narrative* begins with Douglass's origins, describing his various experiences with slavery in rural Maryland and in Baltimore, the denial of literacy to him, his inventive means of educating himself, his escape from slavery, his discovery by abolitionist agents who recognized his potential as a speaker, and the beginnings of his public career, culminating in his writing of what would now be seen as a best-selling memoir. According to Henry Louis Gates Jr., Douglass's *Narrative* was compared favorably with the works of other important authors of his day: "Douglass's elevation, as an author equal to the greatest authors of his time and before, was immediate" (1991, 61). Further, Martin argues, Douglass's *Narrative* should be seen "as part of an important black literacy tradition that flourished between 1840 and 1860 and reached at least as far back as 1789 with the London publication of *The Interesting Narrative of the Life of Olaudah Equiano, or Gustavus Vassa, the African Written by Himself*" (1984, 25). As scholars such as Gates and Foster have argued, slave narratives should not be taken as complete and unproblematic accounts of slavery because they were motivated and shaped by the interests of white people—who, however well meaning and altruistic, also imposed limits on what was told. And this is particularly true for Douglass's *Narrative* because it is in a very real sense a simpler version of Douglass's success story than his two later autobiographies.

For my purposes, then, Douglass's *Narrative* is an important case for understanding alternative rhetoric because it provides a detailed account of Douglass's coming to an identity and a voice that allowed him to speak back to a dominant culture that attempted to silence him through slavery and other forms of racism. However, it is equally important to note that because *Narrative* was written before Douglass's contentious and public split with Garrison, the version of his coming to voice that Douglass tells in *Narrative* does not explore the racism he encountered within the abolitionist movement nor the attempts of abolitionist leaders to limit his voice. The story of the racism Douglass faced within the abolitionist movement and the attempts of its leaders to limit his voice is told in the latter chapters of his second autobiography, *My Bondage and My Freedom*. Ten years after he wrote his *Narrative*, Douglass is able to tell this other important part of his coming-to-voice story because of his widely publicized split from Garrison and because his highly successful tour of Great Britain secured his position not only because British friends obtained his manumission from slavery but also because they provided him with seed money to launch his own newspaper. Thus, although the bulk of my analysis is this chapter focuses on Douglass's *Narrative* as the first and most popular telling of his story, I also include the last three chapters of *My Bondage* to flesh out the complications of white abolitionist sponsorship because this part of Douglass's story is particularly important for understanding how engaging in alternative rhetoric may be critical for teasing out oppression even among those passionately committed to working for social justice.

In short, Douglass's journey from obscurity to national prominence and his fifty years of participation in American public life and policy provided him with important insights into the operation of various forms of oppression in American society, even to such nuances as how success in some aspects (i.e., the abolition of slavery and the fifteenth amendment) changed the nature of the struggle against injustice.[4] Given the scope and longevity of Douglass's contributions to American public policy, only a part of his experience and insight into the operation of race-based and other kinds of oppression is captured in his *Narrative* and in the final chapters of *My Bondage*. However, examining these accounts provides considerable insight into the many forms oppression takes in American society as well as an engaging description of what it meant for a marginalized American to speak back to systemic oppression.

In nineteenth-century America, the forms and consequences of the dehumanization of African Americans were varied and powerful. For thousands of black men who had sex (or were accused of having sex) with white women in the antebellum South, it was a matter of life and death as local laws and social customs of the times allowed them to be lynched without a trial. Such attitudes and actions depended up upon a presumption that that these men were not fully human in that they were not seen as capable of having consensual sexual relationships with white women. In a similar way, systematic oppression also worked to dehumanize black women slaves, who were considered property and could be forced to have sex with their masters or overseers. In response to such dehumanizing effects, Douglass's moving accounts of his early struggles with the cruelties of slavery and his struggle to become literate and gain a public voice can be seen as part of a larger movement of black American writers and speakers who sought to expose this dehumanization through alternative rhetoric that embodied the experiences of black Americans. In addition to Douglass, I am thinking here of Harriett Jacobs's recounting the daily sexual harassment inflicted on her by her master, of Ida B. Wells's scathing news articles and editorials on lynching, and of Sojourner Truth baring her breasts at a women's suffrage convention and exclaiming, "Ain't I a woman, too?"

---

4. For example, see Martin (1984, 68) for a description of Douglass's understanding of what the United States government saw its duty toward freed people as complete shortly after the Civil War.

Within this larger context, Martin explains, part of Douglass's appeal was that he fit "the Horatio Alger myth of the late nineteenth-century American fortune: from rags to riches primarily through the individual's own virtuous character and diligence at work" (1984, 256), and this view of Douglass's rise to prominence is most unproblematically presented in his *Narrative*. "Riches" is a relative term for Douglass as the publication of *Narrative* did not make Douglass independently wealthy; indeed, he would need to rely on the patronage of wealthy abolitionist friends to keep his newspapers solvent. However, Moses argues that the ability to "manufacture a public personality was Douglass's bread and butter"; in this sense, Moses contends that Douglass's *Narrative* should be seen as "a creation of self for economic, as well as for moral and ideological ends" (1991, 69). The story that Douglass told in his abolitionist speeches and in his *Narrative* was useful to white abolitionists who needed him to tell his story to dramatize the degradations of slavery and to serve as *prima facie* evidence that African American people were fit for more than being slaves. Gates (1991) argues that Douglass displaced Phyllis Wheatley as the favorite of abolitionists and that he also replaced disgraced slave narrative writer James Williams, whose story was eventually discovered to be fiction. In a very real sense, abolitionists needed Frederick Douglass and his story as an important piece of evidence to further their cause nearly as much as he needed their sponsorship to find a public voice.

The most immediate need for Douglass's *Narrative* was to counter the claim that because he spoke so eloquently it was not possible that he had ever been a slave. However, Gates explains that the embarrassment of the abolitionists over the Williams controversy led to "even more demands for verisimilitude among the slave narrators and, of course, to the need for a suitable replacement figure—someone who was 'presentable' in the most public way" (1991, 61). Given these rhetorical complexities, Moses argues, "Douglass's early development as a writer had been assisted but also hemmed in by white friends, who had strong ideas about what roles black Americans ought to play in American literary and intellectual life, as well as their own emancipation" (1991, 66). Increasingly, as he shared the platform with white abolitionist speakers, Douglass chafed at their attempts to limit his role: "It did not entirely satisfy me to *narrate* wrongs; I felt like *denouncing* them" (2003, 266), and this conflict can be read as an early indication of one of the larger issues that would eventually alienate Douglass from the white abolitionists who had helped to open "upon me a new life" (2003, 264).

In summary, then, Douglass's telling of his own story in his *Narrative* and in the final chapters of *My Bondage* are important for my exploration of alternative rhetoric because they illustrate both the many ways systematic oppression can dehumanize groups of people as well as the many things "taking an ell" may mean in finding a voice that exposes systemic marginalization and argues for change. Further, Douglass's case demonstrates the complexities of understanding agency from a postmodern perspective—how the notion of coming to a voice that allows one to "write freely" is too simplistic, particularly when the goal is to expose and challenge systematic oppression. "If writing freely means writing not only abundantly, but with absolute or impolitic candor," argues Moses, "Douglass did not write freely of himself. Douglass's literary act of self-presentation was skillfully engineered to produce the desired effects on certain sets of white liberals" (1991, 68). Certainly, Moses and others are right to expose the limits white liberals attempted to place on how Douglass's compelling story would be told and to what purposes it would be used. However, it would be a mistake to underestimate the power of Douglass's *Narrative* to speak beyond those limits when it is read explicitly for what it says about oppression, as well as to underestimate Douglass's direct challenges to attempts to limit his voice. Although Douglass does not attempt to write a rhetoric or even to engage in what would today be seen as race theory, his *Narrative* and the final chapters of *My Bondage* are critical for the development of alternative rhetoric when read as opportunities to name the ills that Douglass so aptly illustrated as well as the rhetorical strategies he used to speak back to oppression. Thus, in the pages that follow, I begin unpacking what Douglass has to offer an emerging theory of alternative rhetoric by focusing first on what we learn about how oppression operates from Douglass's accounts, and second on what we learn about what it means to speak back to oppression.

THE OPERATION OF OPPRESSION: UNACKNOWLEDGED PRIVILEGE AND DEHUMANIZATION

Despite the fact that Douglass does not so much as hint at sexual identity issues in his *Narrative*, a queer reading of this text has much to offer because his text tacitly reveals the operation of a version of the epistemology of the closet in that it exposes the interplay between unacknowledged white privilege and the dehumanization of slaves. As I have already argued, much of the power of Douglass's writing comes from his embodiment of persecution in a genre that makes those horrors real to his audience. I turn now to teasing out the various forms of oppression. In a sense, Douglass's *Narrative* can be read as exposing an earlier and more primal version of unacknowledged racial privilege that Peggy McIntosh (1988) has usefully described as "the invisible knapsack," including such items as seeing people of one's race represented in positions of power and popular media, having one's cultural heritage featured positively in accounts of national history, finding easy access to creature comforts designed for people of one's own race (e.g., Band-Aids and beauty salons), and, in general, not having to consider whether race is a factor in a wide variety of interactions. From a twenty-first-century perspective, the operations of oppression that Douglass identifies seem more obvious than those McIntosh includes in her invisible knapsack. However, reviewing those identified by Douglass is important both to bear historical witness to the operation of white privilege in American culture and because the underlying types of oppression he describes have not yet disappeared from our society, even though slavery itself has been outlawed. Thus, my main argument in this section is that Douglass's accounts suggest a range of means used by those in power, whether consciously or not, to dehumanize the oppressed, and that although these means operate for the immediate benefit of the oppressors, they are ultimately detrimental to both the oppressed and the oppressors (although less so to the latter).

Limiting Knowledge and Control of the Self

Douglass's *Narrative* illustrates a number of ways oppression operated to dehumanize slaves; one of the most basic of these was the denial of basic knowledge of self and familial relations that operated to such an extent that new and different people were created. For example, in the first chapter of his *Narrative*, Douglass recounts the erasure of his identity in a number of basic ways, as well as the restriction of basic human interactions and relationships. For example, he noticed that white children knew their ages and wondered why he was denied this privilege: "I was not allowed to make any inquiries of my master concerning it. He deemed all such inquiries on the part of a slave improper and impertinent, and evidence of a restless spirit" (1960, 23).[5] Douglass was also denied traditional parenting and knowledge of his parentage because of his mixed race status:

---

5. Unless otherwise noted, all quotations from Douglass in the remainder of this chapter are from his *Narrative*.

My father was a white man. He was admitted to be such by all I ever heard speak of my parentage. The opinion was also whispered that my master was my father, but of the correctness of this opinion, I know nothing; the means of knowing were withheld from me. (24)

Whether because of possible complications of being the master's son or because of the general practice of splitting slave families, Douglass was also denied contact with his mother: "My mother and I were separated when I was but an infant—before I knew her as my mother" (1960, 24). Although Douglass reports having seen his mother four or five times, he never saw her "by the light of day" because she could only visit at night after making a long walk, and he notes that although he knew of her death, "I was not allowed to be present during her illness, at her death, or burial" (24). Thus, Douglass was essentially an orphan even though during his early years he lived in relative proximity to both his parents. Douglass is clear that these basic kinds of familial identity that white children could take for granted were denied to him as part of a system designed for the economic and personal advantage of white slaveholders:

[S]laveholders have ordained, and by law established, that the children of slave women shall in all cases follow the condition of their mothers; and this is done too obviously to administer to their own lusts, and make a gratification of their wicked desires profitable as well as pleasurable; for by this cunning arrangement, the slaveholder, in cases not a few, sustains to his slaves the double relation of master and father. (26)

In his account of his early experiences with the systemic dehumanization of slaves for the benefit of their owners, Douglass also makes explicit links between what he has personally witnessed and the claims about slavery made in broader cultural contexts. For example, Douglass challenges the claim of "one great statesmen of the south" who predicted the downfall of slavery "by the inevitable laws of population." In contrast, Douglass argues that the reproductive system he experienced was creating a new population: "[I]t is nevertheless plain that a very different-looking class of people are springing up at the south, and are now held in slavery, from those originally brought to this country from Africa" (1960, 27).

The contrast between the rights that accrued to white, slaveholding families and the lack of any concern for family relations among slaves can be seen in the disposition of assets at the death of Douglass's first master, Captain Anthony. At the about the age of ten or eleven, Douglass was returned to the Maryland countryside along with all of his former master's slaves for "valuation" with his other property:

> We were all ranked together at the valuation. Men and women, old and young, married and single, were ranked with horses, sheep, and swine. There were horses and men, cattle and women, pigs and children, all holding the same rank in the scale of being, and all were subjected to the same narrow examination. Silvery-headed age and sprightly youth, maids and matrons, had to undergo the same indelicate inspection. At this moment, I saw more clearly than ever the brutalizing effects of slavery upon both slave and slaveholder. (1960, 74)

Worse than the indignity of the "valuation" was the pending "division" in which the rights of the white heirs to choose their property would be exercised with little attention to the desires and familial relationships of the slaves. Douglass brings this aspect of the dehumanization of slaves into sharp focus with the privilege of white slaveholders in his description of the dread with which he and his fellow slaves held the impending division:

> I have no language to express the high excitement and deep anxiety which were felt among us poor slaves during this time. Our fate for life was now to be decided. We had no more voice in that decision that the brutes among whom we were ranked. A single word from the white men was enough—against all our wishes, prayers and entreaties—to sunder forever the dearest friends, dearest kindred, and strongest ties known to human beings." (1960, 74)

These basic identity issues continued even after Douglass escaped physical slavery. For example, it was not safe for Douglass to be known by his surname of Bailey because of the real possibility that slave hunters would find him and return him to his master. The description of the process by which he comes to be Frederick Douglass illustrates both the sense of identity that was intimately bound up in his taking of a new name and the arbitrariness involved:

> I gave Mr. Johnson [his benefactor in New Bedford] the privilege of choosing me a name, but told him he must not take from me the name of "Frederick." I must hold on to that, to preserve a sense of my identity. Mr. Johnson had just been reading the "Lady of the Lake," and at once suggested that my name be

"Douglass;" and as I am more widely known by that name than by either of the others, I shall continue to use it as my own. (1960, 148)

Douglass's accounts of this version of dehumanization raise two basic questions: How does systemic oppression strip away the human relationships that dominant culture takes as basic and grants as a matter of course to those it enfranchises? And how do such efforts work to create a separate, "other" class of people? The temptation is to assume that such issues are passé in our society; yet, as McIntosh argues (1988), white privilege continues to exist in our society in more subtle ways and, as a number of queer theorists and LGBT activists have argued, such basic issues of familial relationship are still denied to many Americans.

Denial of Voice

A second kind of dehumanization that Douglass addresses is the voicelessness enforced on him and other slaves. In addition to the proscription against inquiring about his paternity, Douglass also reveals a number of ways in which master/slave relationships made such seemingly straightforward ideals, such as telling the truth and offering help to others, impossible or perilous for slaves. In one of the first examples of silencing in his *Narrative*, Douglass highlights the absolute power masters have over slaves. Douglass lived and worked on Colonel Lloyd's plantation for a number of years, and he describes the master's obsession with his horses and his capricious belief that if one of his horses "did not move fast enough, or hold his head high enough, it was owing to some fault of his keepers" (1960, 40); slaves were powerless to respond no matter how ridiculous the master's claims because "Colonel Lloyd could not brook any contradiction from a slave. When he spoke, a slave must stand, listen, and tremble; and such was literally the case" (41). In addition to silencing in daily encounters related to work, slaves also needed to be careful about what they said to relative strangers because their masters often set traps for them. Douglass tells the story of one of Colonel Lloyd's slaves from an out-farm who did not know his master by sight and answered truthfully when asked by his master about ill-treatment. The slave was sold to a slaveholder in Georgia for his honesty: "This is the penalty of telling the truth, of telling the simple truth, in answer to a series of plain questions. It is partly in consequence of such facts, that slaves, when inquired of as to their condition and the character of their masters, almost universally say they are contented, and that masters are kind" (42–43). Later in his *Narrative*, Douglass writes of his need to feign disinterest in the advice given to him by white shipbuilders in Baltimore about how to escape for fear they are seeking to entrap him. Incidents such as these, Douglass reports, led to the maxim among slaves: "A still tongue makes a head wise" (43).

Douglass sees these silencing moves as linked to a social system that allowed slaveholders absolute control and stripped slaves of the right to bear witness even to what would now be seen as murder. In the fourth chapter of his *Narrative*, Douglass tells the stories of three slaves who were killed by white people—none of whom were punished. The most chilling of these examples links the privilege of killing directly to the legal system that disregarded the testimony of slaves. Mr. Gore, a cruel new overseer, kills a slave in cold blood. Douglass's description of Mr. Gore's justification of this killing to Colonel Lloyd illustrates the systemic way in which oppression occurred:

> His [Mr. Gore's] reply was, (as well as I can remember,) that Demby [the slave who was killed] had become unmanageable. He was setting a dangerous example to the other slaves—one which, if suffered to pass without some such demonstration on his part, would finally lead to the total subversion of all rule and order upon the plantation. He argued that if one slave refused to be corrected, and escaped with his life, the other slaves would soon copy the example; the result of which would be, the freedom of the slaves, and the enslavement of the whites. Mr. Gore's defense was satisfactory. (1960, 48)

Douglass notes that his master accepted this explanation (even though he had lost a valuable slave) and that this incident added to Mr. Gore's fame as an overseer. However, he reserves his greatest expression of horror over this killing for the lack of any possible legal action against Gore:

> His horrid crime was not even submitted to judicial investigation. It was committed in the presence of slaves, and they of course could neither institute a suit, nor testify against him; and thus the guilty perpetrator of one of the bloodiest and most foul murders goes unwhipped of justice, and uncensured by the community in which he lives. (48)

Douglass also details how this silencing effect continued to dog him and other fugitive slaves even after they had escaped the immediate control of their masters. For example, he tells very little of the actual details of his escape in his *Narrative* because he does not want to put at risk any who helped him nor to provide the slaveholders with the motivation or means to increase their vigilance against escape.[6] Further, his description of his fear of asking for the help he greatly needed when he finally reached New York dramatizes the continued silencing effects of slavery:

> I dared not unfold to any one of them my sad condition. I was afraid to speak to any one for fear of speaking to the wrong one, and thereby falling into the hands of money-loving kidnappers, whose business it was to lie in wait for the panting fugitive, as ferocious beasts of the forest lie in wait for their prey. (1960, 143)

For my purposes, one of the most important aspects of Douglass's discussion of the effects of this voicelessness is that they continue even beyond seeming escape from the immediate context of oppression. In his discussion of the need he saw for continued secrecy even among escaped slaves, Douglass criticizes "the very public manner in which some of our western friends have conducted what they call the *underground railroad*" making it, in effect, "the *upper-ground* railroad" (1960, 136). In contrast, Douglass proposes what might be read as a principle for sensible closetedness as a response to systemic oppression: "Let us render the tyrant no aid; let us not hold the light by which he can trace the footprints of our flying brother" (137).

Warping Perspectives

A third effect that Douglass presents of the dehumanizing effects of slavery is that the very outlooks of both slaves and slaveholders were warped in peculiar ways. In chapter 5 of *Narrative*, Douglass contrasts the debasing treatment of being denied adequate bedding and decent food with his extreme pleasure at such seemingly everyday acts as receiving his first pair of trousers because it had been decided he would be sent to Baltimore to attend to the Aulds' son, Thomas: "The thought of owning a pair of trousers was great indeed!" (1960, 53). Another simple act of basic kindness that strikes Douglass as utterly remarkable is his initial reception by his new mistress, Sophia Auld: "And here I saw what I had never seen before; it was a white face beaming with the most kindly emotions; it was the face of my new mistress, Sophia Auld" (55). Douglass's description of his response to the most basic human courtesy of another human being's making direct eye contact with him and smiling at him illustrates how slavery had denied him the ability to deal with the most

---

6. For more on this, see chapter 11 especially.

basic kinds of human contact: "I was utterly astonished at her [his mistress's] goodness. I scarcely knew how to behave towards her. . . . She did not deem it impudent or unmannerly for a slave to look her in the face" (57).

Douglass is clear that this system of dehumanization also had negative effects on slaveholders themselves. Although these effects were not nearly as serious and debilitating as those inflicted upon slaves, Douglass deems it important to report how slavery was, in a more limited sense, dehumanizing to white people as well. His most telling example here is the change in Sophia Auld, whose initial kindness because of her inexperience with slaveholding is quickly rooted out by her husband's edicts about how Frederick should be treated. Douglass says,

> Slavery proved as injurious to her as it did to me. When I went there, she was a pious, warm and tender-hearted woman. There was no sorrow or suffering for which she had not a tear. She had bread for the hungry, clothes for the naked, and comfort for every mourner that came within her reach. Slavery soon proved its ability to divest her of these heavenly qualities. Under its influence, the tender heart became stone, and the lamblike disposition gave way to one of tiger-like fierceness. (1960, 63–64)

The dehumanization of both slaves and slaveholders is most dramatically told in Douglass's description of the rare instances of slave beatings he witnessed in Baltimore. He explains that because city slaveholders were more subject to public opinion than their counterparts in the country, slaves in Baltimore were generally better fed and clothed and not usually beaten. However, the exceptions to this rule were Henrietta and Mary, two slaves own by Mr. and Mrs. Thomas Hamilton. Douglass evokes sympathy for Mary: "The head, neck, and shoulders of Mary were literally cut to pieces. I have frequently felt her head, and found it nearly covered with festering sores, caused by the lash of her cruel mistress" (1960, 60). Although Douglass's eyewitness account of these beatings evokes no sympathy for the evil Mrs. Hamilton, it dramatically illustrates the extent to which some slaveholders were dehumanized themselves by their participation in slavery:

> Mrs. Hamilton used to sit in a large chair in the middle of the room, with a heavy cowskin always by her side, and scarce an hour passed during the day but was marked by the blood of one of these slaves. The girls seldom passed her without her saying "Take that, you *black gip*!" at the same time giving

them a blow with the cowskin over the head or shoulders, often drawing the blood. (61)

That such brutal behavior could occur more or less within public knowledge and spawned no attempts to censor Mrs. Hamilton's cruelty suggests that society itself was dehumanized. Douglass's accounts of the operation of slavery in his *Narrative* suggest that the prevailing laws and social practices sought to actively justify such inhuman behavior. Indeed, one of the most interesting observations about the operation of oppression that Douglass offers is that it often claimed justification on religious grounds. Douglass reserves his most vehement invective for those who used Christianity as a veil for evil or self-indulgent intent, calling the use of Christianity to justify slavery "the grossest of all libels" (1960, 155–56). He says,

> Never was there a clearer case of "stealing the livery of the court of heaven to serve the devil in." . . . We have men-stealers for ministers, women-whippers for missionaries, and cradle-plunderers for church members. The man who wields the blood-clotted cowskin during the week fills the pulpit on Sunday, and claims to be a minister of the meek and lowly Jesus. (156)

After his escape, Douglass illustrates the pervasiveness of this skewed value system when he is surprised to find that Northerners enjoy a higher standard of living that slaveholding Southerners:

> I saw few or no dilapidated houses, with poverty-stricken inmates; no half-naked children and barefooted women, such as I had been accustomed to see in Hillsborough, Easton, St. Michael's, and Baltimore. The people looked more able, stronger, healthier, and happier, than those of Maryland. I was for once made glad by the view of extreme wealth, without being saddened by seeing extreme poverty. But the most astonishing as well as the most interesting thing to me was the condition of the colored people, a great many of whom, like myself, had escaped thither as a refuge from the hunters of men. I found many, who had not been seven years out of their chains, living in finer homes, and evidently enjoying more of the comforts of life, than the average slaveholders of Maryland. (1960, 150)

Whether or not this description of the North as a kind of Nirvana is accurate, Douglass's use of it is significant because it illustrates the pervasive nature of the legal and social system that presumed that a degraded and degrading relationship between slaves and their white masters was necessary and natural and because it suggests the potential power that can be derived when one sees through the system of lies that supports systemic oppression.

To my knowledge, I bear no connection to the dehumanization practices Douglass describes; indeed, most of my ancestors were arriving in the United States from Germany at about the same time Douglass's family was being valued and divided. However, I cannot read these accounts without a profound sense of regret that the country I hold dear allowed such injustices, and this speaks to the continuing power of Douglass's rhetoric. To move beyond a vague sense of white guilt, though, requires me to do more than just regret the distant past, and part of my motivation for this project and this chapter is to understand that past better and to seek out what can be learned about rhetoric's role in creating social justice today. But I also feel compelled to respond in kind to Douglass's accounts to the extent that I am able. I feel his call to attend to the ongoing effects of race discrimination in American society, to raise my head from my laptop and look around my favorite trendy little Starbucks to see that we are all white here, except for one black man, a former NFL football player who hobbles in on knees that bear the literal scars his former profession. I am reminded that beyond writing checks to the local food bank and doing my best to help working-class students and students of color to figure out how to manage the discourse demands of dominant culture, I have done little to address class and race inequities in my city and my country.

SPEAKING BACK TO OPPRESSION

In addition to documenting the many forms and effects of the systemic oppression of racism and slavery, Douglass's *Narrative* and the final chapters of *My Bondage* can also be read as illustrating what it means to take voice in response to oppression. Much like Grimké's *Letters*, Douglass's *Narrative* and *My Bondage* illustrate how speaking and writing from a position of oppression are different activities in a number of important ways than doing so within the discourses of power. For example, Douglass reports amazement at the naiveté of white people who saw slaves' singing in the fields as a sign of contentment rather than as relief for the sorrows of their hearts (1960, 38), and this singing might be read as an instance of the oppressed creating resistive genres. Similarly Douglass's description of how he practiced writing in the unused margins of his young master's copybooks (71) can be seen as a literal instance of the oppressed writing in the spaces left by the privileged, and, as I have already noted, the need for the oppressed to tell partial stories because of the strictures of oppression is illustrated by the many details Douglass removed from the story of his escape to the North. Perhaps the most unexpected and perverse lesson Douglass learned about taking voice in response to oppression is that the more successful and articulate he became, the less likely it was that his audiences would believe that he was ever a slave or that his words could possibly be his own, which illustrates how, for Douglass, finding a voice to speak back to oppression required the ongoing negotiation of his identity.

What is critical here for my purposes is considering how Douglass's case illustrates the performative nature of identity by suggesting that the journey from disenfranchisement to voice is much more complicated than simply mastering the conventions of the discourses of power. Although gaining literacy provided Douglass with important tools for finding his voice, gaining and using those skills also transformed his identity in dramatic ways, and continuing to exercise those skills meant much more than code-switching between discourses or critiquing dominant culture. I contend that Douglass's literacy narratives must be read as complex stories of coming to voice that clearly involved ongoing negotiation of his identity, bringing the usual categories of difference into play in ways that illustrate the dangers of thinking of any axis of difference as a single, independent entity. In the discussion that follows, I review Douglass's account of his coming to voice in his *Narrative* and the final chapters of *My Bondage*, drawing out four themes that suggest in larger terms what it meant for him to speak back to oppression. I offer these observations not as definitive statements of what it means for any person who has experienced systemic oppression to find voice, but as indicative of the kinds of issues we must attend to if we hope to develop practices and pedagogies of rhetoric that do more than presume assimilation is the only possible response to the discourses of power.[7]

Coming to a New Understanding of Self

The first of the themes I draw out of Douglass's descriptions of his coming to voice is that this process seemed to depend on his coming to

---

7. I recognize, of course, that I am using Douglass's accounts of his experiences and insights for purposes different from those he intended and, further, that I do so from a position of racial privilege. For this reason, I ground these discussions as concretely as possible in Douglass's actual text, and I attempt to call out any aspects of this analysis in which I am aware of reading against Douglass's expressed perspective.

a new understanding of self. Douglass's case makes it clear that he was not simply joining a Discourse, in the sense that James Gee (1989) uses that term; rather he was participating in the abolitionist counterpublic that was, despite its overarching egalitarian intent, full of its own complexities. I begin with one of the most heartening moments in Douglass's accounts: his description of the mixture of surprise, joy, and trepidation with which he greeted his invitation to become a paid agent of the antislavery movement—to use his story "to publicly advocate its anti-slavery principles" after his first public speech at an antislavery convention held in Nantucket. He said, "Here opened for me a new life—a life for which I had had no preparation" (2003, 264). Although Douglass certainly had none of the formal schooling many of his white counterparts had for such public roles, I propose that Douglass's account of his coming to voice suggests he was prepared for a public role that challenged oppression in ways neither he nor his white abolitionist sponsors realized at the time of his first speech. Douglass reports that early in his abolitionist career he was called upon simply to tell his story, and his white handlers attempted to create a limited ethos for him in their presentation of him: "I was a 'graduate from the peculiar institution,' Mr. Collins used to say, when introducing me, '*with my diploma written on my back!*'" (2003, 264). My reading of Douglass's accounts of the experiences and insights that led him to this new role and new life teases out the ways in which his coming to voice should be seen as coming to a new understanding of self that begins in his childhood and extends throughout his long public career.

One of the most fascinating aspects of Douglass's story is his description of how he learned to read and write. After the brief beginning given him by his mistress, Douglass presents himself as a wily and inventive youth, bribing poor white boys with extra bread from the Auld house (1960, 65) or tricking them into teaching him to write letters of the alphabet he did not yet know (70). A less obvious aspect of Douglass's bootstraps story is how his literacy allows him to become culturally literate, to find names for the phenomena he had experienced, and to join ongoing discourses that helped him understand his own experiences in a larger context and ultimately helped him define a new identity for himself. This first step in Douglass's literacy journey is particularly important because his account of it illustrates his struggle to imagine a different role for himself in society and to free himself from the dominant cultural values that defined his desire for literacy and for freedom as transgressions.

One of the most important of these experiences occurred when Douglass was about twelve, when the "thought of being *a slave for life* began to bear heavily upon my heart" (1960, 66). Shortly thereafter, he obtained a copy of "The Columbian Orator," and it occurred to Douglass for the first time that arguments might end slavery and that someone like him might take part in those arguments. He says, "The slave was made to say some very smart as well as impressive things in reply to his master—things which had the desired though unexpected effect; for the conversation resulted in the voluntary emancipation of the slave on the part of the master" (66). In this case, a literary model provided Douglass with the means to conceive of a role completely absent in his immediate context—an awakening effect familiar to those of us who grew up with no positive local models of people able to openly claim the axis of difference that dominant culture has schooled us to find shameful in ourselves. Thus, one function of literacy for Douglass was giving him access to models for his own role in culture that extended beyond the very limited roles present in his immediate context.

Later, in that same chapter, Douglass describes how literacy helped him take a further step toward voice by both giving a name to his fondest desire—*abolition*—and helping him find meaning for that concept beyond the negative ways in which it was consistently used in his local context. Douglass reports that he first heard the term in conversation as the cause of all problems with slaves:

> If a slave ran away and succeeded in getting clear, or if a slave killed a master, set fire to a barn, or did any thing very wrong in the mind of a slaveholder, it was spoken of as the fruit of *abolition*. (1960, 68)

When Douglass obtained a city paper, the description of petitions supporting the abolition of slavery in the North suggested other, more positive meanings for the words *abolition* and *abolitionist*. Douglass says he "always drew near when that word was spoken, expecting to hear something of importance to myself and fellow-slaves. The light broke in upon me by degrees" (1960, 69). Certainly Douglass's descriptions in these instances illustrate the power of joining a Discourse, which Gee defines as "ways of being in the world; they are forms of life which integrate words, acts, values, beliefs, attitudes, and social identities as well as gestures, glances, body positions, and clothes" (1989, 6–7). However, the change in Douglass's understanding of his own identity and his relationship to dominant moral values suggests that a better description would be that he was joining a counterpublic because doing so involved conceiving of roles for himself and others like him that challenged their usual roles in dominant culture and required the explicit deconstruction of central dominant cultural values.

The transformative nature of Douglass's literacy journey can be seen even more clearly in his description of the effect of reading Sheridan's speeches on Catholic emancipation and denouncements of slavery in "The Columbian Orator." Douglass's account makes it clear that he was learning more than just rhetorical tools; rather, he says this literacy event "gave tongue to interesting thoughts of my own soul, which had frequently flashed through my mind, and died for want of utterance" (1960, 66). Further, he reveals that these insights extended to a new understanding of himself as a slave and to a reversal of the dominant cultural value of the moral superiority of slaveholders:

> The more I read, the more I was led to abhor and detest my enslavers. I could regard them in no other light than a band of successful robbers, who had left their homes, and gone to Africa, and stolen us from our homes, and in a strange land reduced us to slavery. I loathed them as being the meanest as well as the most wicked of men. (67)

Later, after his escape from slavery, Douglass also saw written texts, most notably Garrison's abolitionist newspaper, *The Liberator*, as an important means of learning about how to address the evils of slavery in the terms of the public debate. He says, "The paper became my meat and my drink. My soul was set all on fire," and "I had not long been a reader of the 'Liberator,' before I got a pretty correct idea of the principles, measures and spirit of the anti-slavery reform" (153).

Douglass was not so naïve as to paint this coming to a new understanding of self within a system of oppression as a wholly positive experience. Rather, he reveals that doing so fulfilled the prophecy of his master:

> As I read and contemplated the subject, behold! that very discontentment which Master Hugh had predicted would follow my learning to read had already come, to torment and sting my soul to unutterable anguish. As I writhed under it, I would at times feel that learning to read had been a curse rather than a blessing. (1960, 67)

It would be a mistake to suggest that Douglass (and the country) would have been better off if he had remained illiterate and unconnected to the abolitionist discourses of his day. However, the struggles Douglass faced in dealing with the immorality of the system responsible for his oppression must be recognized as an important complication of his Horatio Alger story.

Taken in this light, the interplay between Douglass's coming to a public voice and his journey to manhood takes on new significance. Describing events several years later, Douglass reveals that his "differences" with Master Thomas led to his master's decision to remove him from the city his master said "had had a very pernicious effect upon me" (1960, 86) and to send Douglass to do field work with notorious slave-breaker Edward Covey—a story in which Douglass twines together the themes of his own coming to manhood with contesting the supposed moral grounds for slavery. The challenge to dominant morality is clearly invoked in Douglass's description of Covey as "a professor of religion—a pious soul—a member and a class-leader in the Methodist church. All of this added weight to his reputation as a 'nigger-breaker'" (1960, 87–88).

After a lengthy discussion of his mistreatment by Covey, Douglass resolved to fight back, and he describes the actual physical conflict in great detail, explaining, "This battle with Mr. Covey was the turning-point in my career as a slave. It rekindled the few expiring embers of freedom, and revived within me a sense of my own manhood" (1960, 104). Douglass biographer William S. McFeely sees Douglass as exaggerating a bit in his description of a two-hour wrestling match with Covey, and he notes that Douglass's own description of the events suggests that he needed the tacit help of other slaves, Bill and Caroline, to achieve his resistance of Covey (see 1991, 47–48). Although the physical encounter may not be quite the epic man-on-man battle that Douglass bills it, the incident clearly marks an important change in Douglass's relationships with slavery and the people and social institutions that upheld it. Ironically, this physical resistance, based on a new understanding of the immorality of slavery and Covey himself, is an important step in Douglass's coming to voice.[8]

In short, I read Douglass's account of his process of coming to voice as challenging the value structure that, as a child, seemed natural to him, and as involving a change in his own value structure

---

8. It is significant to note here that this physical resistance to slavery is not the last time Douglass would be called upon to physically defend himself against those who sought to silence him; as he describes in *The Life and Times of Frederick Douglass* (1962), Douglass and his abolitionist colleagues Mr. Bradburn and Mr. White were attacked and forced to physically defend themselves during a meeting they held in Pendleton, Indiana (230).

that extended into his very identity. However, I should also note that Douglass's autobiographies describe other, more positive instances of what it meant for him to have a public voice, to join the public discourse about slavery. For example, after he and Anna escaped to New Bedford, Douglass attended several churches, and he began to discover there were communities that not only welcomed him as a member but also provided a context in which he could speak publicly. In this regard, McFeeley cites Bishop Christopher Rush of New Bedford's Zion Chapel giving Douglass "authority to act as an exhorter" (1991, 82), as well as noting that although Douglass eventually became "restless for something more than the respectability of black New Bedford," such churches were important in Douglass's development as a speaker because they "not only gave their members religious nourishment but also provided them with the opportunities to raise their confidence by talking together of both personal and public concerns—moral improvement, it was called" (83). Here, Douglass's experiences suggest that safe havens for those who have been brutalized by systemic oppression may be important contexts for continuing to develop a sense of identity that heals previous wounds, and for practicing rhetorical skills in a relatively safe context.

A final lesson about what it meant for Douglass to come to an understanding of himself that allowed him to take a public voice is that, despite varied kinds of preparation, the act of taking that voice for the first time was a traumatic experience for Douglass because it involved crossing a cultural threshold. Much like Angelina Grimké's description of her surprise that nothing untoward happened when she first spoke to an audience of men and women, Douglass faced his first public speech outside the comfortable black New Bedford community with some trepidation. His accounts of this first speech at the Nantucket antislavery convention differ somewhat in *Narrative* and *My Bondage*. His description in *Narrative* clearly indicates his discomfort on the occasion but also provides a brief and mostly positive assessment of his performance: "The truth was, I felt myself a slave, and the idea of speaking to white people weighed me down. I spoke but a few moments, when I felt a degree of freedom, and said what I desired with considerable ease" (1960, 153). In contrast, his more detailed description in *My Bondage* reveals more about the discomfort he felt in his first public address to white people:

My speech on this occasion is about the only one I ever made, of which I do not remember a single connected sentence. It was with the utmost difficulty that I could stand erect, or that I could command and articulate two words without hesitation and stammering. I trembled in every limb. I am not sure that my embarrassment was not the most effective part of my speech, if speech it could be called. (263–64)

This second description suggests that for the oppressed, taking public voice in venues that include those who are members of their oppressor class may be a momentous and daunting task, even when the speaker is likely to receive a positive hearing. Indeed, Douglass's description of his difficulty speaking and of the way his bodily presence was an important part of his message is strikingly similar to French feminist Hèléne Cixous's description of what it often means for women to take public voice for the first time:

Listen to a woman speak at a public gathering (if she hasn't painfully lost her wind). She doesn't "speak," she throws her trembling body forward; she lets go of herself, she flies; all of her passes into her voice, and it's with her body that she virtually supports the "logic" of her speech. Her flesh speaks true. (1976, 881)

Managing Varied Forms of Sponsorship

A second important theme I see in Douglass's description of the process by which he came to voice is the critical and, at times, problematic roles his sponsors played. Deborah Brandt defines literacy sponsors as "any agents, local or distant, concrete or abstract, who enable, support, teach, model, as well as recruit, regulate, suppress, or withhold literacy—and gain advantage by it in some way" (2001, 556). This definition suggests that although sponsors may be critical for obtaining literacy, or access to what Gee calls Discourses more generally, one cannot presume such sponsorship is always a wholly positive thing or that it is offered without ulterior motives. In Douglass's case, examining his literacy sponsors suggests that for the oppressed seeking to gain voice, sponsorship may come from unlikely sources and it may also come with strings attached, as it did for the Grimké sisters. As the following discussion illustrates, sponsorship of various sorts was critical for Douglass's development of his voice; however, sponsorship was also something he had to actively manage to get what he needed and to avoid having his voice limited by those who provided the necessary help.

As I have already noted, Douglass credits his mistress with providing him the initial inch that enabled him to take an ell, and he describes how he bribed and tricked white boys his own age into helping him gain literacy skills. Further, Douglass credits his master's adamant stance against Douglass's literacy learning as ultimately beneficial to Douglass because it made clear the value of learning to read and write:

> Whilst I was saddened by the thought of losing the aid of my kind mistress, I was gladdened by the invaluable instruction which, by merest accident, I had gained from my master. Though conscious of the difficulty of learning without a teacher, I set out with high hope, and a fixed purpose, at whatever cost of trouble, to learn how to read. (1960, 59)

Thus, in an unintended way, Hugh Auld serves as an unwilling sponsor of Douglass's development of a public voice by making clear to Douglass the importance of gaining the literacy skills he would later use to read newspapers and "The Columbian Orator" in order to join the larger discourse about slavery and ultimately redefine himself in relation to slavery.

In this sense, Douglass's story can rightly be read as showcasing the crucial power of literacy to give access to ideas and communities that allow for the kinds of personal growth that make resistance to oppression possible. However, as I have already indicated, it would be a mistake to read his literacy story in such simple and wholly positive terms. Even the sponsorship of Garrisonian abolitionists widely recognized as critical for Douglass's developing a public voice to oppose slavery and racial discrimination ultimately proved problematic as well. Indeed, Douglass's description of John A. Collins's initial invitation for Douglass to become a paid antiabolitionist agent indicates that from the outset the abolitionists understood Douglass's usefulness in ways Douglass himself could not conceive at the time:

> I was reluctant to take the proffered position. I had not been quite three years from slavery—was honestly distrustful of my ability—wished to be excused; publicity exposed me to discovery and arrest by my master; and other objections came up, but Mr. Collins was not to be put off, and I finally consented to go out for three months, for I supposed that I should have got to the end of my story and my usefulness, in that length of time. (2003, 264)

Douglass reports quickly learning two lessons about how he was being used in this larger public role. First, he learned about the persistence of oppression; he describes how his initial idealism about being treated as a person with an important message did not translate into full acceptance by white society:

> For a time I was made to forget that my skin was dark and my hair crisped. For a time I regretted that I could not have shared the hardships and dangers endured by the earlier workers for the slave's release. I soon, however, found that my enthusiasm had been extravagant; that hardships and dangers were not yet passed; and that the life now before me, had shadows as well as sunbeams. (2003, 265)

Further, much like the Grimké sisters, Douglass reveals that he came to understand that his freak value was being exploited, to some extent, by his handlers. His abolitionist sponsors were not only depending on the prejudices of white Americans to increase interest in a slave who was able to tell his own story effectively; they deliberately played up this prejudice to make Douglass seem an interesting novelty:

> Much interest was awakened—large meetings assembled. Many came, no doubt, from curiosity to hear what a negro could say in his own cause. I was generally introduced as a "*chattel*"—a "*thing*"—a piece of southern "*property*"—the chairman assuring the audience that *it* could speak. Fugitive slaves, at that time, were not so plentiful as now; and as a fugitive slave lecturer, I had the advantage of being a "*brand new fact*"—the first one out. (2003, 265)

Certainly, white abolitionists deserve much credit for their direct advocacy against one of our nation's most despicable social, cultural, and economic evils. In addition, their work was important for a young Douglass in coming to see slavery in a different moral light, and their initial sponsorship of him as a speaker was critical in helping Douglass come to see that he could have a larger public role. However, as I indicated earlier, Douglass quickly began to chafe at their attempts to limit his role:

> During the first three or four months, my speeches were almost exclusively made up of narrations of my own personal experiences as a slave. "Let us have the facts," said the people. So also said Friend George Foster, who always wished to pin me down to my simple narrative. "Give the facts," said Collins, "we will take care of the philosophy." (2003, 266)

Even his "then revered friend, William Lloyd Garrison" sought to limit Douglass's role to simply telling his story, but Douglass "was growing, and needed room." Douglass acknowledges that these friends "were actuated by the best of motives, and were not altogether wrong in their advice" but that he still found he must speak "just the word that seemed to *me* the word to be spoken *by* me" (2003, 266). Fortunately, Douglass's resistance to his white handlers' attempts to limit his role and his subsequent articulate performances occasioned the need for his first autobiography to answer the claims that because of his eloquence he could never have been a slave.

In a very real sense, then, white abolitionists also served as sponsors for this first published account of his coming-to-voice story, although they did so out of the necessity of providing a wider public testimony to his slave origins and to further feed the novelty of his chattel-come-advocate status. In *My Bondage*, Douglass reveals that he was aware of the role the oppression of his early life played in making him a person of interest: "A man is sometimes made great, by the greatness of the abuse a portion of mankind may think proper to heap upon him" (2003, 280–81). However, as McFeely notes, Douglass was troubled by white abolitionists' attempts to dehumanize him by making him a spectacle of sorts:

> He knew he was a glorious specimen, but not of fallen humanity, and he was tired of all the conjecture about his not having truly been a slave, and not being able to write his own speeches. He could damned well read and write; he had been a slave, but slavery had not left him a beast to be displayed; he was not a black dummy manipulated by a white ventriloquist. (1991, 113)

As I have already mentioned, Douglass reports gaining a different and more wholly supportive brand of sponsorship from the friends and fans he made during his twenty-one-month tour of Great Britain, which was occasioned by the possibility that the details revealed in his *Narrative*, coupled with his publicly announced speaking engagements, would make recapture by his slaveholding masters possible. Of course the most direct evidence of this sponsorship were his manumission—Mrs. Henry Richardson raised the 150 pounds sterling necessary to buy Douglass's freedom from his master (2003, 276)—and the 2,500 dollars in seed money provided for him to buy a printing press and printing supplies (286). However, McFeeley argues that Douglass's account of his experiences in the British Isles also suggests that his popularity and reception by moneyed people helped develop his sense of independence :

> In Britain, Douglass had achieved an independence that he would never be willing to yield. In Cork with the Jenningses, in the rest of Ireland, and in Scotland and England as well, he had come to know himself. He gained

enormous self-confidence from being treated with public respect. He had been paid full attention. (1991, 145)

Apparently Garrison and his supporters had been worried about just such an effect. Martin reports that Douglass's speaking tour in Great Britain "occasioned another conflict illustrating the inability of Garrisonians to tolerate a self-styled Douglass." Richard G. Webb was asked to keep an eye on Douglass so he wouldn't be subverted to some of the beliefs of the "London committee"; Douglass found this patronizing and resisted it (1984, 29).

Given the ongoing paternalistic attempts of the Garrisonians to control Douglass, Douglass's account of his surprise at their resistance to his plans to launch his own newspaper upon his return from Great Britain must be read as a bit disingenuous:

> Intimation had reached my friends in Boston of what I intended to do, before my arrival, and I was prepared to find them favorably disposed toward my much cherished enterprise. In this I was mistaken. I found them very earnestly opposed to the idea of my starting a paper, and for several reasons. (2003, 289–90)

However, his recounting of the reasons for their opposition makes their self-interest in the matter clear: "First, the paper was not needed; secondly it would interfere with my usefulness as a lecturer; thirdly, I was better fitted to speak than to write; fourthly, the paper could not succeed" (2003, 290).

Reflecting on these first concrete steps away from his initial Garrisonian sponsors and toward independence, Douglass admits that his newspaper ambition might have been a bit adolescent as he had only been nine years out of slavery, but he greatly appreciated the encouragement of his British friends and chafed at the kinds of derogatory and paternalistic claims made against his abilities:

> My American friends looked at me with astonishment! "A wood-sawyer" offering himself to the public as an editor! A slave, brought up in the very depths of ignorance, assuming to instruct the highly civilized people of the north in the principles of liberty, justice, and humanity! The thing looked absurd. Nevertheless I persevered. (2003, 290)

The identity issues here are unmistakable in the use of class and race to denigrate Douglass and try to keep him in his place.

Douglass also reveals that his fledging independent status as a publisher led him to reject some tenets of Garrisonian abolitionism, particularly as it related to Garrison's position that abolition work should eschew political action because the government that allowed slavery was by definition immoral:

> My new circumstances compelled me to re-think the whole subject, and to study, with some care, not only the just and proper rules of legal interpretation, but the origin, design, nature, rights, powers, and duties of civil government, and also the relations which human beings sustain to it. (2003, 292–93)

Not surprisingly, Douglass's former Garrisonian allies were not pleased with his repudiation of one of the main tenets that distinguished Garrison's version of abolitionism from other versions. What is shocking, though, is the racism inherent in their assessment of reasons for Douglass's defection. Martin explains:

> As with Douglass's shift to political abolitionism, any shift in his thought away from Garrisonian dogma was not, from their perspective, the result of his own reflection, but rather the result of the influence of some white colleague, such as Smith or Griffiths. They implied that he was their intellectual inferior, and that he primarily absorbed his thoughts from them and other whites. (1984, 42)

Douglass's account of the operation of sponsorship in his coming to voice suggests that joining abolitionist discourse was a complicated business in which, ironically, he continued to face racism and classism from some of the most liberal white people of his day. From the standpoint of alternative rhetoric as I have defined the term, Douglass's white abolitionist sponsors may be read as not having sufficiently interrogated their own racial privilege so they could be aware of how the dehumanizing effects of their of initial use of Douglass, and their later direct opposition of him, were based in a more subtle form of racism than the more blatant forms they worked so hard to challenge.

One important parallel for current rhetoric and composition is that we must carefully consider our own roles as sponsors for literacy, both in terms of what limits we set for student writers in our enforcement of our curricula and in the more general assumptions that we bring about the very cultural practices and values that comprise the content of the academy. We need to see ourselves as just one set of literacy sponsors that our students will use for their purposes, and we need to consider carefully the ways in which we may seek to limit the development of our students' voices due to our own blindness or self-interest. As I write these last few sentences, I am aware that my analysis here calls on me to reevaluate my own previous understanding of Garrison, to acknowledge that I can no longer see him only as a wholly laudatory crusader on behalf of slaves who did more than any other white American to bring an end to slavery, and that I must also acknowledge that my own whiteness and its attendant privilege makes me vulnerable to the same blindness to the subtle operations of racism. However, I also worry a bit that my discussion has not substantively examined the ways in which Garrison must have engaged in some version of alternative rhetoric himself, and, by extension, that my focus on writings of those who were compelled to speak from the margins does not adequately attend to how the rhetoric of those in positions of privilege who work to unseat inequities in American society may also contribute to our understanding of alternative rhetoric. Yet, my own experiences of marginalization because of my homosexuality prompt me to focus on the experiences and perspectives of the marginalized rather than those of the privileged.

Managing Representative Status

A third important theme that emerges in Douglass's accounts of how he comes to voice is the difficulty he faced in managing his representative status in a number of ways: the initial risk of making his slave status public, the need to actively engage in acts of disidentification, the possibilities and problems of using celebrity in the service of social justice, and finally the power of social fashion to sweep away social prejudice. Like many members of minoritized groups who gain a public role, Douglass was keenly aware that he served as a role model and that his positions and behaviors were subject to great scrutiny, and that scrutiny put him at some risk. As I have already discussed, Douglass's status as an escaped slave able to articulate his own story made him not simply a novelty but also a spokesperson for the personhood of African Americans. McFeely explains that this public role was thrust upon Douglass from that first speech in Nantucket, and he argues that Douglass understood and embraced this role from the beginning of his public career:

> This was a lot of christological weight for a young man from Talbot County to carry, but more than willingly, Douglass shouldered it. . . . For the whole of

his life, Douglass would have to appear as a man more admirable than other men. (1991, 91)

The most obvious way Douglass's representative status became an issue not only for him but also for the abolitionist cause was the challenge that no one who was so articulate could ever have been a slave. As I have already noted, these claims occasioned the writing of Douglass's *Narrative*, and Douglass's comments about publishing the details of his background illustrate that the power disparities in a system of oppression like slavery can put a public advocate such as Douglass at real risk:

> In a little less than four years, therefore, after becoming a public lecturer, I was induced to write out the leading facts connected with my experience in slavery, giving names of persons, places, and dates—thus, putting it in the power of any who doubted, to ascertain the truth or falsehood of my story of being a fugitive slave. This statement soon became known in Maryland, and I had reason to believe that an effort would be made to recapture me. (2003, 267)

Because of this risk, Douglass took the precaution of not revealing his former name, his master's name, or the state or county from which he came. However, Douglass's description of what it meant for him to take up publicly the role of an escaped slave also illustrates that doing so not only exposed him to the dangers of recapture but also required him to actively disidentify with social prejudice in dominant culture:

> Up to that time, a colored man was deemed a fool who confessed himself a runaway slave, not only because of the danger to which he exposed himself of being retaken, but because it was a confession of a very *low* origin! Some of my colored friends in New Bedford thought very badly of my wisdom for thus exposing and degrading myself. (265–66)

Ironically, escaping his slave status through manumission also brought another kind of critique; Douglass explains:

> Some uncompromising anti-slavery friends in this country failed to see the wisdom of this arrangement, and were not pleased that I consented to it, even by my silence. They thought it a violation of anti-slavery principles—conceding a right of property in man—and a wasteful expenditure of money. (277).

Douglass does not provide details about who exactly raised these objections. Given the pending rift with the Garrisonians, it may be that this objection was raised by white abolitionists seeking to control or discredit Douglass. If this is the case, then unexamined white privilege may have been operating: how could white abolitionists truly understand what it meant for Douglass to face a return to slavery? If raised by other escaped slaves, then the critique might be seen as more palatable. However, it should be noted that in his role as the most visible escaped slave of his day, Douglass put himself at great risk of recapture in the service of abolition, and thus, few, if any people were in the position to understand what it would have meant for Douglass to refuse the security his manumission represented. No matter from what quarter these critiques originated, they forced Douglass to articulate a defense which highlights Douglass's ability to engage in a more subtle form of disidentification in which he shifts the moral grounds away from an attack on the purchase of his freedom and back to the larger issue of the underlying inequities and evils of slavery itself:

> On the other hand, viewing it simply in the light of a ransom, or as money extorted by a robber, and my liberty of more value than one hundred and fifty pounds sterling, I could not see either a violation of the laws of morality, or those of economy, in the transaction. (277)

Another lesson about the complexities of being a public representative of an oppressed class can be drawn from Douglass's accounts of his attempts to use his celebrity to challenge continuing forms of racism. Douglass often sought to challenge Jim Crow laws and other institutionalized discriminatory practices against blacks. For example, in the final pages of *My Bondage*, Douglass tells engaging stories of his struggles to sit in the first-class carriage of trains, including the dramatic story of how he clung to his seat so tightly that he tore it out as he was forcibly removed from the first-class carriage (2003, 298). On his passage to Great Britain, he was denied first-class passage, and on the return voyage he was initially refused the right to buy a first-class ticket. However, playing on the considerable notoriety that his British tour had afforded him, Douglass challenged this instance of discrimination in the British press and received not only a public apology from the owner of the steamship line but also a pledge against discrimination on his line in the future (287–88). Douglass's discussion of the lesson to be drawn from such experiences emphasizes the personal costs involved and the uncertainty of success:

It is not very pleasant to be made the subject of such insults; but if all such necessarily resulted as this one did, I should be very happy to bear, patiently, many more than I have borne of the same sort. Albeit, the lash of proscription, to a man accustomed to equal social position, even for a time, as I was, has a sting for the soul hardly less severe than that which bites the flesh and draws the blood from the back of the plantation slave. (288)

Although the ill treatment Douglass describes here has its roots in racism, it is complicated with a class issue. Indeed, Douglass's description suggests that a part of his outrage was fueled by a sense that his social position had been challenged. It is doubtful that plantation slaves who were suffering the whip regularly would have agreed that the "sting" to Douglass's soul in this instance was "hardly less severe" than the privations and physical abuse they too often suffered. However, it would be a mistake to write off this less-severe form of discrimination simply because it is less caustic than the overseer's whip.

Sorting out the interplay between race and class here is important, first because it illustrates the challenges of identifying the continuing effects of discrimination even after major battles have been won, in this case the end of slavery and the fifteenth amendment. As we now know, even the civil rights legislation that overturned the Jim Crow laws that attempted to bar Douglass from first-class railway coaches has not erased racism and its effects upon our society, but the important steps our society has taken to address race and other discriminatory issues makes expressing the kind of outrage Douglass felt a more rhetorically complicated task. For example, several years ago, the faculty union at my university forced the university administration to add sexual orientation to the university's nondiscrimination policy. However, I and many of my LGBT colleagues feel a continued sense of outrage that the university has not yet offered domestic partner benefits, in part because it claims not be able to afford them. Like Douglass, I feel a sense of class mistreatment as queer professors at other universities, and the queer professionals who work for most of the companies represented on our university's board of governors, receive domestic partner benefits as a matter of course. However, since I have been appointed chair of my department, I have become more acutely aware of how many adjunct professors teach in my department for pitiful salaries and no benefits at all, and the personal sense of rage I feel about domestic partner benefits feels out of proportion to the much larger issue of the two-tiered class system operating in my own department. Further, my sense of outrage at my class mistreatment because of my sexual identity feels a bit too akin to the many examples of outrage expressed by straight, white, relatively economically privileged men I encounter regularly in my workplace: white male honors students who are furious that there are minority scholarships for which they cannot apply and full professors railing that budget cuts require a reduction of their travel funding or that three students must be added to their classes normally capped at fifteen. Of course I would like to see my university make progress on both of these issues, but in my day-to-day work, for which I have limited time and energy I sometimes have to choose on which cause I will spend my time and energy on. Sorting out the complexities of the underlying issues can be a tricky business as my advocacy for the underpaid adjuncts in my department may conflict with my advocacy for fair treatment of LGBT people on campus, particularly given that in recent years our university has faced round after round of cuts in state funding.

Douglass's description of his ill treatment in railway carriages also hints at the importance of enclaves for marginalized people. That is, the relative privilege of escaping the degrading effects of racial prejudice he experienced routinely in the United States also illustrates the importance of enjoying respite from prejudice. Indeed, Douglass writes of his open reception in all places during his tour of Great Britain and contrasts this with the repeated "We don't allow niggers in here!" he routinely faced in similar settings in the United States (1960, 273). He exclaims, "Thank heaven for the respite I now enjoy!" (274). As a gay man, I feel a similar sense of relief from the nearly omnipresent press of heteronormativity when I sit in a gay bar and see same-sex couples free to touch each other in a public setting without the fear of disapproving stares or physical attacks that might occur in other settings, and I also find myself taking vacations to urban centers where queer people have created enclaves in which same-sex desire can be expressed publicly without fear of reprisal. Although there is much to be gained from the substantive negotiation of difference in education, the underlying melting-pot metaphor is problematic if it reduces to such things as cultural whiteness and heternormativity. In rhetorical terms, the lesson here is that while it is important to continually engage the discourses of power and discrimination, working to tease out the ever-more-subtle forms discrimination can take as well as the complex intersections of difference issues, it is also important for those in marginalized groups to escape to settings and to maintain discourses in which the struggle against oppression need not be the dominant issue. The lesson here is that one cannot be a public representative for difference all the time and in every context of one's life.

Yet another important lesson Douglass provides about the challenges of serving as a representative who consistently challenged oppression is the irony of the fact that the success or failure of his acts seemed to depend much more on shifts in the fashion of beliefs and practices than it did on his own actions. For example, after Douglass was no longer forcibly removed from first-class train carriages, he was often met by a more subtle form of racism in which white passengers refused to sit next to him, even when the seat next to him was the only open seat. He describes his surprise at the sudden change in this seemingly intractable prejudice of white fellow travelers after two powerful white men—Governor George N. Briggs and Colonel John Henry Clifford (later governor of Massachusetts)—sat with him on trains and treated him with respect. These stories lead Douglass to conclude that part of the underlying prejudice was based on pride and fashion: "With such facts as these before me—and I have many of them—I am inclined to think that pride and fashion have much to do with the treatment commonly extended to colored people in the United States" (2003, 298).

Douglass's descriptions of what it meant for him to publicly challenge racial oppression in its many forms illustrates the difficulties and uncertain effects of serving as a public representative of a disenfranchised minority. It is significant, then, that Douglass concludes *My Bondage* with a statement committing himself to continuing to use his celebrity in that service:

> Believing that one of the best means of emancipating the slaves of the south is to improve and elevate the character of the free colored people of the north I shall labor in the future, as I have labored in the past, to promote the moral, social, religious, and intellectual elevation of the free colored people; never forgetting my own humble origin, nor refusing, while Heaven lends me ability, to use my voice, my pen, or my vote, to advocate the great and primary work of the universal and unconditional emancipation of my entire race. (2003, 298)

Negotiating the Complexities of Agency

The final theme I draw out of Douglass's descriptions of what it meant for him to come to a public voice explores the complications of negotiating agency. As I argued in chapter one, engaging in alternative rhetoric requires attention to the intersections of one's identity features rather than just arguing from within a single binary relationship of power. As I have already noted, even Douglass's attempts to speak simply as an escaped slave became quickly complicated when his eloquence was read through race and class beliefs that led many to conclude that he could never have been a slave. As I have already noted, race and class issues surfaced when Douglass's former Garrisonian colleagues disparaged the plan for a former slave and wood sawyer to become the publisher of a newspaper. For Douglass, the intersection of identity issues was called into even more direct relief in two other important aspects of his public role: his uneasy alliance with women's suffrage advocates and critiques of his assimilationist stance on race from other African American leaders.

Douglass saw his support of woman's rights as his most selfless work (Martin 1984, 147–48), and Foner reports that during the 1850s, few women's rights conventions were held in which "Douglass was not a featured speaker and whose proceedings were not fully reported in his paper" (1976, 16). Indeed, it is widely noted that at the Seneca Falls Convention for woman's rights, Douglass seconded Elizabeth Cady Stanton's controversial resolution to include woman's suffrage in the convention's official positions, and his support of the measure was critical in its passage because many of the women's rights advocates present thought it too radical a step to propose (Foner 1976, 14). However, the tension between Douglass and women's rights leaders over support for the fifteenth amendment, which would enfranchise black men but not women, made this at times an "uneasy alliance" (Martin 1984, 164). Indeed, Douglass made the sexist argument that white women should be willing to support black male suffrage before women's suffrage because white women were, to some extent, represented through their husbands or other male relatives, and some of the leaders of the women's movement made the racist arguments that white women were, as a group, better educated than black men and thus deserved the vote first. Douglass was not shy about challenging this racism publicly and caustically. For example, McFeely reports that in his last major public speech, Douglass chastised Frances Willard for statements in which she pitied Southerners because they had to deal with the colored race, who, she said, multiplied like the locusts of Egypt and made things unsafe: "[W]ith his lethal sarcasm in full use, Douglass turned to "the sweet voice of Northern women, of Southern principles . . . the good Miss Frances Willard, of the W.C.T.U.'" (1991, 378). Douglass was also disappointed that leading woman's suffrage advocates such as Stanton never apologized for their racist comments; however, to be fair, there is no evidence that he publicly acknowledged the paternalism of his own arguments. Despite this unresolved tension, it is notable that on the day President Ulysses S. Grant announced the passage of the fifteenth Amendment, Douglass immediately called for a new campaign to enfranchise women, and he continued to work for women's suffrage (Foner 1976, 37).

Despite Douglass's considerable importance in challenging race and, to a lesser degree, gender inequities in American society, it would be an oversimplification to read him as unerringly progressive in all his beliefs. Indeed, Douglass is probably best read as an assimilationist whose own discomfort with working-class blacks led him to see limited value in African American culture (McFeely 1991, 315–6; Moses 1991, 78). His identification with dominant culture as the path to success, and his distance from advocates for the value of African American culture in his own day, are probably best read as due, in part, to his own considerable abilities to challenge dominant culture using its own discourse conventions, his unpopular second marriage to a white woman (Moses 1991, 78), and his mixed racial background. Martin sees Douglass's mulatto status as an important part of the reason for Douglass's placing "the politics of humanity above the politics of race, the hierarchical distinction was often implicit and at times confusing" (1984, 95). For the purposes of activism, Douglass was often forced to identity as a black man or Negro and was resented when he tried to engage his white heritage, most notably when he married a white women (98–99).

BEYOND CODE-SWITCHING: A HARD LESSON FOR ALTERNATIVE RHETORIC

Although neither Frederick Douglass nor Sarah Grimké explicitly attempted to write rhetorical theory, their practice of rhetoric makes important contributions to rhetorical theory by demonstrating what is involved in finding voice to challenge systemic oppression. Indeed, as I have illustrated in this chapter, Douglass—because of the range of his experiences speaking back to oppression—serves as a unique case for understanding how oppression can work in directly discriminatory ways and in more subtle ways, often masked by egalitarian intent. Also, Douglass's case is useful for exploring the many things that gaining a voice in response to systemic oppression may mean because it begins with the struggle to gain basic literacy and ends with the challenges of managing representative status as a national and international leader. As I discuss in more detail in chapter six, I see one of the primary benefits of Douglass's case as calling for an understanding of rhetoric that explicitly attends to its effects on identity and for an understanding of pedagogy that offers students more than code-switching and tools for the deconstruction of culture.

To conclude this chapter, I turn to the hard lesson Douglass and Grimké offer the theory, practice, and pedagogy of alternative rhetoric: as a field, we have underestimated the costs and complexity of challenging the discourses of power, largely because we have not fully understood the many ways dominant culture dehumanizes those it oppresses and because we have not fully appreciated all that it means for the oppressed to take voice in response to this dehumanization. Douglass's case is particularly useful in this regard because it sketches these issues in dramatic fashion: detailing how systemic oppression attempts to deny a sense of self to those it oppresses, undermining the possibility of agency by imposing voicelessness in the denial of basic literacy, limiting legal rights, and fostering a warped outlook for both the oppressed and their oppressors. Further, Douglass's journey to voice illustrates that speaking back to oppression is a different act than we have imagined in our rhetorical theory and that the means we have envisioned for doing so in our pedagogy—code-switching, cultural critique, and embodied writing—although useful in some situations, cannot be seen as ends in themselves. Indeed, Douglass's case illustrates that speaking from a position of oppression is fundamentally different than speaking from a position of privilege because speaking back to a culture requires more than just joining a new Discourse, in Gee's terms; rather, it likely means developing a new understanding of self based on the redefinition of the fundamental values of society responsible for the marginalization. Douglass's case suggests that speaking back to systemic oppression means that critical concepts will likely need to be redefined against dominant cultural values, new roles for the oppressed must be envisioned, relatively safe places for training and growth may be necessary, and despite all such efforts, first attempts to speak/write from oppression will likely still be traumatic. Further, Douglass's case highlights the necessary but problematic nature of sponsorship, the challenges of managing representative status, and the likelihood of conflicts among those advocating for social justice based on the competing perspectives and needs of those who are marginalized by differing axes of oppression. There are, of course, many more interesting questions for the theory, practice, and pedagogy of alternative rhetoric; for example, to what extent should those writing from positions of oppression exploit their freak value and what is our responsibility if we encourage our students to do so? To explore how the issues raised in Douglass's case apply in our current disciplinary practice, I conclude this chapter with an example from our disciplinary discourse.

The scene is the 2009 annual business meeting at the Conference on College Composition and Communication in San Francisco. I have dragged myself out of bed early on this Saturday morning because my friends from the CCCC Queer Caucus are bringing several sense of the house motions from the floor. The first two ask for CCCC to take a position that supports the civil and professional rights of lesbian, gay, bisexual, transgendered, and transsexual people, and to establish a task force to address queer issues in the organization and the profession).[9] These two resolutions pass unanimously. The third, quoted below, asks that the executive committee reexamine CCCC's Scholars for the Dream Program that provides financial support for first-time minority members of the organization to present at the annual conference:

> To ensure that CCCC actions parallel its policies on diversity, the CCCC Executive Committee should re-examine the Scholars for the Dream policies to include LGBTQ people as an under-represented class of individuals within our organization (e.g., LGBTQ people, first-generation academics, people with disabilities).

This resolution was the culmination of rumblings in the Queer Caucus for several years about the paucity of sessions at the conference attending to issues of sexual identity and the executive committee's lack of action to try and correct this problem.

The room is tense now. An African American woman who is a CCCC officer comes down from the dais to speak from one of the microphones provided for the regular members to address those assembled. Her concerns are that she believes the resolution pits one diversity group against another and that the resources necessary to increase representation of one minority group should not come at the expense of another. As she

---

9. For more on this, see http://www.ncte.org/cccc/resolutions/2009.

returns to the platform, an Asian American man whose work I have read eagerly for help in understanding a set of difference issues I have not experienced stands to second the concerns raised by the officer. The resolution passes, but a number of hands, including those of the officer and the Asian American scholar, are raised in clear protest. A fourth resolution calls for CCCC to provide more and better quality childcare during the annual conferences and is supported by a number of parents, mostly mothers, who testify at some length about how the organization has made them feel unwelcome by failing to attend to their needs. This resolution passes without dissenting votes.

In the break after the resolutions pass, the queers caucus angrily:

"I can't believe she came down from the platform to say that!"

"All we asked was for them to 'reexamine' the program."

"The Scholars for the Dream Program says it's about diversity. If they mean only 'racial diversity,' then they should say so."

"It's typical: the resolutions that don't cost CCCC anything pass unanimously, while the one that might require some to give up something is controversial."

I listen and then draw one of my friends aside; he is one of our leading queer composition scholars. I say, "How does she [the officer] make that statement without at least saying 'I know LGBTQ and disabled CCCC members face ongoing problems, and it is important for our organization to address them.' I am so tempted to take her aside and tell her that I voted for her and that I expect better leadership on diversity issues."

It is a real question for me; I can't fathom how anyone who has experienced discrimination could take such a position without some gesture toward others who have been discriminated against, and how anyone elected to a position of leadership in an organization devoted to the teaching of rhetoric could fail to look out at the queer people in room and choose not to even pause to acknowledge that a significant part of her audience has a legitimate concern.

There is pain and anger in my friend's face as he responds to my question: "It's prejudice; they don't really want us here." His response stuns me; my first instinct is to respond, "No, not here; she, he, they just felt surprised and attacked," but the words die before I can form them because his interpretation—even if it is posed in the heat of anger and disappointment—seems to fit the facts better than mine: until that day, the organization had not taken a stand on LGBTQ issues; concerns raised by the Queer Caucus about the lack of attention to LGBTQ issues in the program were heard politely but no action was taken, and an elected leader in the organization refused to even acknowledge the substance of the concerns when they were brought to her attention. We deserve better from the leadership of our professional organizations.

I raise this example to illustrate that the kinds of diversity tensions that Douglass experienced between those primarily affected by different axes of discrimination still exist. And my larger point is that I think we have underestimated the difficulty of rooting out prejudice and injustice, even within the supposedly liberal and egalitarian confines of the professional organizations we control. In the end, I think my friend overstated the case: I want to believe no one at that annual meeting wanted to make queer people go away; rather, I think they simply don't care if we are present or not. Further, the statements by the officer and the Asian American scholar suggest a desire to hang on to a tangible benefit that helps to offset the systemic oppression people of color have struggled against in our society and our discipline. With some effort, I can understand how the two scholars of color could feel attacked by the resolution to reconsider the Scholars for the Dream Program. However, I am also profoundly disappointed that their comments gave no hints that they needed to understand the experiences of another marginalized group, and that they spoke against even the possibility of the redistribution of resources based on such an understanding. In the end, I suppose I was naïve to expect there would be a substantive discussion of the complexities of the differences between race and sexual identity discrimination in such a setting, but a token acknowledgment of the struggles faced by others does not seem too much to ask.

Interchapter

PICKLES

The surgeon appears at the glass door that separates the waiting room from the operating suite, clad in dark blue-green scrubs, a surgical mask untied and hanging below his chin, and a loose puffy paper hat gathered by a thin elastic band that reminds me of my mother's shower cap clinging absurdly to his mostly bald head. We stand as a group, moving toward him, Dad in the lead. The doctor opens the door and stands half in and half out, one hand holding the door three-quarters open and one hand resting on the door jamb, his head and torso in the waiting room with us but his hips and legs holding back, ready to pull the rest of him back into the safety of the operating suite. "We were able to remove the main tumor," he begins without greeting or preamble, "but Betty's abdomen was seeded with small tumors." I lose focus; this was not the news I expected; I hear the words but can't understand them. " . . . inoperable . . . without treatment she might live a year . . . but you knew this, didn't you?"

"Yes." My Dad says *yes* in response, and I stand there amazed; my linguistics training notes that the surgeon used the tag question "Didn't you?" to encourage Dad to agree that he knew the news would be bad, and, at first, I assume Dad is just agreeing to be polite; how could Dad have known this when I didn't?

"After she's recovered from the surgery, we'll talk about treatment options . . . chemotherapy . . . radiation . . . she's in recovery now . . . see her in her room in a few hours."

The surgeon is gone, and I look into Dad's eyes and I know he did know, even though I did not. As a minister, he had sat with too many families in waiting rooms not to know that a recurrence of cancer within two years is never good. The family sits and hopes the man in blue-green scrubs will stride into the room smiling and announce "We got it all," but that is not what happens and so their pastor needs to be there, to comfort them, to pray with them. Dad moves into minister mode, shepherding us down to the hospital chapel, where we kneel on the carpeted floor, arms and bodies resting against the simple wooden altar rail. Dad prays in his Sunday morning voice, "Our Father . . . thy will . . . thy love . . . we trust ourselves to thee . . . we ask for thy healing hand for Betty" and I weep for the first time in my life, sobs shaking my shoulders, wiping my dripping nose on my sleeve because it had not occurred to me that I would need Kleenex or a handkerchief that day.

Mom lived more than five years after that second surgery—through chemotherapy, a third abdominal surgery, and radiation. There was time for me to stand at the kitchen counter with her, our hands coated in flour as she taught me to make her flaky pie crust. There was time for her to see my sister get married and for her to meet the woman my brother would eventually marry. Time to watch her slide away little by little, to get ready for the night when she took her last breath and Dad prayed again, "Dear God, thank you for this life." But it was the trauma of the second cancer surgery that changed me in some chemical way; the tears I wept that day altered me emotionally, made me susceptible to tear-jerking movie scenes in ways I had never been before, made me face the possibility of real loss for the first time and created an emotional depth that became the basis for writing I was compelled to do.

Five years later I sit in a small classroom at Iowa State University with the six new teaching assistants I am guiding through their first semester of teaching. It is September, so the windows are open to catch what breeze can be caught. I open my backpack and plunk down a jar of the pickles I made a few months ago, using the recipe passed on to me by my mother and my grandmother. My stated purpose for the class session is to show my new TAs a little description activity—you bring in a provocative object, have the students examine and write descriptions of it and then write about anything it evokes. "It's a good filler exercise for a day when you don't have much planned, and students sometimes find interesting things to write about." Following good National Writing Project protocol, I write with my students:

Murky green brine.

Shiny new brass ring (a sign of a novice canner).

Ragged-edged chunks of pickled cucumber with somewhat whiter meat and split centers.

This jar of pickles connects me with my Grandma Rehnke. When I was growing up, Grandma Rehnke was more of an event to me than a person. Every summer we piled into the family station wagon for a 1200-mile trip from Homer City, PA, to Milbank, SD. At the last stop of that all-night and all-day drive, I'd plot to get a window seat on the passenger side so that when we pulled into Grandma's driveway I would be the first to burst into her house and feel the soft warm folds of flesh on Grandma's arms as I hugged her as only an 8-year old child can.

For two weeks every summer, Grandma was sweet rolls and pickles and a red bowl filled with the biggest strawberries I'd ever seen. Grandma was a 1952

Chevy sedan, a box of marvelous farm toys in the closet, and a consistent source of reasons to stop at the Dairy Queen. In October, she was a birthday card with a dollar or two. Finally, she was a stroke victim in a nursing home bed.

At her funeral, my sister, Judy grieved long and hard; I tried to grieve, feeling that I should, but I couldn't.

Grandma became a real person to me only recently in the long talks I've had with my mother who's dying of cancer. Mom remembers Grandma as a shrewd business woman who managed two farms with only a third-grade education and as a woman who carefully and privately managed her Washington wheat farm income so that she kept her friends and neighbors wondering how Lottie Rehnke managed to make ends meet.

After Mom's first cancer surgery, I realized that she wouldn't be around forever to make the pies and pickles that I loved. I learned to make Grandma's sweet pickles and Mom's fruit pies so that I could continue eating them (Grandma would have approved of this motive) but also so that I could make sure that I had something of my mother and grandmother to carry on.

I never really knew Grandma Rehnke, and I'm losing my mother just when I'm really getting to know her (or maybe I'm getting to know her because I'm losing her). But every year when good baking apples are in season or when cucumbers are fresh and plentiful, I can recreate smells and tastes that connect me in very tangible ways with my past.

After our writing session we share our pieces, and I was a little emotional when I read mine. "Sometimes you need to let your students know that you're a person, too. I guess that's what I'm doing today." I am a little surprised and embarrassed by the emotions bubbling up, but I continue. "I'm going to disappear at some point in the semester, because my mother is going to die. I guess this," I lift the paper on which I have scribbled about pickles, "is my way of telling you that." About five hours later, my mother died, and I flew back to Pennsylvania for the funeral the next day.

The second lesson that day—the one I hadn't planned—was to illustrate that we are people as well as writing teachers—that the two can and should sometimes mix. I have begun perhaps two dozen writing classes by reading the pickles piece I wrote that day to my students. I can do so now without the risk of tears, but there is still an emotional vulnerability that begins to make me accessible to my students, that signals to them something of what it means to engage in alternative rhetoric before we begin to discuss the term.

4

GLORIA ANZALDÚA
Borderlands and Fences; Literacy and Rhetoric

Why am I compelled to write? Because writing saves me from this com-
placency I fear. Because I have no choice. Because I must keep the spirit
of my revolt and myself alive. Because the world I create in the writing
compensates for what the real world does not give me. By writing I put
order in the world, give it a handle so I can grasp it. I write because life
does not appease my appetites and hunger. I write to record what others
erase when I speak, to rewrite the stories others have miswritten about
me, about you. To become more intimate with myself and you. To discov-
er myself, to preserve myself, to make myself, to achieve self-autonomy.

Anzaldúa, 1981

We are used to thinking that we can be responsible only for that which
we have done, that which can be traced to our intentions, our deeds.

Butler, 2005

Here Gloria Anzaldúa suggests that writing is more than communicat-
ing, that it is about the creation and negotiation of identity that challenges the pejorative ways American society defined her and about filling in and filling out the gaps dominant culture created. Her words
remind me that until my mother's second cancer surgery, I did not
write anything that mattered. Although there were a few articles and
book chapters on my vita by that point, none of those were things I
was compelled to write—things that were necessary for my survival, for
articulating myself to a society that had marginalized and erased my
sexual identity and improverished my life. I was closeted and voiceless in a leftover *Leave-It-to-Beaver* family/world that provided a kind of
safety at the cost of incompleteness—a tradeoff that seemed sufficient
until cancer threatened to take my mother, to pull the lynchpin and
send me spinning off, rolling like a loose hubcap along the side of the
road, moving but no longer attached to a vehicle that could bring me
to a destination.

As I write this brief account of the first real trauma of my life, I realize now that it is suffused with privilege I must tease out, that my whiteness, my happy mostly middle-class home life, and my academic successes insulated me from real pain for the first twenty-seven years of my life, and that although there were costs to such an existence for me, I enjoyed a kind of safety and privilege not offered to all in American society. I come to this understanding both because of the arguments Anzaldúa makes about the need to reconsider the functions of literacy, writing, discourse, and rhetoric in American culture and because she situates these arguments concretely in her life and her experiences with dominant culture in a substantive enough way for me to do the same. From the standpoint of Butler's argument about the opacity of self-knowledge I introduced in chapter one, the lesson Anzaldúa helps me learn is that I am responsible not just for my deeds—for what I have consciously intended—but also because I have participated in a system in which I experience marginalization but also enjoy considerable privilege. As I have argued in this book, as both individuals and as a discipline, we must account for our positions and their attendant responsibilities if we are to transform our theory, practice, and pedagogy of rhetoric to attend to difference in ways that substantively address the inequities that plague our society. In short, my most basic argument in this chapter is that Anzaldúa shows in rhetorical practice Butler's theoretical point—that responsibility obtains on the basis of our relationships with others in addition to our direct actions.

Anzaldúa can easily be read as calling for the expansion of the usual neo-Aristotelian rhetorical canon because she mixes not only narrative, descriptive, and expository genres but also code-switches among multiple languages and dialects. However, beyond this, Anzaldúa's work provides a much more explicit and sweeping call for the unsettling of dominant cultural values than did the work of Grimké or Douglass. Indeed, an emerging body of work in rhetoric and composition has begun exploring how Anzaldúa's work provides the basis for a Mestiza rhetoric, and, more generally, how her work can be seen as part of an even larger movement amongst rhetoricians of color to challenge the Greco-Roman roots of American rhetoric as well as the continued dominance of Western thought and Anglo discourse practices. As I argued in chapter one, these efforts are critical for unseating what Damián Baca (2008) calls the Eurocentric fallacy and its attendant valorization of the Anglo version of history and marginalization of indigenous and other minoritized languages and discursive traditions. As Baca and others have demonstrated, Anzaldúa provides one of the most compelling cases for the reexamination of Anglo cultural dominance in American rhetoric; however, these readings have focused primarily on race and, at times, also acknowledged gender and spirituality. However, the contributions that Anzaldúa's work makes toward a better understanding of the marginalization due to sexual identity and differences from presumed physical and mental/emotional norms have largely been ignored in our scholarship.

In one sense, the focus on race in scholarship about Anzaldúa's work is understandable because she often pitches her arguments first as resistance to Anglo dominance. However, issues of gender, class, spirituality, sexual identity, and difference from presumed physical norms are present in her work to such an extent that our field's failure to address them must be read as a failure to grapple with the kind of unacknowledged dominance Anzaldúa sees at the heart of Anglo dominance in the United States. In Butler's terms, readings of Anzaldúa that focus only on race fail to account for their own opacity, and, thus, I argue that Anzaldúa's work will continue to be misread in our field if we fail to consider the complex ways many of the axes of difference and discrimination that operate in American society are addressed in her work.

Of course my own reading cannot hope to unpack everything that can be learned from Anzaldúa. However, in offering a queer reading of her work, I sketch the broader terms in which I contend her work must be understood and illustrate how such a reading further fleshes out the contributions that queer theory can make to understanding and enacting rhetoric that substantively addresses the problem of opacity. Specifically, Anzaldúa's work is highly intersectional—illustrating how the multiple and contested nature of her own identity provides a dramatic picture of ways the disenfranchised can use disidentification strategies to create a substantive copresence in discourse for those who are usually dismissed as others in our culture. In addition, her description of her own coming to voice suggests an incubatory function of closeting that does not erase the oppression inherent in the epistemology of the closet but also does not stigmatize the experiences of those who have been closeted. However, before I take up exploring these aspects of her work, I review Anzaldúa's identity journey. She begins as a poor Tejaña girl marked as queer by her family and community because of a hormone imbalance that made her begin menstruating at three months, and she achieves a kind of elder status within feminism, postcolonial criticism, and queer studies. The main focus of my analysis is Anzaldúa's *Borderlands: La Frontera: The New Mestiza*, but I also review her other major publications.[1]

FROM QUEER GIRL TO ELDER STATUS: SUBVERTING GENRES AND MESTIZAJE ÉCRITURE

Gloria Evangelina Anzaldúa was born on September 26, 1942, to sixth-generation immigrants in the Rio Grande Valley of southern Texas, and she died suddenly of complications related to diabetes on May 15, 2004.[2] In one sense, her life could be read as an academic version of a Horatio Alger story similar to Douglass's, as she begins life as a working class Tejaña girl whose family has lost their landholdings and who subsists by sharecropping, but because of her intelligence and drive, she becomes one of the most influential critics of race and other prejudices in American society. Indeed, she would likely bristle at my identification of her as the child of immigrants because her work challenges the Anglocentric reading of the history of what is now known as South Texas, and, more generally, it calls for what might be seen as a return to a pre-Columbian understanding of what it means to be "American." As the opening epigraph hints, Anzaldúa feels compelled to write to find her identity in ways that reflect a more complex understanding of how difference operates in American society than is seen in Douglass's work. Like Douglass, Anzaldúa calls for a redefinition of basic American values, but her work addresses more directly the complex ways that difference issues such as gender, race, class, sexual identity, spirituality, and physical differences from perceived norms must be accounted for in such an effort. Further, her understanding of the nature of writing and the role of rhetoric in American society requires a more thorough critique of the discourses of power than Douglass saw as necessary; she writes "to rewrite the stories others have miswritten about me, about you" (1987, 169).[3]

---

1. Frost and Hogue report, "In her later writings Anzaldúa no longer chose to italicize Spanish or other so-called foreign words, preferring not to mimic our culture's official ranking of one 'majority' language over others" (2006b, 28). To respect Anzaldúa's practice, I italicize "foreign" words in this chapter only in direct quotes or when introduced as a concept.

2. See Frost and Hogue (2006a) for more details about her life.

3. Unless otherwise noted, all quotations from Anzaldúa are from *Borderlands/La Frontera: The New Mestiza* (1987), third edition.

By her own account, Gloria Anzaldúa was seen as a queer little girl who was lazy because she was more interested in reading than ironing her younger brothers' shirts, because she began menstruating at three months and developed breasts long before the usual age of puberty, and because she was much smarter than a poor Tejaña girl was supposed to be. Although Anzaldúa's mother was frustrated by her stubborn daughter's refusal to slide into traditional gender roles, she also saw Anzaldúa's physical differences from the norm as a punishment for her own sin, for having sex and conceiving Anzaldúa before marriage and marking her daughter with a queerness she went to great lengths to hide:

> Mixed with this power struggle was her guilt at having borne a child who was marked "con la seña," thinking she had made a victim of her sin. In her eyes and in the eyes of others I saw myself reflected as "strange," "abnormal," "QUEER." I saw no other reflection. Helpless to change that image, I retreated into books and solitude and kept away from others. (1983, 199)

Early in her life, school was also a source of shame and queerness. Anzaldúa writes of sharing the degradations experienced by Chicano/a children in schools run by whites: "I had one teacher, Mrs. Garrison, who encouraged me. The rest thought Mexicans were dirty and dumb" (Keating 2000, 90). She tells other school stories of shame, of eating "lonches"

> behind cupped hands and bowed heads, gobbling them up before the other kids could see. Guilt lay folded in the tortilla. The Anglo kids laughing—calling us "tortilleros," the Mexican kids taking up the word and using it as a club with which to hit each other. My brothers, sister and I started bringing white bread sandwiches to school. (Anzaldúa 1983, 201)

However, for Anzaldúa, school was not just an occasion to be denigrated because of her race and class but also to be singled out as freaky because she was smart and physically different:

> I was such an outsider and felt so abnormal. I was super skinny and tall for my age because of the hormones. (I was born with a hormone imbalance, and it made me grow really fast.) I was a freak and had only two loves—books, literature, learning, and dogs. I also loved people, and I think I let them copy to get them to love me or accept my freakiness but also because I didn't want them to be dumb. (Keating 2000, 91)

Later in life, school played a more complicated role for Anzaldúa, serving as both a place for her to explore and begin to accept her queerness but also as a site of continued discrimination. For example, in an interview with AnaLouise Keating, Anzaldúa unpacks the personal history behind her poem "Del Otro Lado," explaining that encounters with differences outside her own experiences—accidentally encountering two lesbians having sex and her college roommate's epileptic seizure—began to help her look at her own queerness in a new light:

> So I started looking at both kinds of queerness: the queerness of making love with another woman and this strange energy that a person could go into convulsions. I started connecting with differences then. I no longer felt like I was the only one on the other side. In some way I had an affinity to the queer women and to the epileptic woman. I realized that I wasn't the baddest girl in the world. Before I thought that I was the worst, that there was something really wrong with me, that I must be so sinful to have this happen to me, that I must *deserve* to have this kind of pain and problem and that there was nobody else like me. (Keating 2006, 23)

It would be a mistake, however, to read Anzaldúa's postsecondary experiences with education as wholly positive. She received encouragement from rhetorician and progressive educator James Sledd, "who got me started to write about my experiences" when she was a graduate student (Keating 2000, 52). However, she also recounts many other incidents in which she continued to be marginalized: forced to smuggle in Chicano/a literature as a public school teacher, refused permission to do her dissertation on Chicana literature in her PhD program, and marginalized as a lesbian even after she gained a visible public role in the academy (Keating 2000, 143).

Despite these struggles with academia, Anzaldúa achieved the kind of success that landed her books on PhD comprehensive readings lists, made her a star in women's studies circles, and resulted in numerous speaking invitations. In her 1998 *Journal of Advanced Composition (JAC)* interview with Andrea Lunsford, Anzaldúa reveals that one of the most shocking of these invitations came from the Conference on College Composition and Communication: "The very same discipline, the very same teachers who had marked me down and had said that I was writing incorrectly, all of a sudden invited me to speak" (1998, 275). Given Anzaldúa's problematic history with higher education, including our own discipline, we need to exercise care in our use of her work, making sure not to "mark it down" again by failing to engage in its complexities, and we need to consider carefully how her work suggests we should deal with students like her, so we don't mark them down either.

Although Anzaldúa did not achieve the same kind of public national standing as Douglass, her elder status allowed her to move beyond her early struggles to gain a hearing and get her innovative work published to a stance that allowed her to decide with whom she would engage in bridge-building efforts. In an interview with Jamie Lee Evans about the difficulties of making alliances and building bridges, she explains that she began to question the motives of those who invited her to speak, rejecting those who wanted her "to be a visible third-world person, a token" and accepting those from people who wanted to be bridges themselves:

> Often those who invite me to be a bridge are bridges themselves—like pro-gressive whites, working-class whites, who've been working with civil rights movements and are part of the multicultural movement. Very rarely do I get asked by a conservative white male heterosexual. (Keating 2000, 198)

Anzaldúa is clear, however, that despite the choices her elder status allowed her, academia itself remains an essentially conservative institu-tion that demands assimilation of those without such status:

> It's a power struggle: Am I going to influence you or are you going to influ-ence me? I don't usually run into that problem. I have a credible reputation as a writer, so they're respectful. I'm an elder to them. They listen to me. But does the school listen to its undergraduates, to its community people who don't have a standing in their community? No, it tries to win them over, seduce them into mainstream ways of thinking. (Keating 2000, 199)

Anzaldúa's skepticism about the motives of those attending to diver-sity issues in academia was not restricted to those who invited her to speak about diversity; indeed, she was also critical of the very feminist, postcolonial, and queer theory to which she is now seen as a major con-tributor (Espinoza 1998, 45; Franklin 1997, 50), arguing,

> We need to de-academize theory and to connect the community to the acad-emy. "High" theory does not translate well when one's intention is to com-municate to masses of people made up of different audiences. We need to give up the notion that there is a "correct" way to write theory. (1990b, xxvi)

She notes, "some Feminist theorists-of-color write jargonistically and abstractedly, in a hard-to-access language that blocks communication, makes the general listener/reader feel bewildered and stupid," and she is suspicious of her own participation in theory, even though she sees it as worthwhile:

> I too am seduced by academic language, its theoretical babble insinuates itself into my speech and is hard to weed out. At the same time I feel that there is a place for us to use specialized language addressed to a select, professional, vocational or scholarly group. (1990b, xxiii)

In summary, Anzaldúa's comments on academic theory suggest that she was suspicious of academic theory, and the convergences of her work with feminist, postcolonial, and queer theory are not direct; indeed, she comments, "I didn't even know I belonged in this postcolonial thing until Patricia Clough said in a bookflap that I'm a feminist postcolonial critic" (Keating 2000, 255).

Given Anzaldúa's suspicion of academic theory and wariness about engaging in building bridges, I am keenly aware of the dangers of appropriating Anzaldúa's work for purposes beyond those for which she may have originally intended it. Indeed, the complex interplay of Anzaldúa's race, gender, sexual identity, ethnicity, class, religion, and other features of her identity that enrich her work also makes using her work without reducing it a challenging proposition. As I noted in chapter one, Baca's reading of Anzaldúa focuses almost exclusively on race. Further, it has always bothered me that Lunsford's interview with Anzaldúa focuses largely on race and, to a lesser extent, gender issues in exploring how Anzaldúa's work helps us further a much-needed postcolonial understanding of the work of rhetoric and composition. Anzaldúa's physical differences from the perceived norm because of her hormone imbalance are not discussed at all in the interview, and sexual identity is mentioned only in passing—in a question in which Lunsford compares linguistic code-switching to "injecting the discourse of lesbianism or alternative sexuality of any kind into traditional heterosexuality" (1998, 21). As a gay man, I am troubled by these and other discussions of Anzaldúa's work that pay what I see as limited attention to sexual identity issues as important subject matter in her work. Yet I must also carefully attend to the ways in which my maleness, my whiteness, my Christian background, and other factors, such as my position in the academy, affect my use of her work. I take seriously the warning Anzaldúa makes in the introduction to her edited collection *Making Face, Making Soul/Haciendo Caras; Creative and Critical Perspectives by Feminists of Color* against the rhetoric of academic scholarship posed by teachers who are "unaware of its race, class and gender 'blank spots.' It is a rhetoric that presents its conjecture as universal truths while concealing its patriarchal privilege and posture" (1990b, xxiii).

Given these concerns, I proceed cautiously, aware that Anzaldúa expected those who occupy positions of privilege such as mine to hear her, to engage with her and her work to challenge the inequities inherent in systems of privilege[4] and that, in her interview with Lunsford, Anzaldúa reveals that she sees the relevance of her work for rhetoric and composition. Indeed, she had been working on a book in which she explores how composition also means "taking it over into how one composes one's life, how one creates an addition to one's house, how one makes sense of all the kinds of coincidental and random things that happen in one's life" (Lunsford 1998, 9). Further, Anzaldúa and those who have written most carefully about her work see her as making substantive efforts to subvert traditional genres and to develop what has been dubbed "mestizaje écriture," which Keating defines as "nonsymmetrical oppositional writing tactics that simultaneously deconstruct, reassemble, and transcend phallocentric categories of thought" (1996, 122). As the title of Lunsford's interview suggests, within rhetoric and composition, Anzaldúa is increasingly being read as providing the basis for a "mestiza rhetoric"; however, the substance of what such rhetoric entails has yet to be explored in much depth.

The main body of Anzaldúa's work relevant for my purposes includes *Borderlands*, a book of essays and poetry published in 1987; *Gloria E. Anzaldúa: Interviews/Entrevistas* (2000), a collection of her interviews edited by Keating; and three edited collections of the work of women of color: *This Bridge Called My Back* (1983, edited with Cherríe Moraga; *Making Face, Making Soul/Haciendo Caras: Creative and Critical Perspectives by Women of Color* (1990a); and *This Bridge We Call Home: Radical Visions for Transformation* (2002), edited with Keating. Although *Borderlands* is my main focus here, much can also be gleaned about Anzaldúa's contributions to alternative rhetoric from the interviews in the collected volume and from the five essays she wrote for the edited collections: "La Prieta" and "Speaking in Tongues: A Letter to 3rd World Women Writers" in

---

4. For more on this, see Anzaldúa (2002b).

This Bridge Called My Back; "Haciendo Caras, una Entrada," her introduction to *Making Face*, and from *This Bridge We Call Home*, the "Preface:
(Un)natural bridges, (Un)safe spaces" and the eightieth chapter, "now
let us shift . . . the path of conocimiento . . . inner work, public acts."

MESTIZAJE ÉCRITURE

Even a cursory examination of this body of work suggests that at the
level of genre and style, Anzaldúa can be read as engaging in alternative
rhetoric and expanding the rhetorical canon because she aggressively
mixes genres, includes considerable code-switching between the numerous languages and dialects she speaks, and brings controversial topics
such as spirituality into direct dialogue with more usual academic issues.
For example, Keating argues that in *Borderlands*, Anzaldúa "combines
autobiography with contemporary and historical accounts to describe
diverse forms of oppression in twentieth-century U.S. culture" (1996,
128). Similarly, Jennifer Browdy de Hernandez suggests that like Audre
Lorde's *Zami: A New Spelling of My Name*, Anzaldúa's *Borderlands* is seen
as subverting "the normative space of autobiography" by turning it to
"radical purposes" by infusing this "traditionally conservative, masculine
mode of sublime writing" with a "lesbian sublime" (1998, 245). Certainly
such innovation is an important part of what makes Anzaldúa's work a
prima facie example of alternative rhetoric as I have defined it in this
book. However, as I illustrate in this chapter, Anzaldúa's work must also
be understood as mounting a thorough challenge to the many faces of
privilege, as demanding attention to the intersections of multiple fac-
ets of one's identity, and as describing a new understanding of identity
negotiation that not only provides the most substantive description of
what it means to find a voice that challenges what Sedgwick as calls the
epistemology of the closet but also identifies a number of concepts critical for alternative rhetoric.

A good beginning place for understanding the nature of the contributions Anzaldúa makes to alternative rhetoric is the similarities and differences between her *mestizaje écriture* and Hèléne Cixous's *écriture féminine*.
Like Cixous, Anzaldúa emphasizes women's need to write their bodies, to
ground their writing in lived experiences, and to reject the false Cartesian
dichotomy between body and mind. As Keating explains, "Anzaldúa's
fluid movements between 'body' and 'soul' destabilize conventional
meanings; the Cartesian mind/body dualism breaks down as consciousness circulates throughout the body" (1996, 135). However, Anzaldúa

attends to a wider range of issues (particularly race and class) than does Cixous, and she is directly concerned about the challenges writing poses for women who are disenfranchised because of race and class:

> Forget the room of one's own—write in the kitchen, lock yourself up in the bathroom. Write on the bus for the welfare line, on the job or during meals, between sleeping and waking. I write while sitting on the john. (1981, 170)

It is also important to note that Anzaldúa took direct action to create meaningful contexts in which women could write. As an editor of three important anthologies, she worked not only to create places for women of color to publish their work but also to provide a body of examples to be used in higher education. For example, Cynthia G. Franklin says of *This Bridge Called my Back*:

> Anzaldúa and Moraga are specific about the women they address, and these are the very women Cixous leaves out. Also, unlike Cixous, they foreground and thematize the material conditions for writing, and, in employing the collective format of an anthology, they give women the space and place to try out this writing of their bodies. (1997, 42)

Anzaldúa's mestizaje écriture also provides three important concepts for helping women of color (and others) to understand what it means to challenge the Cartesian body/mind distinction and to move toward a grounded sense of self that can serve as the basis for discourse that challenges the problematic identity constructions inherent in dominant culture.

Conocimiento

The first of these Anzaldúa calls *conocimiento*, "an overarching theory of consciousness . . . an epistemology that tries to encompass all the dimension of life" (Keating 2000, 177). Conocimiento, as Anzaldúa conceives it, is a meeting of theory and lived experience that has real consequences for one's understanding of self that encourages, among other things, exploration of one's spirituality: "The work of conocimiento—conscious work—connects the inner life of the mind and spirit to the outer worlds of action. In the struggle for social change I call this particular aspect of conocimiento spiritual activism" (178). Further, conocimiento seems to provide a basis for beginning to understand the opacity of one's own identity and position because it requires an assessment of self in relation to others: "It means to place oneself in a state of resonance with the other's feelings and situations, and to give the other an opportunity to express their needs and points of view. To relate to others by recognizing commonalities" (178). It would be a mistake to read conocimiento simply as a call for mutual respect and empathy; rather, the concept must be understood in the context of Anzaldúa's explicit calls for accounting for the operation of marginalization and privileging within dominant culture and, more specifically, the need to unseat the problematic assumptions that maintain the systems of inequity both in the culture at large and in education. As Keating explains, conocimientos are potentially transformative because they are "alternate ways of knowing that synthesize reflection with action to create subversive knowledge systems that challenge the status quo"(5).

Nepantla/Borderlands

The two other concepts from Anzaldúa's work critical for alternative rhetoric—*nepantla/borderlands* and the *Coatlicue* state—are discussed more directly in *Borderlands* than is conocimiento. As I discuss in more detail later in this chapter, these concepts are critical for conceiving of rhetoric that moves beyond binary power differences in accounting for identity, and Anzaldúa's *Borderlands* also illustrates how to engage in rhetorical practices that refuse to be defined by the dominant social values and discursive practices that create and seek to maintain pejorative binary relations. Briefly, Anzaldúa argues that both the physical spaces in which cultural contact and clashes occur, and the underlying binary difference distinctions necessary to those clashes, need to be reconceptualized as borderlands: "This liminal, borderland, terrain or passageway, this interface, is what I call *Nepantla* . . . the space in between, the middle ground" (Lunsford 1998, 17). She explains that nepantla "is a Nahuatl term meaning 'el lugar entre medio,' el lugar entre medio de todos los lugares, the spaces in-between" (Keating 2000, 238). Rather than being definitive and unchallengeable markers of difference or borders than cannot be crossed, nepantla/borderlands are generative places that make change possible: "When you're in the place between worldviews (nepantla) you're able to slip between realities to a neutral perception" (Anzaldúa 2002a, 569).

Coatlicue

The Coatlicue state is more personal, one's own wrestling with the effects of living in nepantla. As Anzaldúa explains, it is both "an intensely negative channel, you're caged in a private hell" (2002a, 569) and a generative position:

> When you come out of the Coatlicue state you come out of nepantla, this birthing stage where you feel like you're reconfiguring your identity and don't know where you are. You used to be this person but now maybe you're different in some way. You're changing worlds and cultures and maybe classes, sexual preferences. (Keating 2000, 225)

As I explore in more detail in the following section, Anzaldúa's understanding of what it means to engage in mestizaje écriture demands accounting for the operation of systemic oppression in American society and for negotiations of identity at both the personal and cultural level. This work has been read as laying the groundwork for a Mestiza rhetoric, a new understanding of writing that requires a different kind of investment and entails considerable personal risk. Anzaldúa can be read as arguing that there is risk involved in creating the copresence of the other in dominant discourse; she argues that exposure is a critical aspect of her writing—"The meaning and worth of my writing is measured by how much *I* put myself on the line and how much nakedness I achieve" (1981, 172)—and that failure to engage at this level results in inferior writing that works only on the surface, while more substantive writing "means getting into emotional states and facing truths about yourself when you would rather not" (Keating 2000, 240). I believe that one of the reasons we have been slow to understand the implications of mestizaje écriture for a Mestiza rhetoric, or alternative rhetoric in my parlance, is that we have been unwilling to account for our individual and disciplinary privilege, because we have been unwilling to put ourselves at risk. Lunsford reports that when she asked Anzaldúa if Mestiza consciousness could be taught, "she said, yes, though with great difficulty and pain" (1998, 3). The body of her work makes it clear that such learning is important for both those who have been marginalized and for those who are privileged, and, further, that such work involves sorting out unacknowledged privilege to assess its effects on both groups:

> The people who practice Racism—everyone who is white in the U.S.—are victims of their own white ideology and are empoverished by it. But we who are oppressed by Racism internalize its deadly pollen along with the air we breathe. (1990b, xix, *sic*)

In my case, taking up Anzaldúa's challenge means daring to tell about my experiences in the Coatlicue state because of my closeting as a homosexual because these experiences provide much of the basis for connection to Anzaldúa's work and lead me to a decidedly queer perspective in my attempts to develop a Mestiza consciousness. Specifically, I read Anzaldúa through Sedgwick's notion of the epistemology of the closet because of my interest in understanding what it means for the marginalized to move from invisibility or stigmatized identities to public voices that expose the means used in the discourses of power to create marginalization. However, as a physically abled, white, middle-class man from a Christian background, I must also account for the ways in which I have unwittingly contributed to the maintenance of systems of privilege both personally and professionally, and, for me, this is the more difficult task.

BUILD THE FENCE FIRST!

> The U.S.-Mexican border *es una herida abierta* where the Third World grates against the first and bleeds. And before a scab forms it hemorrhages again, the lifeblood of two worlds merging to form a third country—a border culture. (Anzaldúa 1987, 25)

Although I had read these words from Gloria Anzaldúa's *Borderlands/La Frontera: The New Mestiza* several times, I did not understand their importance for alternative rhetoric until I saw the people in the park protesting the pending immigration reform bill and carrying signs that said "Stop the Invasion," "Learn English," and "Build the Fence First!" I had spent the morning puzzling about Anzaldúa's metaphor of borderlands as a different kind of underlying metaphor for identity and language/ literacy, and my jog through the protest in the park forced me to see that the white people carrying the signs wanted both a physical and a sociocultural fence—a crisp, clean border that separates the legitimate from the illegitimate with both barbed wire and clear, unaccented English. Vastly outnumbered, I kept my head down as I jogged on, but inwardly I hoped one of these people would shout out to me, force me to stand my ground and explain that millions of Spanish-speaking people were annexed into this country as the result of wars and treaties, that the protestors had better be prepared to pay higher prices for their produce if millions of illegal migrant workers are deported, and that freedom of speech does not apply only to those who speak English as their first language. What I came to understand on my silent seething run was that shedding the notion of physical and sociocultural borders as distinctions that can and should be clearly demarcated is difficult work that requires not just the unseating of cultural values—such as the nineteenth-century notion that it was immoral for women to speak in public to mixed-gender audiences, or that African Americans who were slaves were not capable of creating engaging public discourse—but that the underlying bases for such fundamental concepts as literacy, citizenship, and identity must be radically reconstructed.

Given Anzaldúa's uneasy relationship with the academy in general and theory specifically, I suspect she would be, at least initially, suspicious of my appropriation of her notion of borderlands/nepantla in the service of further defining alternative rhetoric. As I have already argued, I do so with caution, attending as carefully as I can to the ways in which my experiences and position within culture at large create both possible points of connection and occasions for misreadings due to the differences that separate my experiences from hers. For this reason, I began this section by grounding its central insight in my moment of discovery, because I want to suggest the ongoing relevance of her work in current political debates about immigration and the American Southwest and because I want to provide some context for readers to judge what it means for me to engage in this argument: I do so mostly from a position of economic and racial privilege, as one of the relatively few compositionists to whom the academy grants the leisure to engage in such ruminations. Also, I ground my discussion as clearly as possible in the text of *Borderlands* itself to provide readers with a sense of the ways in which I am adapting Anzaldúa's ideas for my own purposes.

Anzaldúa redefines *borders* not as simple geographical lines but as designations used to mark "the places that are safe and unsafe, to distinguish *us* from *them*," and she defines a *borderland* as "a vague and undetermined place created by the emotional residue of an unnatural boundary. It is in a constant state of transition. The prohibited and forbidden are its inhabitants" (1987, 25). It is this constant clash of values and discourse practices that makes borderlands so critical as both physical and metaphorical places for change, and consequently critical also for defining alternative rhetoric in both theory and practice.

Like Douglass, Anzaldúa suggests how colonialist aggression and its attendant cultural values and language practices can create new peoples. This is one reason that borderlands and the people who live in them are critical concepts for Anzaldúa's rereading of the history and culture of her homeland—a valley in what is now referred to southern Texas. Anzaldúa begins *Borderlands* by tracing the physical/geographical creation of her homeland as a borderland, beginning with the Spanish invasion of Mexico that literally created a new race: "*Mestizos* who were genetically equipped to survive small pox, measles, and typhus (Old World diseases to which the natives had no immunity), founded a new hybrid race and inherited Central and South America" (1987, 27). She also rereads the history of Texas as an invasion of Anglos who "drove the *tejanos* (native Texans of Mexican decent) from their lands, committing all manner of atrocities against them" and the Alamo as "a symbol that legitimized the white imperialist takeover" (28). Further, she brings the rereading of history to bear on her own family: "My grandmother lost all her cattle, they stole her land" (31).

Anzaldúa links this historical reaccounting of how she and her people come to be to the formation of underlying cultural notions of race and cultural power in American identity: "The only 'legitimate' inhabitants are those in power, the whites and those who align themselves with whites" (1987, 25–6). She links this history to culture as well:

> Culture forms our beliefs. We perceive the version of reality that it communicates. Dominant paradigms, predefined concepts that exist as unquestionable, unchallengeable, are transmitted to us through culture. Culture is made by those in power—men. Males make the rules and laws; women transmit them. (38)

Further, Anzaldúa sees language as a critical part of this identity formation: "Chicano Spanish sprang out of the Chicanos' need to identify ourselves as distinct people" (77), and she identifies education as one of the important cultural means used to enforce these values: "I remember how the white teachers used to punish us for being Mexican" (89).

The concept of borderlands, as Anzaldúa uses it, is intimately tied to notions of personal and indigenous spirituality. She began using *nepantla* rather than *borderlands*, even though she sees the terms as nearly synonymous, because the former suggests more clearly the "connection to the spirit world. There's more of a connection to the world after death and to psychic spaces between air and water" (quoted in Keating 2006, 27). Keating reports that spirituality is one of the aspects of Anzaldúa's work that scholars find unsafe and tend to ignore (2000, 8), and Anzaldúa herself reports that one of her concerns when she first got her writing out into the world was that people would dismiss it because of the spirituality involved (138–9). In one sense, this emphasis on spirituality might usefully be read as encouragement for all in the academy and in wider professional life to claim their spirituality; that is, Mestiza rhetoric can and should embrace more than the rational. She says,

> I think that most of us, all of us men and women of all colors, go around thinking that this is who and what we are, and we only see maybe three-quarters or not even three-quarters of ourselves. There's a component that is very much part of the unconscious—part of the spirit world—that's also part of the us, but we've been told it's not there, so we don't perceive it. (2006, 13)

However, as I illustrate a bit later, it is also important to note that she sees this spirituality struggle as rooted in the history of this continent—a history in which some forms of spirituality erased, co-opted, or otherwise marginalized indigenous forms of religion. Thus, even though she sees spirituality as a "means of support and sustenance" for groups of people who have been "oppressed historically," she worries that *spirituality* may not be the right word because of its wider cultural associations (2000, 73).

The major question that Anzaldúa's work raises for alternative rhetoric is: how does one respond to a system in which morality is entwined seamlessly into the basic cultural concepts by which the oppressors maintain their cultural and economic power? Anzaldúa offers two main answers to this question. The first answer is that the marginalized must have a substantive enough copresence in culture to force an accounting of previous injustice and the ongoing benefits derived from physical and cultural imperialism:

> We need to say to white society: We need you to accept the fact that Chicanos are different, to acknowledge your rejection and negation of us. We need you to own the fact that you looked upon us as less than human, that you stole our lands, our personhood, our self-respect. We need you to make public restitution: to say that, to compensate for your own sense of defectiveness, you strive for power over us, you erase our history and our experience because it makes you feel guilty—you'd rather forget your brutish acts. (1987, 107–8)

In essence, Anzaldúa calls for a deconstruction of the culture of the dominant, for an understanding of the other that entails challenging such fundamental American notions as *whiteness* and *freedom of speech* as well as what it means to "remember the Alamo." Make no mistake, such an effort requires change to the seemingly unquestionable American values that led those protestors in the park to want to fence off not only the American Southwest but dominant culture and some privileged version of American English as well as change to my own sense of comfort within the discourses of power.

In later interviews, Anzaldúa more explicitly links systemic oppression to identity negotiation:

> For me, identity is a relational process. It doesn't depend only on me, it also depends on the people around me . . . the class you come from, the collective unconscious of your culture and aquí tienes a little body of water I call "el cenote." El cenote represents memories and experiences—the collective memory of the race, of the culture—and your personal history. (Keating 2000, 239–40)
>
> Identity is very much a fictive construction: you compose it of what's out there, what the culture gives you, and what you resist in the culture. . . . You create reality. But you're going to need some help, because it's all done in relationship with other people. (Lunsford 1998, 18)

This relational notion of agency fits well within postmodern understandings of identity in which one must see oneself both as dependent on the mores and history of extant culture—the collective memory of the culture—for the context that gives means to one's contributions to discourse but also as able to draw on that body of cultural knowledge in ways that allow one to challenge its problematic aspects. As I discuss next, Anzaldúa's *Borderlands* provides one of the most substantive discussions of what it means to develop the agency that allows one to engage in such cultural dialogue beginning from a marginalized position. However, it is critical to note that Anzaldúa also requires explicit accounting of the history of systemic marginalization by those who benefit from the values of dominant culture:

> Your whole life as a Mexican you're dumb, you're dirty, you're a drunkard, you can't speak correct English, you're not as intelligent as whites, you're physically ugly, you're short! ¡Todo! . . . From kindergarten through college we were bludgeoned with these views. (Keating 2000, 244)

Her words here remind me that although my homosexuality has subjected me to marginalization in many ways, my whiteness has also insulated me by, among other things, making school a relatively safe and encouraging place for me, a place that reflected my gender, race, and religious background in fairly unproblematic ways. My point here is that a postmodern understanding of agency is not enough; we must also be consciously postcolonial, feminist, queer—attending to the many ways in which systemic privilege requires unpacking the privilege that too often goes unacknowledged in the systems (including rhetoric) that sustain dominant culture.

Anzaldúa's second answer to the question of how the cultural values that support systems of marginalization can be challenged is that we must imagine how both the marginalized and the oppressors can take voices for change—can, in my terms, engage in alternative rhetoric. Indeed, while others have helped us see that culture must be deconstructed for change, Anzaldúa provides what may be the most detailed description of what taking up a voice from a position of marginalization might entail. In *Borderlands*, she recounts her own coming to a voice that allows her to identify the ways in which dominant culture marginalized her and stripped away many important cultural values, as well as recounting the process and discourse moves she uses to gain a voice in response to that oppression. Although she does not explicitly set out to create alternative rhetoric, her work can be read as setting a basis for a rhetoric that seeks to deconstruct the master's house and to develop tools for the reconstruction of the lives and identities that were bulldozed in the building of that house.

La Facultad

One critical contribution Anzaldúa's work makes to the formation of a new concept of literacy and rhetoric is her insistence that we must understand both the complex ways in which dominant culture works to strip culture, identity, and language from those whom it marginalizes and the potential power that speaking from such a marginalized position has to transform dominant culture. The notion that people in marginalized cultural positions are forced to have a kind of cultural insight that provides us with a tool for unpacking the workings of dominant culture is not original with Anzaldúa. For example, Butler argues that injury may lead to consciousness (2005, 10–11), and Anzaldúa's concept of *la facultad*—"the capacity to see in surface phenomena the meaning of deeper realities"—is reminiscent of W.E.B. DuBois's concept of the double consciousness of African Americans. She says, "Those who are pushed out of the tribe for being different are likely to become more sensitized (when not brutalized into insensitivity)" (1987, 60). In an interview originally published before *Borderlands* appeared, Anzaldúa emphasized the queer roots of la facultad but also the underlying sense of oppression that makes it common to many oppressed groups:

> I think lesbians and faggots have access to this other world. . . . It's almost like cultivating an extra sense that straight people don't have, or that straight people who are insane or persecuted, or poor whites or creative people have. Most lesbians and faggots have it because it's a matter of survival. You're caught between two worlds. You're half and half. You allow yourself to have the qualities relegated to the male—assertiveness, independence, going out into the world—you use those qualities, yet you're a women. A faggot uses the emotional qualities of a woman—the feminine stuff. . . . It's not because we cultivated it; it's because the world forced it on us. And blacks, street people have it too. (Keating 2000, 122)[5]

In a sense, la facultad is similar to linguist James Gee's notion of liberating literacies because both concepts require cultural knowledge based on perceived differences that are potentially transformative. Gee argues that the acquisition of secondary discourses can be "*liberating* ('powerful') if it can be used as a 'meta-language' (a set of meta-words, meta-values, meta-beliefs) for the critique of other literacies and the way they constitute us as persons and situate us in society. Liberating literacies can reconstitute and resituate us" (1989, 9). As Jonathan Alexander and I (Wallace and Alexander 2009) argue elsewhere, Gee's underlying notion of primary discourses as largely unitary and safe fails to account for the ways in which broad cultural constructs such as heteronormativity operate across many primary discourses and make "home" discourses inherently unsafe for LGBT people and others whose identities are erased, truncated, or otherwise marginalized in what Gee would call their primary discourses. Further, Gee's notion of literacy as the addition of secondary discourses to one's primary discourses, with liberation possible through metacognition, fails to explicitly consider that one's primary discourses may be in sore need of deconstruction, and that assimilation to the discourses of power without transformation of the inequities that form those discourses may be far from liberating, no matter what kinds of metaconsciousness may be gained in the process. In contrast, Anzaldúa's la facultad is grounded in experiences of difference gained by the oppressed throughout life, which require insight

---

5. Anzaldúa uses *faggot* in this interview as a synonym for *gay man*, not in its usual pejorative sense.

about the operation of power and which may or may not be called to conscious attention. Further, the kind of cultural vision central to la facultad clearly reflects the inherent power of such insight as well as the real need of the oppressed to deconstruct problematic cultural values and discourse practices: "Our strength lies in shifting perspectives, in our capacity to shift, in our 'seeing through' the membrane of the past superimposed on the present, in looking at our shadows and dealing with them" (Anzaldúa 1990b, xxvii).

While Gee and Anzaldúa share a discursive understanding of language, literacy, and identity, Gee's position is essentially a kinder, gentler, and more theoretically sophisticated version of the assimilationist stance that presumes learning the conventions of dominant discourses, however imperfectly, is simply the price of entry into the discourses of power, and that the metacognition gained in the clash of discourses is an important tool for the disenfranchised to use in that pursuit. While Gee realizes discourses often clash, he sees the primary issue in such clashes as their impact on the possibility of acquisition of a secondary discourse: "When such conflict or tension exists, it can deter acquisition of one or the other or both of the conflicting Discourses, or, at least affect the fluency of a mastered Discourse on certain occasions of use (e.g., in stressful situations such as interviews)" (1989, 9). In contrast, Anzaldúa does not set gaining access to the discourses of power as the primary goal; rather, she actively engages what Gee calls "dominant Discourses" to challenge the presumed naturalness of the values, logic, and language of dominant culture.

Anzaldúa is not naïve about the implications of such a stance. Like Mina Shaughnessy, who for practical reasons convinced our discipline to take an assimilationist stance so as not to deny disenfranchised students access to the discourses of power, Anzaldúa understands the consequences of refusing to learn to speak and act in the ways dominant American culture expects: "Chicanos and other people of color suffer economically for not acculturating" (1987, 85). Yet, Anzaldúa refuses to accept an assimilationist stance; instead, as Keating notes:

> Anzaldúa builds a new culture, *una cultura mestiza*. Her words incite readers to actively create a complex mixed-breed coalition of "queers"—outsiders who, because of ethnicity, gender, sexuality, class, position, or whatever, begin transforming dominant cultural inscriptions. (1996, 144)

Code-Switching

One way the difference between the assimilationist stance and Anzaldúa's culture-challenging position can be seen in practical terms is in Anzaldúa's conception of code-switching as a critical strategy in the clash of discourses. The assimilationist position sees switching between linguistic codes, between nondominant home discourses and the discourses of power, as a critical strategy for the disenfranchised. The intent here is that encouraging code-switching allows the progressive assimilationist teacher to respect the home discourse and demystifies academic/professional discourse as just another code that can be learned. Despite the egalitarian intent, such a position carries the danger of tokenizing the nondominant discourse by relegating it to a position of providing ethnic spice to a multicultural stew that does little to challenge the underlying tastes and values of dominant culture. Like the assimilationists, Anzaldúa recognizes that language is critical to identity, particularly, as I have already discussed, that Chicano/a Spanish is intimately bound up in a larger Chicano/a identity. Further, her brief analysis of the differences between Chicano/a and Tejaño/a language from other forms of Spanish claims linguistic legitimacy by showing the underlying linguistic systematicity in ways similar to what William La Bov and Geneva Smitherman did for Black English Vernacular.[6] However, Anzaldúa's version of code-switching is much more invasive and radical; she conceives of code-switching into standard English as a challenge to other identities and notes that, in practical terms, code-switching into nondominant language/dialects is not welcomed in dominant culture:

> To speak English is to think in that language, to adopt the ideology of the people whose language it is and to be "inhabited" by their discourses. *Mujeres-de-color* speak and write not just against traditional white ways and texts but against a prevailing mode of being, against a white frame of reference. Those of us who are bilingual, or use working-class English and English in dialects, are under constant pressure to speak and write in standard English. Linguistic code-switching, which goes against language laws and norms, is not approved of. (1990b, 22)

What Anzaldúa adds to well-intended attempts to understand the complexities of literacy and rhetoric in American culture is a refusal to whitewash language, literacy, and rhetoric by accepting dominant

---

6. For more on this, see Anzaldúa (1987, 79).

discourse practices out of necessity or practicality. Instead, as I have already argued, she demands a rereading of history (as many post-modern, postcolonial, and feminist scholars have), but she sees this rereading as linked in very practical ways to a new understanding of what it means to take voice in society. For example, Anzaldúa makes much of the loss of spirituality that dominant culture attempted to force upon her and upon Chicano/a culture. She recounts the process by which María Coatlalopeuh becomes identified by the Spanish with the Guadalupe, patroness of Central Spain (because the names sound alike) and eventually is renamed the Virgin Mary by the Catholic Church in 1660 (1987, 51). She argues that institutionalized religion, as a tool of western culture, encourages "a split between the body and the spirit and totally ignore(s) the soul; they encourage us to kill off parts of ourselves. We are taught that the body is an ignorant animal; intelligence dwells only in the head" (59). Further, Anzaldúa argues for a spiritual, a shamanistic, understanding of what it means to take voice (88), and she sees this as a response to the "tyranny of Western aesthetics" (90), challenging even the Western European basis for higher education: "Let's all stop importing Greek myths and the Western Cartesian split point of view and root ourselves in the mythological soil and soul of this continent" (90). In short, the kind of accounting of straight, white, male, Eurocentric, Christian privilege Anzaldúa envisions requires the reexamination and unseating of values fundamental to higher education in the United States—even the detachment inherent in the sense of objectivity that has been the basis for Enlightenment moral sensibilities.

Losing Her Homeland and Moving into Coatlicue

Anzaldúa is not naïve about the difficulties of such sweeping changes; indeed, her second critical contribution to alternative rhetoric is her careful description of what it meant for her to gain the kind of voice that can speak back to dominant culture in a way that calls that culture to account. Anzaldúa's account of her struggle to gain voice is particularly instructive because as a lesbian Tejaña seeking to reclaim a sense of indigenous spirituality not only in her life but also in her scholarly writing, she was forced to deal with multiple aspects of marginalized identity. Thus, even though it would be dangerous to read her particular struggles as indicative of what it means for all others to speak/write from the margins, the breadth of her experiences with oppression, and the considerable insights she provides about them, suggest useful starting places for distilling what practicing alternative rhetoric may entail.

Perhaps the most interesting starting place for considering Anzaldúa's practical contributions to the practice of alternative rhetoric is her discussion of her sense of the loss of her homeland because this discussion both illustrates the complexities of identity and challenges the often too-simplistic notion that gaining new insights or discourse practices is automatically empowering. Her comments here reflect a functional intersectionality that attends to both the real ways dominant culture marginalizes those who it labels as other but also how varied aspects of identity combine to create other kinds of connection and community:

> As a *mestiza* I have no country, my homeland cast me out; yet all countries are mine because I am every woman's sister or potential lover. (As a lesbian I have no race, my own people disclaim me; but I am all races because there is the queer of me in all races.) I am cultureless because, as a feminist, I challenge the collective cultural/religious male-derived beliefs of Indo-Hispanics and Anglos; yet I am cultured because I am participating in the creation of yet another culture, a new story to explain the world and our participation in it, a new value system with images and symbols that connect us to each other and to the planet. (1987, 102–3)

Here Anzaldúa captures the difficulties of becoming aware of multiple identities: the loss of the simple cultural narratives often associated with homes and homelands, the intersections of aspects of her identity that isolate her from dominant culture and from her home culture but which also provide a basis for connection outside her home culture, and the generative place this tension leads her to. What is particularly important for literacy and rhetoric here is that Anzaldúa links this liminal state directly to how she understands what it means to be a writer:

> Being a writer feels very much like being a Chicana, or being queer—a lot of squirming, coming up against all sorts of walls. (94)

> Living in a state of psychic unrest, in a Borderland, is what makes poets write and artists create. It is like a cactus needle embedded in the flesh. It worries itself deeper and deeper, and I keep aggravating it by poking at it. (95)

> I cannot separate my writing from any part of my life. It is all one. When I write it feels like I'm carving bone. (95)

For Anzaldúa, getting to this state—to a place where she could imagine having the kind of voice that would give her substantive copresence in dialogue with dominant culture—required a journey which is suggestive of the process other speaker/writers who need to engage in alternative rhetoric may experience. In this sense, my reading of Anzaldúa here begins to flesh out the epistemology of the closet in rhetorical terms by identifying several kinds of disidentification moves that Anzaldúa describes as part of the process of coming to a new kind of voice.

One contribution Anzaldúa makes to the process of coming to understand one's subjugated identity in a manner that will eventually lead to a new kind of voice is her description of the means she used to deny her own identity. She writes of the danger of mirrors to the closeted person because these windows to the soul provide glimpses at "the secret sin I tried to conceal—*la seña*, the mark of the Beast" (1987, 64). Here, she seems to be speaking not of real sins but of aspects of herself such as her love of reading and learning, her desire for women, and her speaking Spanish in school that she was led to see as sinful. This denial led her to isolate herself—"I locked the door, kept the world out; I vegetated, hibernated, remained in stasis, idled" (66)—and to use rage as an active means "to drive others away and to insulate myself against exposure"—"I have reciprocated with contempt for those who have roused shame in me" (67). Further, she describes this denial state as dependent on addictions—rituals that "help one through a trying time; it's repetition safeguards the passage, it becomes one's talisman, one's touchstone" (68).

Anzaldúa describes the culmination of these denial strategies as "the *Coatlicue* State," which may be best seen as a kind of preparation for the crossing in which "paralysis" and "depression" of denial are also accompanied by glimpses of understanding: "I must take small sips of her face through the corners of my eyes, chip away at the ice a sliver at a time" (1987, 70). Coatlicue is an Aztec goddess, known as the mother of the gods and also linked to serpents, whom Anzaldúa recalls not only in an attempt to return to indigenous spirituality but also to link this sense of spirituality to a rebirth from a position of marginalization and silencing into a new identity. As Browdy de Hernandez explains, "Coatlicue functions as a sort of midwife in this process of self-birthing, at once coaxing and threatening Anzaldúa, forcing her to look in the mirror and confront the 'truth about herself'" (1998, 251). In a sense, Anzaldúa's Coatlicue state takes some of the stigma out of closetedness, redefining it as a difficult but ultimately generative state—a necessary precursor to entering nepantla. In a 1994 interview with Debbie Blake and Carmen Abrego, Anzaldúa explains:

> When you're in the midst of the Coatlicue state—the cave, the dark—you're hibernating or hiding, you're gestating and giving birth to yourself. You're in the womb state. When you come out of that womb state you pass through the birth canal, the passageway I call nepantla. (Keating 2000, 225)

This description of the pain and necessity of the Coatlicue state as a precursor for crossing into nepantla helps explain why, as I noted earlier, Anzaldúa sees Mestiza consciousness as something that can be taught only with "great difficulty and pain," as those who do not come to some version of it through the systemic oppression that is part of their daily lives must learn it through conscious effort that requires acknowledging and taking responsibility not only for their unearned privilege but also for tacit participation in the marginalization of others. Of course, it is important not to whitewash Coatlicue, arguing that oppression is really a blessing, that oppressors have really done the oppressed a favor by creating the conditions that allow for insight and enlightenment, as few would choose to be oppressed. However, it is equally important not to unduly pathologize the Coatlicue: while experiencing the oppression that creates the state is far from pleasant, the state can lay the groundwork for a new understanding of self if, as Anzaldúa notes, one is not "brutalized into insensitivity" (1987, 60).

Travesîa/Crossing

Anzaldúa describes the crossing itself, the coming to understanding, not as a bold step out of a closet but as incremental: "Every step forward is a *travesîa*, a crossing. I am again an alien in new territory" (1987, 70). Crossing is costly and incomplete: "Every time she makes 'sense' of something, she has to 'crossover,' kicking a hole out of the old boundaries of the self and slipping under or over, dragging the old skin along, stumbling over it. It hampers her movement in the new territory, dragging the ghost of the past with her" (71). Further, crossing does not lead to a state of grace in which one receives perfect enlightenment and remains forever free of the Coatlicue state. Indeed, in an essay published in 2002, Anzaldúa identifies the Coatlicue state as one of the seven stages of conocimiento, but her description makes it clear that she does not envision a once-and-for-all lockstep progression. Even though the first crossing out of Coatlicue may be dramatic and critical for developing a new identity, movement among the positions she describes continues:

> All seven are present within each stage, and they occur concurrently, chronologically or not. . . . You're never only in one space, but partially in one, partially in another, with nepantla occurring most often—as its own space and as the transition between each of the others. (2002a, 545–6)

Even though Anzaldúa sees crossing as critical for transforming one's borderland status to a constructive liminal state, the journey does not end with the crossing. Instead she describes this new Mestiza state as requiring "a tolerance for contradictions, a tolerance for ambiguity" (1987, 101). She also suggests that such crossings require a careful inventory: "Just what did she inherit from her ancestors? This weight on her back—which is the baggage from the Indian mother, which the baggage from the Spanish father, which the baggage from the Anglo?" (104).

In *Borderlands* and her other writings, Anzaldúa provides a number of critical concepts for alternative rhetoric: embracing the spiritual as counterpoint and complement to the rational; the link between the concepts/myths that bind us and reclaiming those myths to move toward crossing; the costs of denial and the means of doing so; the necessity of crossing but its pains as well; the promise of healing but the ghosts of oppression carried bodily and the struggle to free oneself from the very mental/emotional boulders that were necessary to survival before crossing. It is important to note that Anzaldúa describes these denial and crossing states as precursors to claiming one's wild tongue, as necessary before she was able to no longer "be made to feel ashamed of existing" and to claim "my serpent's tongue—my woman's voice, my[her] sexual voice, my poet's voice" (1987, 81).

Anzaldúa's work can be read as describing the process of accounting for one's own opacity while holding dominant culture accountable for its collective unacknowledged opacity and the marginalization and violence that this lack of knowledge engenders. Her work serves a similar function for rhetoric and composition: she provides a much more nuanced understanding of the complexities of what it means for those in marginalized positions to move to voice, tacitly challenging the overly simplistic models proposed by Gee and others, and she turns the usual notions of the discursive tools that make such interactions possible inside out (e.g., her use of aggressive code-switching to make reading her work problematic for Anglos). Anzaldúa does not provide much substantive description of what it would mean for the dominant to account for their failure to deal with their own opacity and the attendant marginalization. However, her descriptions of moving from Coatlicue to nepantla hint at what such a crossing might mean for our discipline. Indeed, if we wish to create a broader, disciplinary notion for alternative rhetoric, we must understand that we are engaged in a struggle to identify our personal and collective denial and we must prepare for a crossing that will lead not to a state of instant grace but to an ongoing struggle to sort out these new voices. Anzaldúa also provides a description of possible stances to take in such a move as well as sage advice to the oppressed about how much responsibility to take in such an endeavor. I turn to this topic in the final section of this chapter.

EMBRACING SUBJECTIVITY

> But it is not enough to stand on the opposite riverbank, shouting questions, challenging patriarchal, white conventions. A counterstance locks one into a duel of oppressor and oppressed; locked in mortal combat, like the cop and the criminal, both are reduced to a common denominator of violence. The counterstance refutes dominant culture's views and beliefs, and for this, it is proudly defiant. (Anzaldúa 1987, 100)
>
> Our goal is not to use differences to separate us from others, but neither is it to gloss over those differences. (Anzaldúa 2002b, 3)

For nearly a quarter of a century, Gloria Anzaldúa worked and wrote for equity in American society, and while the foundation for her contributions to alternative rhetoric is laid primary in *Borderlands,* her larger body of work also suggests a number of important insights about how she imagines that change might occur. As she suggests near the end of *Borderlands,* breaking the duel between oppressor and oppressed will not be accomplished by a shouting match; yet allowing those in power to set the terms of the discussion is not an adequate solution because it requires those who have been marginalized to assimilate or find ways to argue for change within the terms set by the oppressors.

Near the end of the prose section of *Borderlands,* Anzaldúa suggests what might be taken as a general principle—that the oppressed should not feel obliged to do all the work of rapprochement: "I, for one, choose to use some of my energy to serve as mediator. I think we need to allow whites to be our allies" (1987, 107). However, *Borderlands* itself does not offer much insight into how that confrontational stance can be productively broken. Indeed, much of *Borderlands* is angry, and its primary concern is articulating forms of systemic oppression, calling dominant culture to account. Like Audre Lorde (1984), who has argued for the usefulness of anger, particularly in her essay "The Uses of Anger: Women Responding to Racism," Anzaldúa explains in an interview more than a decade after the publication of *Borderlands* that "sometimes it's really healthy to be angry or sad" and that "*Borderlands* needed that angry voice." However, she also notes the potential dangers: "When the emotion possesses you and becomes a way of life, you have no autonomy," and "in the last twelve years I started getting disembroiled from these emotional states" (Keating 2000, 287). Thus, while expressions of anger or other powerful emotions may be necessary to create a substantive copresence of the oppressed in public discourses to keep difference from being erased, Anzaldúa is also clear that difference must not become an abyss which cannot be bridged.

As a white person trying to be Anzaldúa's ally, I take seriously my need to account for my own privilege, that as a white man who teaches rhetoric and composition I am, in one sense, standing on the other side of the river, and I need to reciprocate the generosity Anzaldúa and others have extended to me. Yet as a gay man I often feel I am standing beside Anzaldúa shouting across a river as well, hoping someone will hear what I am struggling to say—that I believe as a discipline we have not lived up to our moral obligation because we have tolerated homophobia and heterosexism in our classrooms, our composition programs, and our universities. We have been insightful in our theories of difference and language, but slow to see the need to address our own privilege within the discourses of power and quick to fall back on the assumption that assimilation to those discourses is ultimately in the best interests of our students. In addition, we have had too simple an understanding of what engaging with the discourses of power means for ourselves and our students—not fully reckoning the costs of assimilation and embracing such things as code-switching as easy solutions. Our own, still-vulnerable disciplinary position in the American academy robs us of the courage to recognize that oppression is a complicated business implicating all of us to some degree, and, thus, we must all make it our business to address it; those of us who theorize and teach rhetoric bear an additional responsibility to set forward a morally responsible means for using rhetoric to seek justice in American society. One of the most important lessons from Anzaldúa then is that as a discipline we have set too modest a goal; we have settled for either a de facto conservative position or a shallow liberalism in which we refuse to put ourselves at further risk, hiding behind our good intentions and satisfied with shallow versions of code-switching and other kind-hearted assimilation efforts.

Anzaldúa's work demands a more aggressive and nuanced goal for rhetorical theory, practice, and pedagogy, one that takes social justice seriously. We must explicitly admit that, no matter what approach we take to rhetoric and pedagogy, we are engaging in the construction of subjectivities, of notions of self and society capable of negotiating personal identities as well as discursive practices and cultural values that shape them, and we must take responsibility for the effects of our efforts. In this sense, Anzaldúa's work requires more than a theoretical understanding that dominant culture and discourse still carry the status of objectivity, even though postmodern, postcolonial, and feminist theory have rejected the very notion of objectivity. In short, my argument is that Anzaldúa helps us see how we must not only reject the notion of a privileged objective stance but must also embrace subjectivity and work actively to deconstruct dominant discourse practices and reconstruct them in ways that move beyond shallow multiculturalism. Her larger body of work identifies a number of issues critical for attempts to make such a crossing, to work for substantive equity.

Issue #1: Getting Beyond Additive Models

One of the most important ways Anzaldúa's work suggests for moving from an understanding of the need for alternative rhetoric toward enacting such a stance is her insistence that the goal for such change cannot simply be additive; rather, transformation is necessary—the inequities inherent in social conventions that maintain the status quo must be challenged and changed. As Keating explains, Anzaldúa "uses oppositional tactics to break down, rather than simply reverse, western culture's hierarchical dualism" (1996, 126). Like other feminist, critical race, and queer theorists, Anzaldúa argues that the basic binary categories defining much of Americans' identities (e.g., male/female, white/person of color, straight/queer, abled/disabled) must be unseated and that without such deconstruction, discussions of identity issues that invoke center and margin positions may reify the existing hierarchies.

What Anzaldúa adds to this increasingly common critique of shallow inclusion is her absolute insistence that privilege must be accounted for and that pain and loss will be involved in such work. For example,

Anzaldúa's understanding of race requires the recognition that simply to be white in American society is to enjoy at least some privilege and to participate, even without explicit intent, in the systems of racism that operate in our culture. She says, "The refusal to think about race itself (itself a form of racism) is a 'white' privilege" and that most white people do not understand "the racism inherent in their identities, in their cultures' stories. They can't see that racism harms them as well as people of color, itself a racially superior attitude" (2002a, 564). The corollary for rhetoric and composition here is telling: those of us fluent in the discourses of power may also experience a kind of linguistic privilege that often goes unacknowledged and is even less often substantively addressed. Further, Anzaldúa suggests that the insight necessary to understand the need for unpacking the usually invisible operation of oppression in culture may come only through shock or violence:

> With me it always happens with a traumatic shock of some kind that opens me so brutally—I'm cracked open by the experience—that for a while things come inside me, other realities, other worlds. (Keating 2006, 14)

Anzaldúa's discussions of what it meant for her to develop a voice that allowed her to participate in the deconstruction and reconstruction of problematic cultural constructs also suggest that such work may require hard choices about loyalties, straining important personal and sociocultural ties: "I'm constantly asked by my family to choose my loyalty; when I choose who I'm going to be loyal to, myself or them" (Lunsford 1998, 12).

As I discuss further in chapter six, the obvious question that arises here is who would choose to do such work? Why should the privileged choose to understand the ways in which culture has advantaged them/ us; why would I want to understand the ways unacknowledged privilege has contributed to what I have always seen as successes due to my own ability and initiative? For the disenfranchised, the motive to unpack the operation of privilege is more obvious but perhaps no less dangerous because understanding the array of cultural values and conventions that must be unseated is itself daunting and because few do not benefit from at least one of the axes of privilege in American society. My most basic answers to the question of why anyone should want to engage in such hard work are "because it's the right thing to do" and "because it's the next important task." For me, what is fundamentally good about the American ideal is the commitment to equity, and despite the real problems of higher education in our nation, its ongoing commitment to intellectual progress remains engaging. The question of why rhetoric and composition should be interested and engaged in such hard work is also important, and, fortunately, Anzaldúa's definition of writing provides a fairly direct answer to this question: "Writing is an archetypal journey home to the self, *un proceso de crear puentes* (bridges) to the next phase, next place, next culture, next reality" (2002a, 574). In short, then, we should engage in this struggle to deconstruct privilege and reconstruct new identities despite the pain and danger involved because it is the only place for growth, for real change, and, as Anzaldúa argues, writing—both in the individual immediate sense and the larger cultural sense—is the critical tool for engaging in such change.

Issue #2: Accounting for Difference Without Reifying Oppressive Relationships

A second way Anzaldúa's work helps us understand what it means to move from a desire for equity toward a rhetoric that does the hard work involved in the necessary transformations is by teasing out several of the complexities of creating commonality without erasing difference. In the introduction of her 1990 collection *Making Face, Making Soul/Haciendo Caras: Creative and Critical Perspectives by Feminists of Color*, Anzaldúa identifies shallow multiculturalism as "a way of avoiding seriously dismantling racism." She explains that the motivation for such shallow engagement in the ongoing problems of racism is not explicitly racist itself; rather, "We want so badly to move beyond Racism to a 'postracist' space, a more comfortable space, but we are only prolonging the pain and leaving unfinished business that could liberate some of our energies" (1990b, xxii). Thus, the first, and perhaps most important lesson Anzaldúa provides about moving toward commonality while honoring difference is *calling out the danger of presuming that we have moved beyond racism* and that, by extension, our society, at least in its more enlightened elements, is also postfeminist and equitable in terms of class, religion/ spirituality, age, physical and mental/emotional abledness, and sexual identity. It is critical to note that Anzaldúa does not presume that this problematic presumption of "post" status is restricted to the uninformed masses, to the people who say such things as "I'm not racist, but. . ." and then nearly always proceed to provide evidence of their racism in the second part of the sentence. Instead, Anzaldúa raises the dangers of presuming a postracist society in the context of feminism, amongst both "whitewomen and women-of-color" (1990b, xxii). I believe the lesson she offers here is that one of the primary challenges faced by those of us who want to work for equity on many fronts is our presumption that we are not, cannot be, part of the ongoing problem.

A second lesson Anzaldúa offers about creating commonality out of difference is that *bridge building is hard work*. Indeed, in her 1993 interview with Evans, Anzaldúa notes, "One of the drawbacks to being a bridge is being walked on, but one of the pluses is that it's two-way— on-coming and outgoing traffic" (Keating 2000, 206). As someone who made a career out of being a bridge in some sense, Anzaldúa speaks tellingly of the difficulty of creating a balance. Her bridge work came with the "perk—of getting my name out, of people buying my books and believing in my work," but it also caused personal damage: "This work bends a person, wastes a person; the wear and tear is stressful" (207). One practical observation Anzaldúa suggests about maintaining balance on bridges is in attending to the direction of the flow of traffic. In another interview she remarks:

> With *This Bridge* [*Called My Back*] we were in direct dialogue with white women and I didn't see much change for many years. All that energy was going out, out, out. The dominant culture—Euro-American women—were sucking all that we had to say, all our experiences, all our writings, symbols, rituals, and we were being drained. (217)

Related to the notions of balance in roles and reciprocity of effort, a third lesson from Anzaldúa's work beyond *Borderlands* suggests that because of the pitfalls of presumed commonality, alliances must be made with care, with cognizance of underlying differences and the dangers of appropriation by those who assume the "post" position. One of the specific dangers Anzaldúa identifies for the oppressed in making alliances is co-optation. For example, in the introduction to *Making Face*, she writes of the dangers she has found as a lesbian working to educate others, of the pulls to "get along" with those who offer alliances without a full understanding of difference:

> The pull to believe we can "belong," that we can blend in, that we can be accepted like any other "American" can seduce us into putting our energies into the wrong battles and into picking allies who marginalize us further. (1990b, xxii)

Anzaldúa is equally clear that the complicity of the oppressed in their own domination must also be understood and acknowledged, asking,

Do we hand the oppressor/thug the rocks he throws at us? How often do we people of color place our necks on the chopping block? . . .I see Third World peoples and women not as oppressors but as accomplices to oppression by our unwittingly passing on to our children and our friends the oppressor's ideologies. I cannot discount the role I play as accomplice, that we all play as accomplices, for we are not screaming loud enough in protest. (1983, 207)

Anzaldúa is clear that serious deconstruction of cultural values and conventions is necessary: "Sharing the pie is not going to work" (1983, 208), and she argues for a more complicated understanding of what it means to create commonalities in alliances intended to work for equity. In her interview with Evans, Anzaldúa contrasts alliances with the island/drawbridge model that presumes largely that we deal with single-difference issues from enclaves of identity. Instead, she proposes a more fundamental and connected notion of alliances: "I now believe alliances entail interdependent relationships with the whole environment—with plants, the earth, and the air as well as with people" (Keating 2000, 195). Here Anzaldúa is not offering a vague, earth-mother, can't-we-all-just-get-along understanding of what it means to build commonality out of difference. Rather, she sees the needed change as substantive and calls for a real accounting of positionality: "Alliance making is therapeutic. You're trying to heal a community or a culture while healing yourself" (199). Further, she sees writing as a critical part of this process: "Writing is my way of making alliances. I say, 'Here is this piece of work, it has these images and ideas. It has these beliefs, it has this perspective. What is your perspective? What is your history?'" (197).

A third lesson about the challenges of building commonality out of difference that can be drawn from Anzaldúa's work is that doing so will likely involve *dealing with internalized violence.* She argues that systemic oppression does violence to the oppressed and that such violence can be internalized:

The violence against us, the violence within us, aroused like a rabid dog. Adrenaline-filled bodies, we bring home the anger and the violence we meet on the street and turn it against each other. We sic the rabid dog on each other and on ourselves. (1983, 205–6)

Her comment here reminds me of a conversation I had with a female colleague when I was a new assistant professor. I often stopped by her office to chat, and in our talks I began to get the first glimmers of how women are socialized differently and, too often, more problematically in higher education than are men. In one of our conversations, I let out a long sigh and said, "I don't think I'll ever really be a feminist." The next day I got an angry e-mail, chastising me for writing off the problems faced by women, and I was surprised by the thinly veiled vehemence of her response. I wrote back that my long sigh was not resignation but a realization of how much I had to learn and how much work there was to do to create equity for women, but I don't think my colleague believed me. After reading Anzaldúa, I read my colleague's response differently, seeing that given the struggles with sexism she had shared with me, I should not have been surprised that she would bristle at the ease with which I could walk away from such an exchange without an explicit acknowledgement of my male privilege, of the ease with which I could step back from the problems of sexism in the academy, attending to the issue later at my leisure. I tell this story not only to illustrate how the internalized violence Anzaldúa discusses may surface in day-to-day to conversations but also to illustrate the dangers of taking too casual an approach to understanding the oppression of others. In this case, my male privilege surfaced as an unintended coolness toward my colleague's lifetime of marginalization because of sexism.

A fourth lesson Anzaldúa's work suggests as important for negotiating commonality and difference concerns *labeling*; specifically, she suggests that labels must be dealt with because the underlying identity issues are always relevant for the exercise of rhetorical agency. Although she thinks we need to "start thinking about a time when labels won't be necessary," she also understands the pragmatic function that difference labels serve: "I use labels because we haven't gotten beyond race or class or other differences yet. When I don't assert certain aspects of my identity like the spiritual part or my queerness, they get overlooked and I'm diminished" (Keating 2000, 77). In a sense, this pragmatic position reflects one of the central conundrums of feminism and other progressive movements— the subalternity problem in which there is a need to posit a coherent difference identity in the service of exposing systemic marginalization, yet doing so reinforces the very problematic binary the movement hopes to unseat. In "La Prieta," Anzaldúa's primary contribution to *This Bridge Called My Back*, she illustrates the reductive nature of labels, how they split identity:

> What am I? *A third world lesbian feminist with Marxist and mystic leanings.* They would chop me up into little fragments and tap each piece with a

label. . . . You say my name is ambivalence? Think of me as Shiva, a many armed and legged body with one foot on brown soil, one on white, one in straight society, one in the gay world, the man's world, the women's, one limb in the literary world, another in the working class, the socialist, the occult worlds. A sort of spider woman hanging by one thin strand of web. . . . Who, me confused? Ambivalent? Not so. Only your labels split me. (1983, 205)

In an interview a dozen years later, Anzaldúa suggests a more generative use of society's labels, recognizing that the individual can exercise some agency in how labels are applied to him/her:

> You can take your identity into your hands recognizing that you don't need a white person or a Chicana middle-class person to tell you who you are. You have some say in it. Constructing identity is a collaborative effort. . . . You can decide what to label yourself. (Keating 2000, 203)

Although it might seem that Anzaldúa is inconsistent in her understanding of the interplay between the constrictiveness of labels and individuals' ability to claim their own identities, this is not the case. Instead, her position is probably best read as understanding both the real challenges posed by society's pejorative labels and the new kind of freedom to redefine one's relationships to those categories after one does the hard work of crossing. As I discussed earlier, Anzaldúa sees emerging from the Coatlicue state as a kind of crossing that provides new insight into self and the possibility of redefining limiting categories for oneself. In one of the last important essays she published before her untimely death, Anzaldúa argues that after crossing (or perhaps as one makes a crossing), "you share a category of identity wider than any social position or racial label." In a sense then, crossing moves you beyond labels, to a position where you are no longer personally bound to all the baggage that dominant culture attaches to such labels. However, this does not mean the implications of those labels, and the attendant cultural values and practices that enforce them, are miraculously erased. Rather, Anzaldúa goes on to explain that crossing brings not only a new understanding of one's relationship to dominant culture's marginalizing labels but also a sense of responsibility to work for equity: "This conocimiento motivates you to work actively to see that no harm comes to people, animals, ocean—to take up spiritual activism and the work of healing" (2002a, 558).

Issue #3: Embracing the Need to Develop a Responsible Voice

A third way Anzaldúa's work helps us understand how we might
move forward in our discipline toward rhetoric and pedagogy that
attends substantively to difference is to suggest strategies for developing
a responsible voice—a voice that understands its place in the ongoing
history of oppression. Indeed, Anzaldúa's work is directly relevant to the
development of alternative rhetoric because she suggests several principles for translating the need for change into discursive practices. As I
have already discussed, in *Borderlands* Anzaldúa mixes narrative, descriptive, and expository genres together with poetry in ways rarely seen in
academic discourse. Also, she engages in code-switching that moves well
beyond sprinkling in some ethnic spice or Gee's notion of mushfaking
one's way into a secondary discourse. Instead, Anzaldúa purposefully
uses Spanish, Chicano/a, Tejaño/a, Nahtual, and other languages and
dialects to create a sense of dissonance in readers, to recreate a sense of
dialogue in the borderland and to challenge the discourses of power. Of
course, Anzaldúa's particular set of transgressive practices is not a recipe
for others to engage in alternative rhetoric; indeed, simply aping her
specific techniques would likely result in parody because it would bypass
the struggle that led Anzaldúa to use these practices. Fortunately, her
later work, as well as others' discussions of it, suggest three underlying
principles for developing a socially responsible voice and, by extension,
a socially responsible rhetoric and pedagogy.

The most critical concept in this regard is Anzaldúa's call for *sorting out our own histories*. Dionne Espinoza sees Anzaldúa as taking on
the issue of what it means to face our histories in the introduction to
Making Face:

> Anzaldúa points out that the project of encountering "our own" histories still
> awaits elaboration. What does it mean to come face to face with "our own"
> histories? Are these histories of the individual or of the collective? Who is
> included in the collective that proclaims ownership and how is she (are they)
> included? (1998, 44)

The range of issues to be examined here is important: we need not
just to tell stories about ourselves but to tell stories that situate our histories within larger collective histories. Anzaldúa's call to account for our
individual and collective histories can be read as an important refine-
ment of the notion of "embodied writing" that I discussed in chapter

one. That is, telling a story about oneself may simply be an exercise in self-indulgence unless that story is connected to some aspect of personal and collective history that brings the operation of culture into relief, unless that story works to situate the self within the discourses of power. Anzaldúa is clear that engaging in such work, even for her, requires effort to escape the expectations of academic discourse: "I have not yet unlearned the esoteric bullshit and pseudo-intellectualizing that school brainwashed into my writing" (1981, 165). And even Keating, who was one of Anzaldúa's closest collaborators, reveals in her introduction to her collection of Anzaldúa's interviews (2000) the difficulty she found in taking up Anzaldúa's urging for Keating to be more present in her work:

> My academic training, coupled with my love of privacy, makes me fear self-disclosure. (1)

> I am a product of the U.S. university system. I have learned to mask my own agenda—my own desires for social justices, spiritual transformation, and cultural change—in academic language. (3)

Despite such discomfort, Anzaldúa is clear that risk, that personal investment, is necessary to move beyond the status quo. For Anzaldúa there was really no choice; she felt marginalized in so many ways by American society, by the academy, and by her own family that, she says, "Writing saved my life. It saved my sanity. I could get a handle on the things happening to me by writing them down, rearranging them, and getting a different perspective" (Keating 2000, 41). For others who are less marginalized than Anzaldúa, the need for embodied writing that accounts for one's place in the histories of oppression may not be as immediately necessary. However, the underlying principle for engaging in alternative rhetoric remains the same: we must substantively account for our places in the discourses of power and oppression and risk allowing others to see where we stand and judge our attempts to take responsibility for those positions.

Expanding the useful range of emotion is a second concept that can be drawn from Anzaldúa's work in that such personal investment may provoke, even demand, a wider range of emotion than we normally see in academic and professional writing. As I have already argued, Anzaldúa sees the value of anger, that when it is honest and linked in substantive ways to issues of oppression, it may serve an important function: "I purposefully allowed negative emotions in, sort of like singing with a full range of notes and with both lungs" (Keating 2000, 287). However, she is equally clear that anger or other negative emotions are dangerous when they become a way of life. It would be a mistake to read Anzaldúa as arguing for the inherent value of all negative emotions. Along with activists/theorists such as Audre Lorde, Anzaldúa's work has also been used to argue for the uselessness of guilt. For example, Keating sees Anzaldúa's work as contributing to the challenge to "traditional human-ist notions of a unitary self and its various forms in conventional iden-tity politics" (1998, 24), and she identifies guilt as "a useless debilitating state of consciousness that reifies boundaries between apparently sepa-rate groups" (38). As a white person reading *Borderlands*, I find it diffi-cult to avoid feeling a sense of collective white guilt for the problematic history that has led to my unearned privilege in American society, and I would argue that Anzaldúa wants me to feel this, perhaps even that she intends to evoke such feelings. However, she is also clear that sim-ply feeling such guilt is not enough: one must enter into dialogue with those who have been disadvantaged by such privilege, acknowledging the history of oppression and working for change. Thus, I would amend Keating's position about guilt to argue that it may have uses but that it cannot be the end state. While Anzaldúa's work suggests that negative emotions may serve important roles in the work for equity, she also sees humor as playing an important role: "Among the strengths working for us is the ability to see through our self-sabotaging behaviors. Our inner *payasa*, clown-face, is always aware of what's going on and uses humor to volley back the racial slurs" (1990b, xxvii). Here Anzaldúa sees humor as a defense strategy, as a means of both freeing oneself from internalizing oppression and taking a position that demonstrates a coolness toward oppression's intended effects. In a sense then, Anzaldúa sees the value in responding to oppression from both the "hot" position of anger and the "cool" position of humor. As I discuss in detail in the next chapter, humorist David Sedaris illustrates the power of a cool, detached position that uses self-deprecatory humor to speak from normally marginalized positions in American society.

A third concept important to developing a responsible voice that can be drawn from Anzaldúa's work is the *problematic but creative tension between embracing the need to publish oneself and recognizing the need for some kind of larger endorsement.* In her interview with Lunsford, Anzaldúa poses this central tension: "The question is, how can you change the norm if

the tide is so tremendous against change? But you can do something"
(1998, 13). While Anzaldúa acknowledges that she needed to get some
level of endorsement of her work from peers and from wider communities to get her message heard, she is equally clear that those who speak/
write from oppressed positions must come to see themselves as sponsors
of their own message and as adjudicators of its forms: "We begin to dis-
place the white and colored male typographers and become, ourselves,
typographers, printing our own words on the surfaces, the plates, of our
bodies" (1990b, xvi). And it is significant that Anzaldúa devoted much
of her professional life and effort to editing three collections of the work
of women of color, essentially proving that such agency can be effective.
Anzaldúa is explicit in arguing that for women of color in the academy,
taking such a position means resisting the rhetoric of dominant ideology
that is "riddled with ideologies of Racism which hush our voices so that
we cannot articulate our victimization" (xxiii).

Anzaldúa is realistic about the difficulties of taking such a resistive
position, even in the supposedly liberal academy; indeed, in a 1982
interview with Linda Smuckler, she notes that she is glad not to be a
"dependent scholar," someone who depends on a school or discipline
to survive (Keating 2000, 18). In that interview she also suggests that
one of the primary impediments to exposing the nontraditional in
one's writing is overcoming one's own sense of censorship. In answer-
ing Smuckler's questions about whether or not revealing her interest in
psychic readings would make her "less respectable," Anzaldúa answers:
"Tough shit! Once I get past my own censorship of what I should write
about, I don't care what other people say" (Keating 2000, 17). Of course
it would dangerous and inaccurate to reduce Anzaldúa's contributions
to alternative rhetoric to taking a "tough shit" attitude toward one's
audience because such an oversimplification would gloss over all the
hard work she does to help us understand the effort it took for her to
come to such a position. Instead, we should read her tough shit comment as a further call for substantive collective accountings of the operation of privilege and oppression in American society and in rhetoric and
for individuals to take responsibility for their own positions within the
discourses of power. However, the tough shit sentiment is an appropriate
final note for this chapter because it illustrates that when one has done
the work Anzaldúa calls for, there is a kind of freedom, dare I say a moral
position, of privilege that works to free a person from the constraints
of unexamined privilege inherent in the discourses of power. Such a

position does not give one the power to magically slay oppression and extract its many tentacles from American culture, but it does provide a sense of distance that allows one to take up a different kind of agency, a different stance in relationship to the discourses of power, and such a position is the basis for the practice of alternative rhetoric.

Interchapter
THE LIGHT OF THE WORLD

I have always wanted to write about that day Dad said that I shouldn't be split, that I should be the same person no matter where I am, that the Bible says we are to be the "light of the world." I sorely wish I could remember his words exactly because I took them as a rebuke, a sermon but I don't know if Dad intended them that way. The conversation happened some time during my teens when Dad and I were working on some project around the house or yard. Although I didn't know it then, these are the times when Dad and I often talk—when we're working on something together, when we're committed to spending time on a task that occupies most of our physical and conscious effort but in which there are also cracks, moments to stand and wipe the sweat out of your eyebrows before it spills out and runs down your cheek, or to lean back in our office chairs and stretch our bad backs as we wait for the computer to reboot to see if our latest theory about why Windows '94 needs yet another change to its config sys file will make the Microsoft gods happy. In these moments, Dad and I have some of our best talks because we are not officially talking, we are working, doing something else, and each of us mulls things in the leftover bits of concentration we don't need for the task at hand.

On this occasion, though, it ended up that we were talking; we stopped whatever our task was for a few minutes, and, in my eyes my dad morphed into my minister and pronounced to me that I needed to be the light of the world. Too shy and insecure to push the conversation forward, I pulled back, feeling rebuffed. I had been trying to explain to Dad, although I did not completely understand it myself, that my home/church and school lives seemed completely separate, almost as though I was a different person in the two settings. I had no friends who crossed contexts, and the worlds seemed separate.

I am sorely tempted to fictionalize this moment. To write representative dialogue as if it were exact dialogue, to sketch the likely moment, me stumbling out the words, "You know, Dad, um." Dad smoothes the heavy gray mortar with the sharp metal edge of the trowel, looking up to meet my eyes briefly as he reaches for a brick. "Yeah," he says, hefting the brick in his hand, lightly tossing it with practiced skill to flip it rough side out in his rough hand as he turns to lower it onto the mortar, carefully aligning it with the string strung from one end of the row to the other and turning his trowel hand up to tap the brick down with the wooden end of the handle. Gray mortar oozes out as he presses the brick down, and then he flips his trowel hand again to scrape the long metal edge across the face of the emerging wall, gathering the excess in one graceful swoop and tossing it back onto the mortar board with a splat, but smearing small mortar leavings on the finished face of the bricks, which I will brush off later after the mortar is dry and flakey but not quite set, scraping my knuckles against the rough bricks.

It was a moment like this, but not this moment that I have constructed out of my many projects with my dad. I want to pretend I can remember such a moment in detail, because I want to give my readers the pleasure of detail and because I want to embody something of my relationship with my father to provide some context for my reconstruction of this conversation. So I have split the difference, trying to capture something of the essence of our relationship but admitting my artifice. As I reread the description, I recognize I have probably represented my father as a more skilled bricklayer than he actually was. I had tended much more skilled masons when I worked with Dad to build the church building he preached in for two decades, so I know he was slow and a bit awkward compared to them. But what has always impressed me about my father is that he could learn how to do this task, for which he had no real training, just by watching. My younger brother is the same way. Sometime later in my college years, the three of us were working on some project that required a small cement block foundation, and Dad showed my brother how to lay the block, turning at one point and saying to me, "Don't you want to learn?" This time I remember the actual dialogue well. I laughed in response, "No, if I learn how to do that then people will want me to do it!" I think Dad laughed at that. But my answer to the question should have been, "No, Dad, I'm just not as good at this kind of stuff as you and Dan are."

My minister-dad is also a jack-of-all-trades, and although I learned to hang dry wall, wire an outlet, and make mortar the right consistency for bricklaying, I did not excel at these things, and I think my dad was genuinely puzzled that his eldest son, who rarely brought home anything other than As on his report cards, couldn't immediately see the component parts of these physical tasks (although my D in seventh grade woodshop should have given him a hint).

I have digressed from my the "light of the world" story because I wanted to show the jack-of-all-trades side of my father and how much I admire him even though this moment was hard for me. I came to my father that day looking for dialogue about my two worlds, not sure what to make of this separation and perhaps a little proud of who I was in school and wanting him to know that other me and be proud of him, too. His response reminded me that we were not equals—that he was my father and my minister. I read my father's response as quite literally paternalistic in that he saw his father/minister job as judging how I might be straying from the Truth as he knew it and urging me to consider my potentially sinful error. It is tempting for me to engage in my own version of post hoc paternalism by suggesting that my father didn't really understand what it would mean for me to turn his Truths into my principles, that in passing judgment on my brief expression of my situation he was overlooking an opportunity to help me build my own beliefs and perhaps even to learn something with me about how the beliefs we shared could be enacted.

Beyond the obvious teenaged-boy-coming-of-age-trying-to-become-his-father's-equal reading of this story, I want to read this story as an instance of being in a Coatlicue state, of the coming together of divergent aspects of my life and my inability to negotiate my identity at those points. For me, the conflict between my school world and my home/religion world was not resolved for many years, until I began reading about the sociocultural construction of texts in graduate school, a concept that provided me with a meaningful discourse from which to understand my own experiences. And the difficulty of this work makes me realize there was no hope that my father would have been able to help me sort it all out in that one conversation. My point here is threefold. First, I cannot help but consider how we writing teachers (myself included) get so caught up in making sure our students learn what we know they need to learn that we don't stop to consider the worlds they are straddling and make it our goal to help them address the implications of their Coatlicue states. And, second, this story makes me wonder about the nature of the journey and what kinds of interventions could be made at any given point. On the day I tried to talk with my dad about my two worlds, even the most supportive informed response could not possibly have helped me come to an understanding of self that would have made my homosexuality articulable that day, so I take this as a cautionary tale about the difficulties of such identity negotiations and a recognition that small steps may be important and that creating real dialogue in such moments may be difficult. This story also reminds me that I am in many ways my father, that though he was a minister and I am a professor, in many ways I still see my job as he did: as being the light of the world. Yet, I have also seen in my teaching and the process of writing this book that I need to curtail my inclination to pronounce and instead to consider what it means for my students or the readers of this book to move forward. In a sense, I'm following my dad's advice to continue trying to be the light of the world, but I'm trying to do so in a way that understands although there are occasionally dramatic conversion moments, most change that matters comes in small increments.

5

DAVID SEDARIS
Expanding Epideictic—A Rhetoric of Indirection

My writing is just a desperate attempt to get laughs. If you get anything else out of it, it's an accident.
David Sedaris in Berquist, 2000

Given that we are vulnerable to the address of others in ways that we cannot fully control, no more than we can control the sphere of language, does this mean that we are without agency and without responsibility?
Butler, 2005

David Sedaris would likely be bemused to know that anyone considers him a rhetorician, much less a purveyor of alternative rhetoric. As the opening epigraph indicates, Sedaris steadfastly refuses to claim his work has any purpose other than humor. Thus, from the outset I must acknowledge that Sedaris is not compelled to speak out against injustice in the same ways as Grimké, Douglass, or Anzaldúa. He is much less direct than the other three authors in using his experiences with marginalization to expose fault lines of difference and discrimination in American society. Yet even a casual reader of Sedaris's work could hardly miss that Sedaris needs to write; he is unabashed about his desire for attention, but more to the point, his writing serves as a means for him to make sense of life and culture on a daily basis. He is an avid, perhaps even compulsive, diary writer, writing every day and filling four diaries a year, which he has professionally bound.[1] However, Sedaris's popularity as an essay writer for such periodicals as *The New Yorker, GQ,* and *Esquire,* and as a best-selling memoirist, depends on more than just his wit and his desire for attention. Without seeming to do so, Sedaris provides keen cultural insights that parse problematic cultural values without engaging in heavy-handed deconstruction. Further, as the Butler epigraph suggests, Sedaris cannot fully control the ways in which he is read, even

---

1. For more on this, see Bergquist (2000).

if he claims that getting anything other than laughs out of his writing is an accident. Indeed, in this chapter, I use my own and others' readings of Sedaris's writing to illustrate that the answers to the questions Butler poses here are yes and yes. That is, despite his inability to control how he is read, Sedaris does exercise agency (beyond his humorous intent), and his writing puts both himself as author and his readers into a relationship of responsibility that can be usefully examined in the service of deconstructing the usual conceptions of Truth and morality.

Sedaris cannot be seen as explicitly seeking to expand the rhetorical canon for the academy or as directly attempting to unsettle problematic cultural values, although his memoir writing can be read as having these effects. In fact, as I argue later in this chapter, Sedaris engages in what I call a rhetoric of indirection, and, in this sense, he provides an interesting counterpoint to Grimké, Douglass, and Anzaldúa because he does not explicitly attempt to change cultural values. However, as I argue in the next section of this chapter, he can be read as expanding the canon of rhetorical practice if one reads him in the light of calls for an expanded understanding of epideictic rhetoric in the last twenty years, and his work can also be read as engaging in nearly as great a range of difference issues as Anzaldúa's work does, but Sedaris's approach is decidedly different. In one sense, he is more successful than any of the other three writers in creating the copresence of the other without falling into the potential subalternity trap of reifying the problematic binary values usually entailed in those differences, in part because he simply refuses to take his work seriously, even though I argue that his writing does serious work.

Sedaris first garnered national attention in the early 1990s when Ira Glass asked him to read his "SantaLand Diaries" (1994) for *Morning Edition* on National Public Radio. Although Sedaris now refuses to read from "SantaLand Diaries" because he considers it poorly written (Bergquist 2000, 55), this exposure led to the publication in 1994 of *Barrel Fever*, a collection of short stories and memoir pieces and, eventually, to a four-book deal with Little, Brown and Company which, in turn, resulted in four best-selling books of memoir: *Naked* (1997b), *Me Talk Pretty One Day* (2000), *Dress Your Family In Corduroy and Denim* (2004), and *When You Are Engulfed in Flames* (2008). In addition, he published a small volume of short stories and memoir pieces called *Holidays on Ice* in 1997 and edited *Children Playing Before a Statue of Hercules* (2008), an anthology of short stories to benefit 826NYC, a writing and tutoring center in

Brooklyn, New York. He has also written several plays, and he regularly reads his work on NPR's *This American Life*.

Despite Sedaris's claim that he is just out for laughs, his work is beginning to receive serious attention. *Sedaris*, a book of criticism on his work written by Kevin Kopelson, was published by the University of Minnesota Press in 2007; his stories are increasingly anthologized in high-school textbooks and college composition readers, and his work has even been the subject of an article on composition pedagogy.[2] There is little doubt that Sedaris is becoming one of the most read humorists and memoirists of his generation; however, sorting out to what extent he can be seen as engaging in alternative rhetoric is a somewhat complicated project.

Given his body of work, I admit it makes more sense to call Sedaris a memoirist and humorist than it does to call him a rhetorician; however, Sedaris's work can be usefully read as an expansion of epideictic rhetoric when considered in the context of a number of rhetorical theorists who have questioned the continuing neo-Aristotelian distinction between rhetoric that explicitly seeks to persuade and rhetoric that seeks to praise, blame, or entertain. For example, Takis Poulakos, among others, has argued that epideictic rhetoric has the "propensity to shape the social sphere" (1988, 148), and, in his article reexamining Gorgias's *Encomium for Helen*, Edward Schiappa argues that Gorgias would not have recognized the distinction Aristotle made between epideictic rhetoric and deliberative and forensic rhetoric (1995, 313). Further, David C. Hoffman argues that epideictic rhetoric serves an important community-building function and that we should not write it off as occasioning some of the worst kinds of empty oratorical showboating and leading to the degeneration of society. Rather, we should see such ritualized discourse as having an important community-building function: "Epideictic is the foundation of rationality and ethicality. It can be used as an instrument to work against the disintegration of social order" (1997, 33).

As I explore in more detail in the next section, Sedaris's work can be read as a further expansion of this enlarged view of epideictic rhetoric because he writes from a position of marginality, exposes systemic oppression, and accounts for his own place within those systems. His work uses his own experiences not simply to reinforce traditional American values but to call problematic aspects of them into question.

---

2. For more on this, see Linden (2004).

Thus, ironically, reading Sedaris's writing as epideictic rhetoric means looking not for the ways it shores up values, which Hoffman suggests is the value of epideictic rhetoric (1997), but for the ways his work seeks the disintegration of problematic aspects of the dominant social order. In this sense, Sedaris can be read as engaging in the kind of recasting of the epideictic as a force for change described by Cynthia Miecznikowski Sheard: "a rhetorical gesture that moves its audience toward a process of critical reflection that goes beyond evaluation and toward envisioning and *actualizing* alternative realities, possible worlds" (1996, 787).

In the body of this chapter, I explore how Sedaris contributes to this wider notion of epideictic without intending to do so and then, more particularly, how, much like Anzaldúa, he performs multiple identities, but, unlike her, makes the other visible and relevant not through direct argument but through indirection, the presumption of normality, and confession, apology, and other forms of self-deprecation. Entailed in this larger effect is an important issue about the role of Truth in expanded genres of epideictic writing. The emphasis on the value of the aesthetic over the strictly factual has been a part of the debate about the value of epideictic rhetoric since Aristotle. Sedaris's writing provides a particularly interesting case in this history because, even in his memoir writing, he often crosses the line from nonfiction into fiction. Indeed, Sedaris has been accused by Alex Heard in a *New Republic* article of "lying through his teeth" (2007, 36). Thus, in the body of this chapter, I explore first how Sedaris toys with the usual notions of Truth in his version of expanded epideictic, and then how he can be read as engaging in a rhetoric of indirection. In doing so, I draw occasionally on his essays published singly in magazines, on a few pieces from *Barrel Fever* and *Holidays on Ice*, and on his many interviews. However, my primary focus in this analysis is *Naked, Me Talk, Dress,* and *Engulfed* (I have shortened the titles for convenience) because they provide the most substantive descriptions of what it means for Sedaris to speak from his positions of marginality in American culture as a homosexual, as an obsessive-compulsive, and as a former drug, alcohol, and tobacco addict within a broader context of commenting on American culture. However, these are not books about being gay or recovering from a drug addiction; indeed, Sedaris hates "the way the word *out* has been sexualized and forced into service for all things gay (2000, 258) and wrote a piece called "Twelve Moments in the Life of the Artist" (2000) that can be read as a loose parody of twelve-step programs. Instead, Sedaris makes humorous comments on American society, and as the title of his 2004 book—*Dress Your Family in Corduroy and Denim*—suggests, the primary topic of his books is, to a large degree, his family.

Sedaris's growing body of work is also interesting as a kind of case study of his evolution as a writer, particularly how he has come to account for his own positionality more explicitly in his later work. As a writer, Sedaris has never been shy about admitting his interest in the grotesque or things often stigmatized, but his work has steadily moved away from the safe: from fiction to nonfiction, from writing about family in fairly easy terms in *Naked* and *Me Talk* (even though the former tells of his mother's cancer death) to being more revealing about his family and the problems his writing about them creates in *Dress* and to more explicit discussions of his relationships with his boyfriends and his struggles with addiction in *Engulfed*. In his latest book, we also begin to see Sedaris's financial success: he can choose to spend "close to twenty thousand dollars" to quit smoking (2008, 313) and has become so accustomed to luxury hotels that one of his primary motivations to quit smoking was so that while he is on book/speaking tours he can stay in luxury hotels with nonsmoking policies.

EXPANDING EPIDEICTIC

Sorting out the ways in which Sedaris's memoir writing can be read as an alternative form of epideictic requires attention to three aspects of the modern debate about the form and function of epideictic rhetoric: the valuing of aesthetic effect over an emphasis on the negotiation of truth status, affirming or challenging traditional values, and blurring the borders between narrative and argumentative genres. In this section, I examine these three issues before I illustrate how they apply to Sedaris's work by exploring claims that Sedaris is lying through his teeth.

Sheard argues that epideictic rhetoric is quite common in modern life and is also important because it serves as the site of negotiation of commonly held values:

> Most of us, however, regularly participate in situations where appropriate conduct is assigned to and followed by us through ritualized uses of words whose authority we take largely for granted. Acts of worship, protest, celebration, and education are some of those in which we find word and deed difficult to separate and generally accept their connection without question. (1996, 765)

This expanded view of epideictic rhetoric runs contrary to the classic distinction made by Aristotle between serious political and legal debates (deliberative and forensic rhetoric) and show pieces (epideictic rhetoric) that were, as Chaim Perelman and Lucie Olbrechts-Tyteca explain, valued in Aristotle's day for "artistic virtuosity" and "regarded in the same light as a dramatic spectacle or athletic contest." Perelman and Olbrechts-Tyteca explain that this distinction was challenged as early as the nineteenth century by rhetorician Richard Whately, and they identify "the absence of the concept of value-judgment" and an emphasis on "intensity of adherence" as the critical underlying issues at stake in the distinction (1969, 48).

Valuing the Aesthetic Over Absolute Truth

As I have already mentioned, this limited view of epideictic rhetoric has been challenged by modern rhetorical theorists for two decades, and one of the critical issues in understanding the larger role of epideictic rhetoric is the underlying balancing act between aesthetic and argument. As Hoffman explains, the emphasis on pleasing aesthetics in epideictic forms makes the relationship between epideictic and argument "a troublesome one" (1997, 2). The presumption is that because epideictic forms give primacy to aesthetic pleasure, the underlying truth value of claims is a secondary issue—a charge that has been leveled against Sedaris.

Sheard argues that epideictic rhetoric should be seen as having a kind of enthymemic relationship with truth—one in which truth issues are more presumed than highlighted. However, she argues that this relationship does not diminish its importance: "I also wish to suggest that epideictic's questionable relationship to truth need not be seen to undermine or diminish its significance" (1996, 774). Similarly, building on Kenneth Burke's notion of "play," Hoffman argues that epideictic should be seen as operating under a different presumption about truth value: "that there is a game afoot, that the speaker has entered a play-world with its own set of rules" (1997, 18).

Affirming or Challenging Traditional Values

Because epideictic rhetoric depends, to some degree, on signaling to its audience that a different kind of truth game is in play—one that favors aesthetic pleasure over detached rationality—it is often dismissed a mere entertainment. However, Sheard argues that epideictic "serves more exigent social and civic functions than simply celebrating, reinforcing, or reexamining values" (1996, 787), and several scholars see epideictic as serving an illuminative function because it blends the universal and the particular, making connections between argument and lived experiences (Hoffman 1997, 19; Poulakos 1987, 323–6; Ryan 1996, 2). Of course, as Sir Francis Bacon so tellingly reasoned, persuasive rhetoric must apply reason to the imagination for the better moving of the will. In this sense, an epideictic/aesthetic function is often critical in neo-Aristotelian rhetoric in that it may help engage the audience's imagination in the hope that such engagement will move them accept new views or take action. However, modern defenders of epideictic rhetoric see it has having significance of its own, as functioning to affirm or challenge traditional values. Thus a second important issue in understanding how epideictic rhetoric can be alternative is understanding how it may work as a force to reinforce or to challenge dominant cultural values.

From the standpoint of alternative rhetoric as I have defined it in this book, the critical issues for determining whether any given act of epideictic rhetoric serves as alternative rhetoric is whether or not the act upholds or challenges social values and conventions that maintain systems of oppression and whether or not that act of rhetoric shows awareness of its own relative standing in systems of oppression. In regard to the former, rhetorical theorists arguing for an expanded understanding of epideictic have been well aware of the social implications of such rhetoric. For example, Pat Ryan argues epideictic rhetoric is "ambi-potent" in that it can serve either to "unite or fracture." Ryan takes the traditional view toward epideictic rhetoric: "Ideally, *epideictic* promotes identification and inclusion by celebrating cultural values that hold a community together, but by defining values too narrowly *epideictic* discourse can also promote division and exclusion" (1996, 7). Similarly, Poulakos notes the elitism inherent in the ancient Greek sophists' purveyance of epideictic rhetoric: "This is not to suggest that the educational activities of the Sophists helped the 'middle class'" (1988, 158) And in her analysis of the "neoliberal epideictic" rhetoric of the 9/11 memorial in New York City on September 11, 2002, Vivian Bradford argues that epideictic rhetoric often serves a conservative, didactic function:

> Epideictic is typically didactic in nature. Encomiasts sustain civic memory from one generation to the next by catechistically instructing audiences in

putatively common accounts of collective origins, experiences, and ideals. (2006, 5)

This value-affirming function of epideictic rhetoric is one reason Sheard calls for it to be reassessed as playing important roles in defining civic responsibility and in understanding its visionary potential: "Reconceptualizing epideictic in order to emphasize these traits will in some sense require that we 'reinvent' not only epideictic but also its relationship to forensic and deliberative rhetorics as well" (1996, 766). My argument is that epideictic rhetoric need not always serve a conservative function. As Bonnie J. Dow (1989) argues, it can be used to define situations, and as I illustrate later this chapter, its enthymemic relationship to truth and its connectedness to human experience can be used in powerful ways to fracture traditional values, challenging the status quo. The extent to which those who engage in acts of epideictic substantively account for their standing within systems of privilege and oppression, and the opacity of their own perspectives, has not been much discussed, and I take it up later as I discuss Sedaris's writing.

Blurring Genre Boundaries

A third aspect of epideictic rhetoric I see as critical for its use as alternative rhetoric is its blurring of traditional boundaries between argumentative and narrative genres. The traditional distinctions among deliberative, forensic, and epideictic rhetoric are based not only on differences in their basic underlying purposes (persuasive for deliberative and forensic and celebratory for epideictic) but also on the usual genres for their expression. Modern rhetorical scholars arguing for an expanded view of epideictic rhetoric have challenged the limiting of epideictic rhetoric to celebratory purposes and a few ceremonial genres. For example, Poulakos uses examples from Isocrates's *Evagoras* to show how this important example of classic Greek epideictic rhetoric illustrates not only the need for a more nuanced understanding of epideictic rhetoric historically but also how genres could be mixed across the three modes of rhetoric: "Not all generic elements included in a given work need belong to that same generic family" (1988, 151). Sheard is even more direct in her argument that epideictic rhetoric should not be and cannot be limited to a particular set of genres: "I have also tried to recast epideictic less as a 'genre' and more as a 'gesture' or 'mode' of discourse, avoiding the term 'genre' intentionally" (1996, 789). Poulakos goes so far as to argue that epideictic rhetoric may usefully blend fact and fiction; in another article examining the *Evagoras*, he argues that not only did Isocrates expand the usual role of the epideictic to include persuasion but that the speech must also be seen both "as fiction and as history" (1987, 322).

This blurring of both purposes and genres is important for understanding how a writer like David Sedaris can be seen as practicing alternative rhetoric because for Sedaris the aesthetic (usually humor) is always primary, but it is also nearly always mixed with critical insight. While Sedaris can be read as often using both praise and blame in such work, he usually turns the two on their heads, reversing values, often in self-deprecatory ways. Before I examine the range of techniques Sedaris uses to create connection with his readers through indirection, I turn to his blurring of fact and fiction, beginning with charges that Sedaris's memoirs frequently move from nonfiction to fiction. In a sense, I am arguing that to understand Sedaris's writing as alternative rhetoric, we must read it in the same way Poulakos argues we must read Isocrates's *Evagoras*, recognizing that the work

> suspends the referential capacity of language by creating a possible world. Such manner of representation provides us with a link between poetry and rhetoric, a continuity that Isocrates boasts to have established through his novel composition. (1987, 323)

The essence of my argument here is that epideictic rhetoric not only gives primacy to the aesthetic but that it also plays with truth-value in a way that might be seen as cheating in other forms of rhetoric. As the scholars whose work I have cited here argue, engaging in this expanded form/function of epideictic rhetoric often depends on signaling to the audience that a different kind of game is afoot and that some kind of means for escape from the usual values and discourse practices is necessary. In this sense, I contend that playful epideictic rhetoric can be used as a powerful form of alternative rhetoric precisely because it plays a different kind of Truth game. Because alternative rhetoric as I have defined it requires accounting for one's positionality within the discourses of power, it must be understood that doing so may require publicly owning identities and experiences that have been stigmatized, or admitting culpability in the oppression of others. As the discussion that follows illustrates, truth-value may be difficult to sort out, particularly when one narrates one's attempts to use one's own experiences to expose others' complicity in systemic marginalization.

DON'T MAKE THINGS UP: EPIDEICTIC IN SEDARIS'S MEMOIR WRITING

I begin this exploration with claims by Alex Heard (2007), who argues in an article appearing in *The New Republic* that Sedaris's memoirs are factually inaccurate, that Sedaris breaks the fundamental rule of autobiography: don't make things up. While Heard may be right that Sedaris crosses the line between fiction and nonfiction, in some cases without signaling the shift clearly, Heard's own account of his fact-checking mission illustrates that the underlying issues are more complex than they first appear, specifically that applying a journalistic notion of verification with sources has limited value in assessing playful epideictic rhetoric.

For his part, Sedaris readily admits that strict historical accuracy is not his primary concern when he writes memoir. In an interview, Sedaris suggests, "autobiography is the last place you would look for truth," and he expresses surprise about the controversy surrounding the accuracy of James Frey's *A Million Little Pieces* memoir:

> He [Frey] kind of warned you in advance that he was a fucked-up alcoholic. I can't understand the self-righteousness that goes along with that anger. You can let the truth slide when it comes to the president, but if it's a first-time memoirist, how dare he? How dare he lead us on? (Knight 2007, 80)

Further, Heard reports that in an interview he conducted with Sedaris, the author admitted that in "Dix Hill" (1997b), he made up specific details about his experiences with Clarence, an orderly at the mental hospital, and Heard reasons, "That seems beyond the boundaries of comic exaggeration. . . . It's not fine to pretend—in a long and detailed scene—that you performed outlandish, dangerous tasks at a mental hospital when you didn't" (2007, 36). Heard is similarly concerned about a made-up scene in "Giant Dreams, Midget Abilities" (2000), in which Sedaris admits (to Heard) that he made up his midget guitar teacher's personality quirks and poor teaching methods as well as a scene in which the teacher, Mr. Mancini, mistakenly assumes Sedaris is making a pass at him. Heard reports that his conversations with Sedaris convinced him that "Sedaris honestly doesn't see the difference [between fiction and nonfiction], and his audience isn't complaining," and then raises a critical question: "Should that be good enough for the rest of us?" (36–37).

For Heard, the answer to this question is clearly "no," but I think he has posed too simple a question about the applied truth promises of nonfiction writing that seeks primarily to entertain rather than to directly affect public policy, and he underestimates the role and value of play in epideictic forms. I agree with Heard that if specific scenes did not occur, then these pieces cross from nonfiction to fiction, and this is a line that must be crossed carefully. Also, Heard rightly critiques those who have written about these events in Sedaris's writing as if they were absolutely true, exposing their naiveté in taking Sedaris too literally. However, I have two concerns about Heard's presumption that he has found the truth about Sedaris and his writing. First, Heard presumes that his own journalistic fact-checking methodology allows him to pronounce what has truth-value and what does not without any substantive attempt to account for the subjectivities of those involved (including his own).

For example, Heard claims that even before Sedaris admitted in their interview that the mistaken pass at Mr. Mancini was fictional, "I already felt sure of it, because I'd found a man, who, like Sedaris, took guitar lessons from Mancini when he was a child" (2007, 37). Heard writes at some length to establish the credibility of his source and the superiority of this source's perspective on the guitar teacher:

> The former student is 49-year-old L.M. (Sam) Hawkins, and he seems quite credible. He works on the Executive Security Branch of the Kentucky State Police, which means he protects Governor Ernie Fletcher and his wife, Glenna. The teacher's name was George Sage, and, though I was unable to locate Sage, alive or dead, Hawkins says he was an excellent instructor. The lessons worked: to this day, Hawkins makes extra money playing jazz guitar on the side, and Sedaris's description of his old mentor bothers him. "'My recollections of the character represented as Mr. Mancini are not the same as David Sedaris's' he says. 'George Sage was a very serious-minded guitar teacher. I am indebted to him, because without his patience with me as a student, guitar would not be the integral part of my life that it is today.'" (37)

Hawkins's use of the term "character" hints that he understands Sedaris is up to something different than writing a factual review of his guitar teacher—that Mr. Mancini is a character who is different from the "real" George Sage. While Heard may be justified in his critique of Sedaris's invention of a whole scene that did not occur, his acceptance of the testimony of his source as the true account fails to acknowledge both that the perspective of a successful guitar student and a failed one might differ greatly and that Sedaris might have a different purpose than the one Heard attempts to impose on him.

A more dramatic example of failure to consider differences in subjectivities occurs in Heard's critique of "Go Carolina" (2000), a piece which
Heard claims is an even more egregious example of departing from reality. In the piece, Sedaris somewhat satirically implies a conspiracy among
his elementary school teachers to identify latent homosexuals and send
them to speech therapy with "agent" Chrissy Samson:

> "One of these days I'm going to have to hang a sign on that door," Agent
> Samson used to say. She was probably thinking along the lines of SPEECH
> THERAPY LAB, though a more appropriate marker would have read
> FUTURE HOMOSEXUALS OF AMERICA. We knocked ourselves out trying
> to fit in but were ultimately betrayed by our tongues. At the beginning of the
> school year, while we were congratulating ourselves on successfully passing
> for normal, Agent Samson was taking names as our assembled teachers raised
> their hands, saying, "I've got one in my homeroom," and "There are two in
> my fourth-period math class." Were they also able to spot the future drunks
> and depressives? Did they hope that by eliminating our lisps, they might set
> us on a different path, or were they trying to prepare us for future stage and
> choral careers? (2000, 10–11)

Heard contacted the retired principal, whom he presents as "confused"
rather than "angry" when he read this piece, and as commenting, "'I
don't understand why he thinks we would make decisions about a
speech class based on such factors . . . I'm sorry it seemed that way to
him'" (2007, 37).

That Heard and (apparently) the retired principal miss the over-
the-top exaggeration of this piece surprises me given that when I teach
this essay, few of my students have difficulty understanding that Sedaris
is exaggerating to the point of absurdity here. However, I am not surprised that neither Heard nor the retired principal can imagine the
purpose for this exaggeration because neither of them comments on
the possibility of systematic but unacknowledged homophobia. Neither
of them seems to take the principal's implied question seriously: why
would Sedaris think school officials made decisions based on "such factors?" My best guess is that their inability to read this text as my students
and I do is because they are unable to see its playful absurdity, to sort
out when Sedaris is teasing them because they can't conceive that men
like them could have played a role in the kind of heteronormativity that
underlies the story or that an author would choose to poke fun at it (and
them) rather than to be outraged. In the terms I have used in this book,

Heard and the principal's limited reading is a problem of their failure to consider the opacity of their own perspectives in that they are blind to their own potential participation in heteronormativity and homophobia. Although Heard is likely right to criticize Sedaris for making up the critical scene with Mr. Mancini, I would argue that he misses the larger Truth because he plays too literal a truth game and because he refuses to substantively explore the question his own analysis raised about the operation of heteronormativity.

Of course, I may be misreading Heard and the principal, particularly the principal whose comments are available only through Heard's lens. However, in Heard's case, I think there are only two possible readings: either the complexity of Sedaris's purpose is beyond him, in part because he cannot appreciate the underlying cultural truth/experience being satirized, or he understands the underlying dynamic and chooses to ignore it. In the former case he should be seen as woefully uninformed and unimaginative, and in the latter as irresponsible if he refuses to explore the issues his own research raised. In either case, I contend that the problem with his analysis is that he takes a stance as the arbiter of truth and presumes his perspectives and journalistic methods are sufficient for such a task without considering the limits of his own understanding.

My point here is not to defend Sedaris; indeed, when I teach these essays, I counsel my students to be more cautious than Sedaris is about changing the characteristics of the people they write about or inventing incidents that did not occur. Rather, I want to illustrate that the underlying presumptions about what constitutes truth are not as simple as Heard presumes; his "fact checking" is itself neither inherently objective nor a sufficient basis for sorting out truth-value because it fails to account for the inevitable differences of perspectives of those involved in such negotiations and for how those involved are positioned within the discourses of power and marginalization. In the terms I introduced in chapter one, Heard must be read as failing to consider his own opacity in that he does not explicitly acknowledge his own place within systems of inequity such as heteronormativity that affect his reading of Sedaris or within the standards for such judgment—journalistic fact checking—that he presumes are an unproblematic basis on which to judge truth. Such kinds of judgment, as Butler explains,

> can be a way to fail to own one's limitations and thus provides no felicitous basis for reciprocal recognition of human beings as opaque to themselves,

partially blind, constitutively limited. To know oneself as limited is still to know something about oneself, even if one's knowing is afflicted by the limitation that one knows. (2005, 46)

In contrast, Sedaris can be read as at least acknowledging some of his relationships with the discourses of power. To be fair, Sedaris does not often directly acknowledge his positions of privilege nor provide substantive discussions of how they affect the stories he tells. However, he does not claim to be adjudicating truth, as does Heard, and his description of his primary means for addressing potential problems created by his narratives emphasizes maintaining relationships with his family and friends and, at least implicitly, recognizes the underlying differences in perspectives:

> It's important to me that the people I love aren't hurt. If I write about anyone in my family, I give it to them first and say, "Do you have any problem with the way you're portrayed? Is there is anything written here that you don't want people to know?" That's important to me, but the clock being oak or walnut is not important to me. (Knight 2007, 80)

Sedaris's practice here is reminiscent of the kinds of participant checking that are often part of ethnographic research, with the notable exception that Sedaris makes no claim that he is taking care for those he does not love (e.g., Mr. Mancini), or that the family members he writes about might choose to represent themselves and their relationships in other ways if given the chance. To his credit, Sedaris writes about these tensions in *Dress* (2004), representing himself as a scavenger of sorts, rooting through his family's lives for things to write about in "Put a Lid on It" and recognizing that he sees himself as "a friendly junkman, building things form the little pieces of scrap I find here and there, but my family's started to see things differently" in "Repeat After Me" (147). Among the things I often ask my students to try to emulate in Sedaris's writing are his willingness to consider multiple perspectives, his deconstruction of traditional values, and his reflexiveness about his own understanding of a given situation. That Heard fails to comment on any of these aspects in his analysis of the truth-value of Sedaris's writing is indicative of the second problem I see in his critiques.

My second concern with Heard's pronouncements of the truth-value of Sedaris's writing is that he bases such judgments on a very traditional set of culturally dominant values, and, in a very real sense, he misreads

Sedaris's writing because he cannot or, perhaps, will not step outside those values. Ultimately, this failure to engage with a perspective that understands and represents systemic difference in American culture makes Heard, in my view, an irresponsible reader and an example of privileged resistance to the possible subversive functions of expanded epideictic rhetoric. The basic problem I want to explore here is the imposition of a particular set of value judgments that are not only taken as objective without any substantive accounting of the subjectivity of the user, but also are based on unexamined cultural privilege. Such a position presumes both that the rules of the game are fixed and that the values by which those rules are interpreted and applied are consistent with those of dominant culture.

From my perspective, an important aspect of Sedaris's genius as a writer and commenter on American society is that he refuses to be bound by such assumptions; indeed, at the heart of Sedaris's humor is keen cultural insight by which he deconstructs traditional values. He simply plays a different game, and in doing so he not only breaks traditional genre boundaries but he also reverses values. As I have already noted, Heard's failure to recognize Sedaris's comments on the pervasiveness of homophobia and heteronormativity in "Go Carolina" and "Giant Dreams, Midget Abilities" limits his reading of those texts, and his insistence on applying the set of truth-values commonly used in journalism blinds him to the larger implications of the very questions he raises. However, Heard's narrow reading is not limited only to sexual identity issues. His readings of several of Sedaris's characters reflects a rather wooden application of traditional, bourgeois American values to the extent that he misses both the depth of the characters and the ways in which Sedaris challenges traditional values in his use of them. To illustrate how the presumption of traditional values may limit understanding of epideictic texts that value aesthetic effect over clear identification of disputed values, I turn now to Heard's reading of some of Sedaris's characters: the patients of the Dix Hill mental hospital, Sharon (Sedaris's mother), and Mr. Mancini.

In places, Heard's readings of Sedaris seem determined to miss the larger picture, to invoke not only a strict journalistic truth-telling standard but also to refuse to consider that Sedaris might hold nontraditional values. I contend that Heard's failure to engage with Sedaris beyond this limited perspective amounts to more than just a lack of imagination on his part. Instead, I read it as an attempt to impose problematic dominant values, and, thus, it serves as an example of a misreading of alternative rhetoric based on unexamined privilege. For example, as I have already mentioned, Heard is concerned that Sedaris made up the scenes where he worked with Clarence, the orderly at Dix Hill (1997b). However, his critique does not stop there; citing evidence from the letters Sedaris wrote to Libby Currence, one of his adolescent friends, Heard suggests that, in college, Sedaris was actually much more kind-hearted toward the mentally ill and that the later stance he takes in writing "Dix Hill" is

> strange. In real life, young David felt more sympathy for mental patients than he would later display in *Naked*. I guess being mean was funnier. Libby and I talked about his tendency, and she said, "David probably sidestepped intimacy with humor." (2007, 38).

Setting aside the pop-psychology-fear-of-intimacy diagnosis, Heard's labeling of Sedaris as being "mean" for the sake of comic effect ignores Sedaris's own positionality with regards to mental/emotional abledness, that before "Dix Hill," another *Naked* essay, "A Plague of Tics," describes in comic detail, Sedaris's own "freakish collection" of obsessive/compulsive behaviors (1997b, 17).

Even the most casual reader could hardly miss the matter-of-factness with which Sedaris speaks of what would likely be diagnosed as an obsessive-compulsive disorder in this essay. For example, when his teacher shows up at his home to discuss such activities as Sedaris leaving his seat in the classroom to lick the light switch, Sedaris describes his mother offering Miss Chestnut a drink and performing an imitation of his compulsion to touch things with his tongue, which Miss Chestnut deems "Priceless!" (1997b, 13). In her comments about Sedaris's compulsive tics (which young Sedaris apparently overhears), Sharon refuses to unduly pathologize them:

> "God only knows where he gets it from," my mother said. "He's probably down in his room right this minute, counting his eyelashes or gnawing at the pulls on his dresser. One, two o'clock in the morning and he'll still be at it, rattling around the house to poke the laundry hamper or press his face against the refrigerator door. The kid's wound too tight, but he'll come out of it. So, what do you say, another scotch, Katherine?" (14)

Of course, from a traditional perspective, Sharon might be read as refusing to deal with her son's mental/emotional disease and denying him treatment, but Sedaris himself does not see it that way. In fact, in later essays he takes the same kind of cool stance toward his compulsions and addictions, representing himself as largely freed of his compulsions when he took up smoking in college: "For people like me, people who twitched and jerked and cried out in tiny voices, cigarettes were a godsend" (2008, 247). Also, he speaks directly and with detachment about the problems and benefits of his compulsions:

> The good part about being an obsessive compulsive is that you're always on time for work. The bad part is that you're on time for everything. Rinsing your coffee cup, taking a bath, walking your clothes to the Laundromat; there's no mystery to your comings and goings, no room for spontaneity. (2004, 114)

My point here is that given this larger perspective on mental/emotional abledness in Sedaris's work, Heard's suggestion that Sedaris is simply being mean to increase the comic effect of "Dix Hill" is, at best, a narrow reading that ignores the wider body of his work and, at worst, an attempt to enforce a traditional set of unexamined values.

A similar misreading occurs in Heard's use of Libby Currence's perspective on how Sedaris represents his mother in his writing. Heard paints Sedaris as presenting a cold caricature of Sharon as a "full-time grouch." In contrast, Libby, whom Heard describes as "a sweetheart," remembers Sharon as a capable mother: "She was nurturing, she was warm, she cooked dinner every night. I thought she was a *marvelous* woman" (2007, 38). This assessment of Sharon's character can be sustained only through the most wooden application of the *Leave-It-to-Beaver* notion of the perfect stay-at-home mom, and the implication that Sedaris does not see his mother as nurturing or marvelous is bizarre, and it misses the reversal of values Sedaris uses. For example, as Kevin Kopelson notes is his 2007 book *Sedaris*, it is possible to read Sedaris's Sharon as lazy: "Her hobbies, to hear Sedaris tell it, were smoking, sleeping, and Sidney Sheldon" (27). While young-Sedaris often chastised his mother for her substandard housekeeping, such claims are always made in a context of his own exaggerated fastidiousness: Sedaris is the kind of boy who "regularly petitioned for a brand-name vacuum cleaner" (2000, 20) and once asked his mother, "Are you sad because you haven't vacuumed the basement yet?" (1997a, 6). As Kopelson notes, Sedaris's sketch of Sharon's departures from the traditional ideals of American motherhood need to be read as operating under a different set of values: "If the smoking, the drinking, the insults, and the aversion to sentiment aren't vices for Sedaris, nor are they virtues. Sharon, however, was basically good. She was both instinctively egalitarian and willfully benevolent" (2007, 31). In addition, Sedaris paints portrait after portrait of the Sedaris children's adoration for their mother. For example, in an essay entitled "Let it Snow" (2004), Sedaris tells the story of Sharon locking the kids out of the house after two snow days off from school and refusing to let them back into the house as she alternates between drinking wine and coffee. In the story, oldest sister Lisa calls her mother a "bitch," and the Sedaris kids devise a plot to shame their mother by laying youngest sister, Tiffany, down in the street to be run over. However, the genuine affection the Sedaris children feel for their mother is amply evident in Sedaris's description of the end of the episode, when Sharon is shamed by a neighbor into coming out into the snow in her loafers to reclaim her children:

> This was how things went. One moment she was locking us out of the house and the next we were rooting around in the snow, looking for her left shoe. "Oh, forget about it," she said. "It'll turn up in a few days." Gretchen fitted her cap over my mother's foot. Lisa secured it with her scarf, and surrounding her tightly on all sides, we made our way back home. (16)

In a number of essays, Sedaris writes similar tributes to Sharon, who appears as the voice of reason, trying vainly to reign in her husband's absurd behavior in "Ashes" (1997b); as a woman who takes decisive action to remove Sedaris from a situation in which he was being manipulated by young girl and her mother in "The Girl Next Door" (2004); and as weeping and apologizing in "Hejira" (2004) when her husband throws Sedaris out of the house for being gay, even though Lou does not have the guts to tell his son the real reason. That Heard misses these obvious tributes to Sharon and suggests that Sedaris presents her as a "full-time grouch" indicates that either he has not read Sedaris's books very carefully or that he applies such a narrow set of bourgeois cultural values that he misses the larger picture. Of course, the answer may be that some of both is at work, and Sedaris's refusal to provide the usual resolutions to conflict in his essays may be also at work; for example in "Let It Snow" (2004), he gives the description of the Sedaris children's search for their mother's shoe rather than a Sunday School moral-to-the-story ending. Thus, Sedaris's brand of alternative rhetoric may be somewhat more susceptible to misinterpretation than more traditional forms, but the example that follows illustrates how Heard's misreadings must ultimately be read as more than just misunderstandings.

The uncritical application of a bourgeois set of values to Sedaris's work is most clearly seen in Heard's critique of Sedaris's representation of Mr. Mancini, in which he notes, "Sedaris once told an interviewer he exaggerates people 'up,' making them better than they are" and argues that it is hard to see how he does so in Mr. Mancini's case as the character is portrayed as a poor guitar teacher and "a badly dressed cornball with a 'high and strange' voice" and ultimately as a homophobe (2007, 37). Pulled out of the context of the essay, such assessments might seem reasonable; however, once again Heard misses that there is a game afoot, that the essay provides plenty of indications that the adult-writer Sedaris is painting a picture of the interplay of the adolescent-character Sedaris's cold-heartedness and vulnerability. For example, the cold-heartedness appears shortly after Sedaris's description of his first meeting with Mr. Mancini, when he and his sisters spend their supposed practice sessions eating potato chips, "scowling at our hated instruments and speculating on the lives of our music teachers. They were all peculiar in one way or another, but with a midget, I'd definitely won the my-teacher-is-stranger-than-yours competition" (2000, 25). Here Sedaris represents his younger avatar as engaging in the troubling but common practice of teenagers judging adults by their failure to meet some mythical norm, and Mr. Mancini is offered up as the freakiest of the freaks solely because of his physical stature. The passage is followed immediately by another troubling but all-too-common effect on those who are seen as other due to physical differences from a supposed norm: being perceived as other, as an object of curiosity, a sideshow. Young-Sedaris wonders where Mr. Mancini lives: "Did he stand on chair in order to shave, or was his home customized to meet his needs?" (2000, 25).

Fortunately, for both Mr. Mancini and for the reader, Sedaris's representation of this character and his own character's interactions with him does not end with this shallow othering. Instead, the reader is offered scenes that feature the intersection of sexual identity and nonnormative physical stature. In fact, the purpose of the next scene in which Mr. Mancini appears is to show the young-Sedaris coming to see Mr. Mancini as a person with whom he might have a substantive connection. At the mall with his mother, young-Sedaris sees Mr. Mancini at a fast-food restaurant, standing on "his tiptoes to ask for his hamburger" and taunted by a group of boys Sedaris's age who say "Go back to Oz, munchkin" (2000, 26). This encounter leads young-Sedaris to reconsider Mr. Mancini:

I'd always thought of Mr. Mancini as a blowhard, a pocket playboy, but watching him dip his hamburger into a sad puddle of mayonnaise, I broadened my view and came to see him as a wee outsider, a misfit whose take-it-or-leave-it-attitude had left him all alone. This was the persona I'd been tinkering with myself: the outcast, the rebel. It occurred to me that, with the exception of the guitar, he and I actually had quite a bit in common. We were each a man trapped inside a boy's body. Each of us was talented in his own way, and we both hated twelve-year-old males, a demographic group second to none in terms of cruelty. (27)

Based on this connection, Sedaris represents his younger self just a few pages later as having his first honest interaction with Mr. Mancini and as being rejected because Mr. Mancini sees him as gay:

He'd used the word *screwball*, but I knew what he really meant. He meant I should have named my guitar Doug or Brian, or better yet, taken up the flute. He meant that if we're defined by our desires, I was in for a lifetime of trouble. (29)

In this essay Sedaris offers readers an opportunity to view intersectionality, to understand how a closeted adolescent boy could come to see a midget as a man, to reach out for a possible connection, and to be rejected. While Heard may be justified in his concerns that the Mancini and young-Sedaris characters are exaggerated to the point of crossing into fiction, his insistence that Sedaris does not cast the Mancini character "up" according to Heard's traditional set of values dismisses a much more complicated interaction between heteronormativity and the presumptions about those who do not fit the usual expectations of physical stature in American society. Taken together, these examples illustrate that beyond playing with traditional genre distinctions, expanded epideictic rhetoric may also find means to reverse values and thus to challenge dominant values without making a direct frontal assault. Further, Heard's misreadings of Sedaris's work suggest a basis by which readings of alternative rhetoric texts might be labeled irresponsible: woodenly applying a traditional set of values without accounting for the exercise of privilege that underlies one's own reading. In this sense, Heard's reading of Sedaris illustrates how failing to acknowledge one's own opacity can, too often, masquerade as common sense or as accepted values presumed to be unproblematic, normative, or morally right. Such masquerades need to be unmasked as exercises of unacknowledged privilege;

they can be more dangerous than overt attempts to marginalize because they hide behind a veil of fairness or rationality.

A RHETORIC OF INDIRECTION

Sedaris reports that when he was twenty, he stared writing a daily diary and reading voraciously, but that his early diaries were terrible: "No one was a worse writer than me. No one was more false" because "[a]t that point, I was trying to be other people" (Knight, 2007, 83–4). Despite the falseness he now sees in his early diaries, Sedaris reveals that his daily diary writing and his desire to share that writing publicly is unusual: "It sometimes helps to remind myself that not everyone is like me. Not everyone writes things down in a notebook and then transcribes them into a diary. Fewer still will take that diary, clean it up a bit, and read it in front of an audience" (2008, 122). Clearly, Sedaris has developed a unique voice not only literally in his NPR broadcasts but also in his memoir and other essay writing. From the standpoint of alternative rhetoric, one important part of that voice is that he refuses to write from a single identity issue. For example, he says he is always surprised to find his books in the gay and lesbian section of bookstores:

> I use the word "boyfriend," so I go next to the fisting manual? . . . It's not that I'm ashamed of being gay. It's just that first on my list right now is that I'm foreign. If my average day-to-day life said one thing, if it said, "What are you?" I'd say a foreigner. Living in France, I feel like a foreigner more than anything else. (Knight 2007, 80)

Sedaris's comment here bristles at the reduction of his identity to his homosexuality, and certainly his work can be read in other traditional categories as well. For example, *Me Talk* has been read as travel writing about France.[3] I read his comment as hinting at a larger debate in queer theory between those who advocate for clear identity positions that reflect the disproportional power relations inherent in heteronormativity (i.e., hetero = normal; homo = aberrant) and those who argue that such clear identity positions simply recreate the very problematic discourse of power they seek to dismantle. As I discussed in chapter one, Karen Kopelson dubs this tension the gay/queer binary, explaining that identity emphasis in the former is often contrasted with the emphasis on constitutive performativity (á la Judith Butler) in the latter.

---

3. For more on this, see Knox (2003).

For example, the gay/identity position would argue for "coming out" as a positive move to create increased visibility for an oppressed group. In contrast, Kopelson argues that queer theorists see that "coming out simply obeys and reinforces the laws of sexual categories, and of their knowable, nameable selves" (2002, 21), recreating the subalternity it seeks to unseat. Kopelson argues that this breach can be bridged and calls for pedagogy that understands that traditional identity categories provide the "raw material" from which performative acts can be made that seek to disrupt the very heteronormative strictures that created those identity categories (2002, 31).

From the standpoint of alternative rhetoric as I have defined it, this debate is instructive because it illustrates that even efforts to engage in discursive performativity—to challenge and change problematic social values and the conventions that support them—are in some sense dependent upon the very structures of the underlying oppression to provide a basis for the meaningfulness of attempts to change that oppression. In Warner's term, the creation of a counterpublic is in some sense dependent upon the existence and values of the public. Citing Althusser, Foucault, Derrida, and Butler, Karen Kopelson argues that a "performative act can only work at all, in other words, to the extent that it is recognizable" (2002, 31). Her argument here reflects the work of several queer scholars who argue that it is "feasible to adopt a subject position while still contesting its coherence, possible to agitate for the rights of certain groups while still calling attention to the multiplicity of differences within that group (21). The question for rhetorical theory that remains largely unanswered is how does one do so, and as I argued in the previous chapter, Anzaldúa's strategies illustrate how a rhetor may write from multiple positions of marginality and privilege to directly challenge the underlying systems of oppression. In contrast, Sedaris's writing provides an example of how one may write from multiple positions of marginality and privilege tacitly challenging the underlying privilege *without* making a direct assault. Through indirection, Sedaris embodies a number of problematized subject positions, but he does not directly claim any of them as an identity, and, in this sense, he provides an important example of how to use the power of identification through narrative representations of one's own experiences to inhabit a stigmatized identity. Again, in Warner's terms, even though Sedaris refuses membership in the traditional counterpublics, he still successfully creates the copresence of the other by unsettling dominant values—what

Warner calls the "Bourgeois Public Sphere" (2002, 165). I contend that what Sedaris's writing adds to this understanding of what it means to create the copresence of the other without recreating subalternity is a different understanding of what it means to take agency in response to oppression—one in which the rhetor simply refuses to play the usual game and works largely through indirection.

Sedaris provides readers with numerous snapshots in his four books of memoir about his experiences with the axes of differences in American culture: what it means for him to be gay, obsessive-compulsive, and addicted to speed, alcohol, and tobacco. However, he never writes a traditional coming-out story or twelve-step confession, and unlike writers such as Nancy Mairs (1986), who claims the term "cripple" in writing about her multiple sclerosis, Sedaris writes about his obsessions without identifying himself as mentally/emotionally disabled. In addition, he writes about his regionalism (moving from upstate New York to Raleigh), his Greek heritage, his class aspirations, his whiteness, his Greek Orthodox religious background, his American nationalism, and his insomnia. Obviously, Sedaris's work is highly intersectional, bringing many aspects of his identity to bear, and, of course, this is not unusual for a memoir writer. What is unusual about Sedaris is that he writes about difference issues primarily through indirection; the broad pattern in Sedaris's work is that he writes about the kinds of difference issues that often serve as the axes of oppression in American culture in the context of other issues, without making them the primary focus. For example, in his fourth book of memoir, *Engulfed*, Sedaris finally tells the story of the first time he said he was gay in a piece that is essentially a road-trip story. The announcement came not to a trusted friend or family member but to a couple who had picked him up when he was hitchhiking and who tried to seduce him. He explains that the man asked him, "'How'd you like to eat my wife's pussy?'" He continues, "Then the woman turned as well, and it was to her that I made my confession: 'I'm a homosexual'" (2008, 65–66).

As I mentioned at the outset of this chapter, Sedaris would likely be surprised to see himself cast as a rhetorician because his primary purpose is to entertain, to get laughs. Yet, I contend that in these four books, Sedaris can be read as engaging in alternative rhetoric because he uses his own and his family's experiences to comment on Americana, exposing the intersections of sexual identity, gender, race, class, regionalism, ethnicity, physical and mental/emotional abledness, religion, and a host of other issues. Through indirection, he normalizes what is usually stigmatized, and writes what often cannot be said either in his own experiences or in society in general. For example, in "Rooster at the Hitchin' Post," the main topic is the story of his younger brother Paul's wedding. However, Sedaris hints at how restrictive gender roles (as well as the quirky relations in the Sedaris family) operate when Paul rebuffs Sedaris's effort to have a deeper moment with Paul and his father as they prepare for the wedding:

> "We're trying to watch some TV here," he said, "Jesus, do you mind?" Over in the bridal suite, they were applying makeup and systematically crying it back off. Noteworthy things were being said, and I couldn't help but feel I was in the wrong room. My father turned my brother to face him and, with one eye on the television, began knotting his bow tie. (2004, 173)

One aspect of Sedaris's skill as a writer is his ability to move deftly from narrative moments into analysis and back again without heavy-handed analysis sections or explicit morals to the story. Although his essays often involve important social issues, Sedaris consistently chooses to show them at work in life rather than to moralize about them. For example, he concludes the essay about his brother's wedding not with a comment about gender policing in American society and in the Sedaris household but with a scene that celebrates life. The essay ends with Sedaris and Paul walking Paul's dogs on the beach after the wedding, using what most readers would see as a rather disgusting description of how his brother had trained one of the dogs to clean up after the other dog by eating its feces.

> "Tell me that was an accident," I said.
>
> "Accident, hell, I got this motherfucker *trained*," he said. "Sometimes he'll stick his nose to her ass and just eat the shit on tap."
>
> I thought of my brother standing in the backyard and training a dog to eat shit and realized I'd probably continue thinking about it until the day I die. Forget the tears and brotherly speeches, this was the stuff that memories are made of.
>
> The Great Dane licked his lips and searched the grass for more. "What was it you were going to say?" Paul asked.
>
> "Oh nothing." (2004, 178–79)

In this aesthetic reversal, Sedaris uses the grotesquely scatological as a setting for the sublime. In the next few lines, Paul's bride, Kathy, calls out to him, and the new couple, together with the dogs, "set forth, spreading a love that could not be found under a tree, beneath a shell, or even in a treasure chest buried centuries ago on the historical islands that surround us" (2004, 179). The romanticized scene serves as a fitting ending for a piece about a wedding, but it also hints at the operation of traditional heteronormativity and the gender roles that support it. In this essay, Sedaris provides readers with a peek into his misfit status, how his desire for female-like interactions with his brother and father are quashed by their traditional maleness. In addition, I read the final scene as a comment on the ascendancy of heteronormative values as the newly married couple walk off together down the beach in celebration of their union, which is not only legally sanctioned but also blessed by the gathering of the Sedaris family perhaps because I have had similar experiences at the weddings of my three siblings.

In his latest book, Sedaris makes it clear that he understands the operation of heteronormativity and provides an example of disidentification in which he takes the sting of out the usually pejorative terms *cocksucker* and *faggot*. In a story about buying pot with his brother Paul from "Little Mike," Paul describes David to Little Mike as "being a faggot and all" and as having "hisself a cocksucker—I mean boyfriend—and everything," and Sedaris sees this not as particularly derogatory: "It was sort of nice listening to my brother, who sounded almost boastful, as if I were a pet that had learned to do math" (2008, 163). The coolness of Sedaris's stance toward the operation of heteronormativity in this instance from his life can be seen even more dramatically in the ensuing conversation in which Little Mike's wife asks which of Sedaris and his boyfriend "is the woman," using the strange analogy that one of them must have been like a murderer and the other a child molester, and that one must be "more like a normal man" (163). In his analysis of this incident, Sedaris-the-writer does not rail against heteronormativity but comments on it, providing an insightful description that applies not only to the immediate situation but also to American society at large:

> They can't imagine any system outside their own, and seem obsessed with the idea of roles, both in bed and out of it. Who calls whom a bitch? Who cries harder when the cat dies? Which one spends the most time in the bathroom? I guess they think that it's cut and dried, though of course it's not. Hugh might do the cooking, and actually wear an apron while he's at it, but he also chops firewood, repairs the hot-water heater, and could tear off my arm with no more effort than it takes to uproot a dandelion. Does that make him the

murderer, or do the homemade curtains reduce him to the level of the child molester? (164)

Of course it is significant that Sedaris does not make the comments about the wedding scene or the "Little Mike" scene that I make here. In the wedding scene, his primary purpose is to create a pleasing aesthetic, and the possible social comment is left for the reader to infer or not. In the "Little Mike" scene, the comment is more overt, but he does not name the underlying problem nor does he stand back from commenting on the particular moment just narrated to make a larger comment about heteronormativity in American society. For this reason, I propose that Sedaris engages in a rhetoric of indirection: his social comments, his contributions to the ongoing negotiations of social values in American culture, are made largely through suggestion. Although such tactics run the risk that some readers will not attend consciously to the important underlying issues, this indirection has the considerable benefit of setting those issues in stories from his life in way that draws readers in, that takes advantage of the natural identification that occurs between a reader and the protagonist of a well-told story. In a sense, Sedaris engages in a rhetoric of stealth, of getting issues on the table in entertaining stories that do not take themselves too seriously but may still do serious work. In the remainder of this chapter I explore three kinds of such stealth strategies as examples of how expanded epideictic may serve as alternative rhetoric as I have defined it: identification as a means of indirection; presuming normality for the usually marginalized; and confession, apology, and other forms of self-deprecation.

Identification and Indirection

Kevin Kopelson argues that one reason readers like and identify with Sedaris is that, despite his satirical excesses, readers "rarely see themselves as targets," and that part of Sedaris's charm is that "to love Sedaris is in a sense to love ourselves" (2007, 225). Sedaris balances stinging satire with frequent self-deprecation, and he scrupulously avoids standing on soap boxes. For example, even when he paints a wholly unlikable character, he shows a remarkable willingness to consider situations from the standpoint of that character. For example, in "City of Angels," readers meet Bonnie, who accompanies Sedaris's childhood friend, Alisha, on one of her annual visits to stay with Sedaris in his New York apartment. Sedaris introduces Bonnie as

a dour, spindly woman whose thick girlish braids fell like leashes over
the innocent puppies pictured on her sweatshirt. She had a pronounced
Greensboro accent and had landed at Kennedy convinced that, given half
a chance, the people of New York would steal the fillings right out of her
mouth—and she was not about to let that happen. (2000, 126)

Using what my students and I have come to call his let-a-character-hang-
herself-with-her-own-words strategy, Sedaris employs a conversation in
which he tries to assure Bonnie that thirty dollars is the standard fare
from Kennedy Airport to Manhattan, and that tipping is customary, to
allow Bonnie to announce herself as unreasonable:

"You didn't tip him?"
    "Hell no!" Bonnie said. "I don't know about you, but I work hard for my
money. It's mine and I'm not tipping anybody unless they give me the kind
of service I expect."
    "Fine," I said. "But what kind of service did you expect if you've never rid-
den in a cab before?"
    "I expect to be treated like everybody else is what I expect. I expect to be
treated like an American." (127)

As the essay progresses, Bonnie is further painted as unsophisticated
and unreasonable when she berates a subway attendant who shorts
her a nickel on her change, drags Alisha to all the usual tourist attractions, and attends high tea at the Plaza Hotel dressed in "'hog wash-
ers,' the sort of denim overalls favored by farmers." Although Sedaris
tries to persuade her to wear something more appropriate, he is "actually thrilled when she rejected my advice" feeling "certain she'd be
eaten alive by troops of wealthy, overcaffeinated society women with
high standards and excellent aim" (130). The essay takes a surprising
turn in Bonnie's favor when Sedaris meets them at the Plaza and finds
Bonnie fitting in nicely with the tourists there; Sedaris becomes the
uninformed outsider in venues peopled with "out-of-town visitors from
Omaha and Chattanooga, outraged over the price of their hot roasted
chestnuts." While Bonnie sees "a glittering paradise filled with decent,
like-minded people," Sedaris hobbles "off toward home, a clear outsider in a city I'd foolishly thought to call my own" (2000, 131). In the
end, Bonnie wins.

In addition to frequent self-deprecating reversals and self-revelations
(e.g., he reveals he got crabs from shopping at second-hand clothing

stores in *Engulfed*), Sedaris has several other strategies for taking the edge off his cutting satirical critiques and wickedly exaggerated caricatures of those he writes about. One of these strategies is to embrace his own low-brow interests to balance the fact that essays often display a kind of upper-class envy. For example, despite his disgust that his brother taught one of his dogs to eat the other's feces, the centerpiece of Sedaris's essay "Big Boy" is "the absolute biggest turd I have ever seen in my life" that he finds in a friend's bathroom during a dinner party: "this long and coiled specimen, as thick as a burrito" (2000, 97). In an essay about his experiences as a first-time adjunct teacher of creative writing, "The Learning Curve," he writes of feeling like a fraud because "it was automatically assumed that I had read every leather-bound volume in the Library of Classics" (86) and of his students' complaints about his use of the soap opera *One Life to Live* as a teaching tool: "I'd taught the Buchanan's Landview just as my colleagues had taught Joyce's Dublin or Faulkner's Mississippi, but that was now over. Obviously certain people didn't deserve to watch TV in the middle of the afternoon" (91). Sedaris also shows a taste for the grotesque and macabre. He reveals that one of his childhood nicknames was "Igor" because as a kid he dug up buried pets (his own and others') to see the decomposition process (2008, 110), and that when Helen, his elderly neighbor in New York, frantically called him to retrieve her dentures that had fallen out as she leaned out the window, he discovered, "It is not unpleasant to hold someone else's warm teeth in your hand, and before returning upstairs, I paused, studying the damp plastic horseshoe that served as Helen's gum" (95). Sedaris's willingness to embrace the macabre is probably most graphically seen in "Nutcracker.com" in which he compares his computer-engineer father's utopian vision of the positive effects of computers on family life with a scene in which he and his sister Amy watch a video clip on Amy's candy-colored laptop. In the clip, a woman in "sharp-toed shoes with high pencil-thin heels" stomped on a man's testicles and "kicked them mercilessly and, just when I thought she'd finished, she got her second wind and started all over again."

> I'd never realized that a computer could act so much like a TV set. No one had ever told me that the picture could be so clear, that the cries of pain could be heard so distinctly. This, I thought, was what my father had been envisioning all those years ago when words failed, not necessarily this scene, but something equally capable of provoking such wonder. "Again?" Amy

pushed a button and, our faces bathed in the glow of the screen, we watched the future a second time. (2000, 148)

Because he eschews any purpose beyond entertainment, Sedaris does not comment directly on the possible underlying issues of social discomfort, using popular culture as a teaching tool, or the Internet as a venue for the proliferation of sexual fetishes, yet by identifying himself with such topics, he tempers his elitist tendencies and makes himself more accessible to a wider audience. The benefit of such a strategy is that it humanizes him for readers; by embracing the queer, the unknown, the unusual, the strange within his own experiences and observations, Sedaris makes the other accessible. Of course, the possible danger is that he may be read as a performing fool—as funny but also as easily dismissed.

One strategy that mitigates against such a simplistic reading of Sedaris as light-weight and dismissible is the depth of insight about his own position, which he frequently displays as the narrator of his own story. In an essay about his sister Tiffany, Sedaris is not only aware that he is appalled by the conditions in which his sister lives but that she is aware of his judgment. In describing this amalgam of issues, he first acknowledges his own stereotypical gayness: "The homosexual in me wants to get down on my hands and knees and scrub until my fingers bleed." He then acknowledges the insightfulness of his sister's critique of him: "She later phoned my brother, referring to me as Fairy Poppins, which wouldn't bother me if it weren't so apt" (2004, 200). However, Sedaris moves beyond the simple stereotype by further commenting on a more usual middle-class American phenomenon—the horror of discovering that one has become one's parents: "She'd wanted to show me her artwork—something that truly interests her, something she's good at—and instead, like my father, I'm suggesting she become an entirely different person" (202). Here the potential homosexual other is linked to the more familiar theme of the horror of discovering one has become part of the bourgeois establishment represented by one's parents, and, thus, to some extent, the queer is rendered as more than just a stereotype.

Sedaris makes similar queer-mitigating connections in comparisons with his siblings. He notes his own lack of a quick and ready wit in describing his sister Amy's cleverness when they are riding Chicago's elevated train together: as she gets out several stops ahead him, she calls out, "So long, David. Good luck beating that rape charge." He instantly becomes a pariah and winds up "getting off at the next stop rather than continue riding alongside people who thought of me as a rapist" (2000, 226–7). He also admires the cool relationship Amy has with their father, Lou, in an essay in which he describes Amy as "capable of getting even" by wearing a fatty suit home for the Christmas holidays one year "without first getting mad" at her father for his years of obnoxious comments about his daughters' weight gains (133). Sedaris exhibits envy of his brother Paul's relationship with his father in "You Can't Kill the Rooster." In this essay, Sedaris introduces us to Paul, who has nicknamed himself the Rooster, and sets up an implicit comparison between himself and his brother, who is eleven years younger, by showing how the rules in the Sedaris household changed:

> When I was young, we weren't allowed to say "shut up," but once the Rooster hit puberty it had become acceptable to shout, "Shut your motherfucking hole." The drug laws had changed as well. "No smoking pot" became "no smoking pot in the house," before it finally petered out to "please don't smoke any more pot in the living room" (62)

Paul is described in crude terms, as unfocused and unsuccessful early in life and as foul-mouthed, but Sedaris also notes Paul's unique relationship with Lou: "Unlike the rest of us, the Rooster has always enjoyed our father's support and encouragement" (66).

Given that Lou kicked David out of the house for being gay, without ever telling him the reason—"I think we both know why I'm doing this" (2004, 88)— it would not be surprising that Sedaris would envy his younger brother's less problematic relationship with his father. However, the portrait of that relationship in "You Can't Kill the Rooster" is characterized more by admiration. For example, Sedaris tells the story of his father's complaining about his feet during dinner when Lou and Paul visit David and Amy in New York:

> When my father complained about his aching feet, the Rooster set down his two-liter bottle of Mountain Dew and removed a fistful of prime rib from his mouth, saying, "Bitch, you need to have them ugly-ass bunions shaved down is what you need to do. But you can't do shit about it tonight, so lighten up, motherfucker." All eyes went to my father, who chuckled, saying only, "Well, I guess you have a point." (2000, 64)

Sedaris-the-writer stands back from this scene and provides analysis that, if anything, hints at admiration rather than jealousy:

> A stranger might reasonably interpret my brother's language as a lack of
> respect and view my father's response as a shameful surrender. This, though,
> would be missing the subtle beauty of their relationship. (64)

In the rest of the piece, Sedaris shows his brother's attempt to support
his father after their mother died and after a hurricane. In the final
scene of the essay, Sedaris paints his brother as rushing "over with a
gas grill, three coolers full of beer, and an enormous Fuck-It Bucket—a
plastic pail filled with jawbreakers and bite-sized candy bars" (67) The
final lines of the piece make it clear, without any direct statement, that
Sedaris intends the piece as a tribute to his brother:

> It was a difficult time, but the two of them stuck it out, my brother placing
> his small, scarred hand on my father's shoulder to say, "Bitch, I'm here to tell
> you that it's going to be all right. We'll get through this shit, motherfucker,
> just you wait." (68)

Taken together, these examples, as well as many others I do not have
space to review here, illustrate both the power of indirection and of
embracing the unusual, the marginalized, the queer, and taking it seriously as a matter deserving attention but not so seriously that a moral
imperative must be overtly drawn. To be sure, serious analysis underlies the seemingly simple stories Sedaris tells. Even though David-the-
character is not capable of the quick-witted, cool revenge in the moment
that Amy-the-character achieves, Sedaris-the-writer exhibits both keen
insight and a willingness to consider perspectives outside his own experience. And his choice to do so through indirection—to tell stories rather
than to make arguments—brings what is usually stigmatized or rendered
invisible to light within the context of the more familiar and accepted
and is an important tool for alternative rhetoric. As I explore in the next
section, the indirect invitations that Sedaris offers readers to identify
with positions and people who are usually marginalized or stigmatized
depend largely on his refusal to buy into the usual binaries that create
marginalization and stigma.

Presumption of Normality

A second means by which Sedaris illustrates how one can embody a
problematized subject position without reifying the underlying social
system that created it is his coupling of a refusal to speak explicitly from
a marginalized identity with his utter irreverence. This stance can be

read as a kind of nonchalant disidentification—a casual creation of the copresense of the other. Sedaris simply expects his readers to accept his homosexuality, obsessive-compulsive behaviors, and drug use (as well as a host of foibles) as a part of what makes him a highly entertaining and insightful commentator on American society. Further, as I have already argued, his use of memoir invites readers to identify with him and his characters without overtly challenging them to address the underlying social issues. Managing such a strategy requires a careful balance of acknowledging and representing his own and others' very real experiences with sexism, racism, homophobia, ableism, and the like, while subtly challenging the underlying problematic value systems.

For example, if readers were introduced to Sedaris, as most of my students are, by reading *Me Talk*, they would learn in the first two essays, "Go Carolina" and "Giant Dreams, Midget Abilities," that Sedaris is gay, but they would learn it in the context of essays about his speech therapy in elementary school and the guitar lessons his father forced him to take. Similarly, Sedaris reveals he was addicted to speed in "Twelve Moments in the Life the Artist," an essay primarily about his failed attempts to become an artist. Three boyfriends appear in this book of memoir. The first is an unnamed boyfriend who accompanies Sedaris when his cat, Neil, must be euthanized, and this boyfriend, like the cat, does not figure much into Sedaris's further accounts of his life. Another is an ex-boyfriend Sedaris describes as "so good-looking, I had always insisted that he must also be stupid" (2000, 202). The most important of the three is Hugh, Sedaris's long-time partner, who appears suddenly in the first sentence of "Today's Special," an essay about absurd highbrow restaurants: "It is his birthday, and Hugh and I are seated in a New York restaurant, awaiting the arrival of our fifteen-word entrées" (120). The casual revelation of his drug addiction and his obsessive-compulsive behaviors, as well as the sudden appearances of boyfriends, illustrate the cool stance Sedaris takes toward normally stigmatized issues. Although Sedaris is somewhat more forthcoming about his struggles with addictions and about his daily life with Hugh in his two latest books, *Dress* (2004) and *Engulfed* (2008), readers of his books of memoir get no painful coming-out stories, no salacious account of his first man-on-man sex, and no step four fearless, moral inventories of Sedaris's soul. Instead, Sedaris-the-writer simply presumes such things can be discussed matter of factly, like the story of his sister Lisa getting her first period in the gallery of a master's golf tournament, a story he tells in "The Women's Open" (1997b).

From the standpoint of queer theory, the danger of such a position is that it could be read as presuming a postoppression stance—that social ills such as sexism, heterosexism, racism, ableism, and the like are no longer problematic. This, however, would be a misreading of Sedaris as many of his essays continue to illustrate such problems by showing Sedaris-the-character as implicated by such problematic social values and conventions while Sedaris-the-writer uses them coolly for comic effect. For example, his essay "Chicken the Henhouse" is ostensibly about his experience at a second-rate hotel while on a book tour, but it illustrates how even as a best-selling author, Sedaris-the-gay-man cannot completely escape the possible stigma of pedophilia. The essay begins in Sedaris's basement room of a hotel without room service, listening to Audrey, who has called into a radio talk show about Catholic priests and pedophilia: "Then, little by little, they'd begin interchanging the words *homosexual* and *pedophile*, speaking as if they were one and the same" (2004, 213). A few pages later, Sedaris, seeking coffee at the hotel's complimentary coffee stand, offers to help a boy struggling to carry coffee back to his parents' room: "I was a stranger, an admitted homosexual traveling through a small town, and he was, like, ten. And alone. The voice of reason whispered in my ear. *Don't do it, buster. You're playing with fire*" (216). The two encounter a man in the elevator who mistakes Sedaris for the boy's father, teases the boy about possible girlfriends, and pats the boy on the head, triggering an obsessive compulsion in Sedaris to do that same—an urge he fights off by stopping to smoke a cigarette before continuing on with the boy. In his comments on this situation, Sedaris reveals his internalized homophobia:

> The closer we got to the end of the hall, the more anxious I became. I had not laid a finger on the boy's head. I have never poked or prodded either a baby or a child, so why did I feel so dirty? Part of it was just my makeup, the deep-seated belief that I deserve a basement room, but a larger, uglier part had to do with the voices I hear on talk radio, and my tendency, in spite of myself, to pay heed to them. (222)

He also hints at the heteronormative privilege of the man on the elevator, who

> had not thought twice about asking Michael personal questions or about laying a hand on the back of his head. Because he was neither a priest nor a homosexual, he hadn't felt the need to watch himself, worrying that every word or gesture might be misinterpreted. (222–23)

In contrast, for Sedaris, wandering the halls with a ten-year old boy "amounted to a political act—an insistence that I was as good as the next guy" (2004, 223). Further, he accounts for the role his obsessive compulsions played in the situation: "I sometimes feel an urge to touch people's heads, but still I can safely see a ten-year-old back to his room" (223), and he acknowledges that by engaging in this act he is trying to prove something "to people whom I could never hope to convince" (223). Although this essay strays farther from the presumption of normality about homosexuality than any other of Sedaris's essays, he chooses not to explicitly make any of the points I have just culled. Rather, the identity issues in the essay are resolved humorously when the boy's mother assumes Sedaris is a hotel employee and hands him a dollar tip, leaving him standing alone "in the empty corridor, examining my tip and thinking, *Is that all?*" (224).

This essay illustrates Sedaris's strategy of showing the very real effects of homophobia and heteronormativity on Sedaris-the-character from the relatively unaffected perspective of Sedaris-the-writer, who is secure enough to write about such encounters. The danger inherent in this strategy is that it most directly locates the problem in stupidly homophobic people such as Audrey and within homosexuals, such as Sedaris, who are directly affected. As Kevin Kopelson (2007) suggests, the average reader is not directly challenged in Sedaris's writing, in this case to acknowledge their participation in the larger societal heteronormativity. While the comparison between Sedaris and the man on the elevator tacitly invites readers to consider the operation of heteronormative privilege, Sedaris-the-writer will not make this point directly.

There are subtle indications in Sedaris's writing, and more direct indications in his interviews, that his decision not to engage in direct confrontations with his intended readers is part of his underlying character. As I have already noted, Sedaris represents himself as not verbally quick witted like his sister Amy, and when asked if he sees himself as courageous because he reveals so much about himself in his writing, Sedaris describes these acts as "the illusion of courage" because he does not really expose himself: "There's the real me that lives inside my diary, and then there's the character of me" (Knight 2007, 89). Further, in an essay in which his mother rescues him from a situation in which he might have been accused of pedophilia, "The Girl Next Door," Sedaris hints that he sees real courage as the ability to face down an opponent directly, in this case to reclaim a pejorative term intended to hurt and minimize. In the final scene of the essay, during which Sharon helps David pack up his apartment to escape the manipulative young girl and her equally manipulative mother, he wonders how the girl, Brandi, "who was certainly watching through the keyhole," would view his mother. In these musings, Sedaris hints at his own admiration for his mother: "A person who shepherds you along the way and helps you out when you're in trouble—what would she call that thing? A queen? A crutch? A teacher?" The essay ends with the answer to this question and a description of his mother as possessing a kind of courage to directly confront the demeaning barbs of the small minded, which he lacks:

> I heard a noise from behind the door, and then the little moth voice. "Bitch," Brandi whispered.
>   I fled back into the apartment, but my mother didn't even pause. "Sister," she said, "you don't know the half of it." (2004, 122)

This example illustrates the history of shame and silence enforced by systemic oppression that even a highly successful author like Sedaris may carry, as well as suggesting that writing itself can serve as a critical tool for gaining distance from such experiences. This kind of speaking back to oppression is a critical part of what it means for me to take authorship, and I contend that if we are serious in our profession about helping the marginalized to find voice in the society that marginalizes them, then we must consider that such agency may also be a critical part of coming to voice for many of our students.

CONFESSION, APOLOGY, AND OTHER FORMS OF SELF-DEPRECATION

In current rhetoric and composition pedagogical theory, inviting students to write confessions is deemed a highly suspect practice. For example, Geoffrey Sirc writes, "I recoil from such a curriculum, one that would extract gut-wrenching confessionals from students in the name of writing instruction" (2001, 521). This suspicion of the confessional is shared even by advocates for the use of the personal in composition pedagogy, such as Candace Spigelman, who seconds the concerns of those who "object to semester-long composition programs that call for writing as personal confession, the cathartic soul-searching narrative of trauma or enlightenment associated with expressivism taken to extreme (2001, 70). Further, Beth Daniell counsels that because we are not priests or psychologists, we must be careful to observe the difference between true-confession assignments and real personal narratives: "Personal-narrative papers ask students to connect ideas to their lived or observed experience. True-confession assignments explicitly ask students to reveal private moments" (2003, 163–64).

As is likely already apparent from my discussion of Sedaris's writing, confession plays an important role in his writing, and I contend that it may also play a critical role in alternative rhetoric because of its potential for allowing writers to account for their positions within the hierarchies of power in American culture as well as their culpability in the attendant oppressions. Because of this, I believe we need a more nuanced understanding of confession, apology, and other forms of self-deprecation. As Sedaris's writing illustrates, not all confession needs to be "gut-wrenching," nor does confession need to occur only in the context of semester-long trauma writing courses, which, as Spigelman suggests, should never be forced on students and should be conducted only by those qualified to do so. Further, while I think Daniell is right to suggest that personal narratives must consist of more than the revelation of private moments for cathartic purposes, to restrict our students from writing such moments robs them of tools that writers like Sedaris use to positive effect. Thus, I conclude this chapter by examining confession, apology, and self-deprecation as a third kind of strategy that Sedaris uses to inhabit problematic subject positions while challenging the underlying power relations—in these cases even more subtly, and mostly to manage his own position as author, to soften a stance which could easily become too caustic or judgmental.

One of the most important examples of confession in Sedaris's writing is his description of his withdrawal from speed in "Twelve Moments in the Life of the Artist." Although Sedaris does not glorify his drug addiction, this essay might be read as normalizing it—because Sedaris speaks so matter of factly about how his drug use was an integral part of his performance art, he, in some sense, makes light of it:

> Quite a few people showed up for the museum performance, and I stood before them wishing they were half as high as I was. I'd been up for close to three days and had taken so much speed that I could practically see the individual atoms pitching in to make up every folding chair. *Why is everyone staring at me?* I wondered. *Don't they have anything better to do?* I thought I was just being paranoid, and then I remembered that I was being stared at for a

reason. I was onstage, and everyone else was in the audience, waiting for me to do something meaningful. (2000, 53)

In describing his withdrawal from speed, Sedaris does not invoke the usual addiction/intervention/treatment narrative. In fact, he quits because "my drug dealer moved to Georgia to enter a treatment center" (55). Instead, Sedaris's confession and his atonement for his comic description of drug addiction is subtle and presented in terms of his own experience:

> Speed's breathtaking high is followed by a crushing, suicidal depression. You're forced to pay tenfold for all the fun you thought you were having. It's torturous and demeaning, yet all you can think is that you want more. . . . Thinking I might have dropped a grain or two, I vacuumed the entire apartment with a straw up my nose, sucking up dead skin cells, Comet residue, and pulverized cat litter. Anything that traveled on the bottom of a shoe went up my nose. (56)

Similarly, in his latest book, Sedaris admits, "All I know is that I drank to get drunk, and I succeeded every night for over twenty years" (2008, 265–66); however, he does not call himself an alcoholic or a drug addict. Rather, he lets one of his characters do so. For example, when his elderly and colorful neighbor Helen refuses to loan him her key to the basement of their building, Sedaris says she is being an "asshole."

> "That's better than being a drunk," she said, and she waited a moment for the word to settle in. "That's right. You think I don't see you with the empty cans and bottles every morning. You think I can't see it in your swollen face?" (97–98).

Confession is often one of Sedaris-the-writer's strategies for examining the operation of the cultural narratives that shaped his life. For example, in "Get Your Ya-Ya's Out," he tells of visits to his widowed grandmother's small apartment, the tension between his mother and father when Lou brings his mother, Ya Ya, to live with them, and the special treatment Sedaris and his younger brother received because they were male: "My brother and I came to view our Ya Ya as a primitive version of an ATM machine. She was always good for a dollar or two" (1997b, 29). Confession plays an important role in this essay; when Sedaris tells of returning home from college for Ya Ya's funeral wearing an earring and of his father's refusal to let him in the house. After spending several hours in the carport and threatening to sleep in the family station wagon, Sedaris sees reason when his mother intervenes, and Sedaris-the-writer confesses his previous bad behavior:

> I removed the earring and never put it back in. Looking back, it shames me that I chose that particular moment to make a stand. My father had just lost his only mother, and I assumed that, like the rest of us, he felt nothing but relief. (39)

A similar pattern of analysis of mixed self-deprecation ending in an apology that is a confession of sorts occurs in "Repeat After Me," an essay about adult-Sedaris's visit to his sister Lisa and her parrot. Sedaris arrives while her sister and her husband are at work, and he describes the note Lisa leaves for him: "The note reflected a growing hysteria, its subtext shrieking, *oh-my-God-he's-going-to-be-alone-in-my-house-for-close-to-an-hour*" (2004, 143). In the discussion that follows, Sedaris tempers his cutting comment about Lisa's failing as the Sedaris sibling "marked Most Likely to Succeed" by admitting, "As far as my family is concerned, I'm still the one most likely to set your house on fire" (144). A few pages later, Sedaris presents himself in a self-deprecating way when he approaches the parrot's cage only to be lunged at through the bars: "I screamed like a girl and ran from the room" (146). Such self-deprecation and reflexiveness about his perspective is critical for maintaining a voice that is at times sharp and uncompromising in its insightfulness about his family and others he writes about, but that does not become strident or self-aggrandizing. In this essay, he examines his own role as a writer when he notes that Lisa is "afraid to tell me anything important, knowing I'll only turn around and write about it." As I have already noted, Sedaris recognizes that although he sees himself as a "friendly junkman," his family, Lisa in this case, see things differently (147). Apology plays a critical role in the conclusion of this essay, when Sedaris relates a story Lisa told him, even though as he "instinctively reached for the notebook I keep in my pocket," she warned, "'If you ever, . . . *ever* repeat that story, I will never talk to you again'" (155). Sedaris, of course, intends to tell the story, and recognizing that in his own words an apology will be meaningless, he depicts himself slipping down to Lisa's kitchen at three a.m. that night, sitting before her parrot with a gift for imitating voices, "repeating slowly and clearly the words 'Forgive me. Forgive me. Forgive me'" (156).

The pattern of self-deprecation extends beyond the few examples I have alluded to here. Kevin Kopelson notes, "Sedaris calls himself an asshole—not to mention scumbag, shithead, and son of a bitch" (2007, 1). In addition, Knox observes that in his writing about France, Sedaris is "quite self-deprecating, referring to himself for example as the 'village idiot'"; further, Knox notes that this self-deprecatory stance is "part and parcel of his skewering of pretentious compatriot behavior" (2003, 17). It is important to note that, to some degree, this self-deprecation is possible for Sedaris because of his positions of economic, gender, and other privilege; for example, Sedaris does not have to argue for the right to speak, as did Grimké, nor does he argue for basic human rights, as did Douglass (although as a gay man he might do so). Although his writing bears witness to multiple aspects of identity oppression, much as Anzaldúa's writing does, he takes a dramatically different approach from hers—choosing to be both vulnerable and aloof. As I have illustrated, this substantive but cool stance allows Sedaris to get a kind of revenge against his homophobic teachers without directly accusing them of homophobia, but confession, apology, and self-deprecation play an important role in creating an inviting persona from which to do so. Sedaris allows us to see him writing what he can't find the words to say to his brother, and he apologizes to Lisa, Tiffany, and other family members in his writing about them—saying the things he cannot say in person.

Although Sedaris certainly does not set out to right the world's wrongs or to serve as a role model for engaging in alternative rhetoric through indirection, his work makes contributions on both of these fronts. In the terms I used to introduce the concept of *alternative rhetoric* in chapter one, Sedaris's work creates copresence of the other by embodying his experiences with the cultural forces that create other status, most notably homophobia, heterosexism, and ableism, but also a host of other issues. In doing so, he takes a clearly intersectional position, rarely representing himself according to a single difference issue, and he refuses to engage in the usual value judgments attached to issues of sexual identity, ability/disability, drug and alcohol addiction, and other issues. The latter strategy denies him the bully pulpit that Grimké, Douglass, and Anzaldúa used so effectively, and, in this sense, he does not directly name the kinds of social ills that they made it their business to challenge. Yet, although we might read Sedaris as a reluctant rhetor, his work illustrates how indirection may be used to create identification with readers. Also, his work illustrates how presuming the normality of problematized stances without ignoring the ongoing effects of marginalization and engaging in nuanced, at times, self-deprecatory authorial stance may also work to create an engagement with the other that humanizes. These are important strategies for engaging in alternative rhetoric.

Interchapter
DAY FOUR IN PARIS

Vitor sleeps in the bed I rent for 155 euros a night. He's the third man to be in that bed with me, but the first to get under the covers and the first man to sleep with me for nearly a year. He lies there, the soft Paris morning light filtering through the gap in the drapes that shade the garret window. He wants to sleep until 11:30 because couture week is incredibly hectic, and he sniffed lines twice yesterday—once to wake up after only three hours' sleep to schedule models until 10 p.m. and once at 11 p.m. for the energy to have sex with me.

I write these lines at the Starbucks in the Marais district of Paris, "the Swamp," the Jewish and now increasingly gay section. My moyen (tall) caffé latte here is 3.70 euros, nearly twice the $2.93 I pay at my Starbucks in Orlando, but I need something familiar after three days of puzzling out the signs, looking for English translations, and trying to remember when to stop saying *bonjour* and begin saying *bonsoir*.

I have been feeling like and unlike David Sedaris on this trip. It began on the flight over, reading from his latest book in which he describes the "brief parody of an evening" that one experiences on transatlantic flights to Paris: "Dinner is served, the trays are cleared, and four hours later it's time for breakfast" (2008, 217). I'd bought a little notebook I could carry, like he does, for Paris, and I wanted to begin writing in it after dinner on the plane, but I didn't want to turn on my reading light because everyone was trying to sleep except the twenty-something girl in the row in front of me, who bounced up and down until she attracted the attention of handsome young man with a shaved head, who soon parked himself in the empty seat next to her, pulled out his laptop and fancy headphones, and began playing the trance house music he was flying to Paris to play at some club. She giggled a lot, which might have been a pleasant sound on a daylight flight, but on a quiet plane flying 600 mph toward dawn over the Atlantic, it boomed through the cabin, dragging my consciousness back to the surface each time I nearly drifted off. After a particularly loud cackle from the row in front of us, the beautiful young woman in the seat next to me sighed heavily and threw her red airline blanket over her head and sank back into her seat. I tried to do the same, but the strangers-when-they-boarded-the-flight-but-soon-to-be-lovers just eighteen inches away flirted and laughed, and flirted and laughed, and then were quiet just long enough for me to start drifting off before they flirted and laughed and flirted some more.

This was my first Sedaris-like moment: sitting in my seat, desperately tired, debating the merits of asking them to be quiet so I could sleep versus being the man who shushed the young soon-to-be lovers for the rest of the flight. I shushed, but it didn't help much, and then I ended up waiting about forty minutes in the immigration line at Charles de Galle Airport behind them and the beautiful young girl who had sat next to me. The three of them chatted; cell phone numbers were exchanged while I stood there amazed at the ease with which the young, beautiful, and straight find friends and lovers, and I understood in a new way why Sedaris wrote that the enthusiasm of his young classmates in his French class exhausted him: "I'm just too old and worn-out to share their excitement over such innocent pleasures as a boat ride down the Seine or a potluck picnic at the base of the Eiffel Tower" (2000, 183).

Walking the streets of Paris, I fantasize that I will see David and Hugh walking along or that they will wander into Starbucks while I sit summarizing notes from his latest book, and I will be the stumbling fan who shyly asks for an autograph, and he will ask about all the post-its sticking out from the pages, and I'll have to explain, in somewhat embarrassed fashion, that I'm writing a chapter in a rhetoric book about him, and he'll be confused at first and then delighted with the attention, and then he and Hugh will invite me over for dinner. I look up from my notes and scan the tables at Starbucks, but there is no sign of him.

I feel like Sedaris again this morning as I lie beside Vitor, pulled into consciousness by the morning street sounds rising up five stories as I feel the warmth of his long body next to mine and let my eyes rest on that place on his neck where the first little black hairs seem to cling to his caramel skin and merge gradually into neatly clipped short hairs on the sides and back of his head and then on up into the thick mat of jet black hair on his head. I drift off again only to be pulled back to wakefulness by the patter of water in the shower in the next room. This time I see Vitor's face, the high cheekbones of a model, the long lashes and dark brown eyes of a Spaniard, and I wonder why this beautiful man is sleeping with me. I think, vainly, that I am unlike Sedaris, because I can get a tall, handsome, former model to sleep with me, but like Sedaris in that I feel completely unworthy of this man.

As pleasant as it is to lie with Vitor and press as much of my body against his as I can, I cannot stay in bed with him. Like Sedaris, I cannot simply enjoy this moment, I need to record it; I need to write, to analyze, to capture, to imagine that I have an audience who wants to know about this moment. This is not the impulse to brag about bagging a handsome man; that would be too crass for me.

Instead, I want to write about finding romance in Paris—a topic so hackneyed as to be boring— but it is as fresh to me as the desire that made the strangers-when-they-boarded-the-flight-but-soon-to-be-lovers flirt and giggle. But even as I open my little journal and uncap my pen, the part of me that is Lottie, my German grandmother who died twenty-eight years ago, pushes into my consciousness and makes me pull on shorts, t-shirt, and sneakers, grab a handful of euros, and head out to find croissants, juice, and bananas to feed my man, my guest. I say only four words in the patisseria, *"bonjour," "deux croissant,"* and *"merci,"* and I think I have passed for French until the clerk says "thank you" instead of *"merci."* I wake Vitor in time for a shower and a croissant before he rushes off to open the modeling agency, and then I come to Starbucks and write because a writer must write in Paris.

Romance and croissants are hardly newsworthy in Paris, but I write this because it is new for me, because there have not been many Vitor-romance-croissants stories told in rhetoric and composition, because there is risk in telling these things, and because—at long last—I have a point to make. Part of that point is about the ease of heteronormative desire—that even in Paris, the gays tend to congregate in havens like Le Marais, where I can sit in Starbucks and see a tall rugged French man with broad shoulders smiling into the eyes of a slim flight attendant in a crisp white dress shirt and tie, his suit jacket draped over the handle of his flight bag, and then turn my head to see a muscle boy in a t-shirt tighter than mine sip his Caffé Americano, watching the parade of queers on Rue du Archives on a Sunday morning. The other part of my point is that this is what it means to be a writer, to sit back from your lover in bed and wonder about him, to regret the loss of both facility and subtlety when you must buy croissants in a language you do not command with ease, to see where you stand in the world and to try to understand it so you can show it to others, and sometimes to find a voice that makes yet another romance and croissant story in Paris at least somewhat relevant in a book on alternative rhetoric.

6

ALTERNATIVE RHETORIC AND MARKED WRITING

Perhaps most importantly, we must recognize that ethics requires us to risk ourselves precisely at moments of unknowingness, when what forms us diverges from what lies before us, when our willingness to become undone in relation to others constitutes our chance of becoming human.

Butler, 2005

Although definitions of what constitutes a better writer may vary, implicit in most teachers' definitions of "writing well" is the ability to produce English that is unmarked in the eyes of teachers who are custodians of privileged varieties of English, or in more socially situated pedagogies, of an audience of native English speakers who would judge the writer's credibility or even intelligence on the basis of grammaticality.

Matsuda, 2006

Put most simply, engaging in alternative rhetoric means, as Butler argues, risking ourselves in moments of unknowingness, loosing ourselves from the moorings of dominant culture and discourse and striking out into uncharted waters. The potential benefit is becoming more fully human, becoming something other than what has been prescribed, and having the opportunity to take up a kind of rhetorical agency that engages dominant culture and discourse rather than accepting their dictates. Doing so is a risk, as it will likely require a redefinition of the self in regard to the discourses of power.

The basic question I address in this final chapter is what would it look like if we embraced alternative rhetoric in our own practice and in our pedagogy? One answer to this question is that one of our fundamental goals—to help students produce "unmarked" writing—would have to change. As Matsuda has argued, we have taken up this goal for ourselves and for our students: producing texts that will not be marked as other in dominant culture. I begin this chapter of examining the practice and pedagogy of alternative rhetoric by suggesting that we all need to produce more "marked" writing—writing that bears some stamp of who we are, writing that understands what dominant culture expects of it and takes a stand in regard to those expectations. In this regard, the four rhetors whose work I have examined in the preceding chapters have much to suggest about how we might do this.

Although few, if any, of us will rise to the sort of national prominence Douglass enjoyed or achieve Sedaris's bestseller status, the somewhat extreme examples I have examined in this book are useful for teasing out the underlying nature of the problem of taking the kind of responsible rhetorical agency Butler and other feminist, postmodern, postcolonial, and queer theorists have helped us to see as necessary. More specifically, reading the work of these four American rhetors as instances of alternative rhetoric allows us to consider what can be done when the dissonance between cultural values and discourse practices brings one to a problematic juncture, and when what one sees as needing to be done at such a juncture is great enough to force a person to consider being, in some sense, "undone in relation to others." Butler sees this as a generative place, indeed as constituting "our chance of becoming human." The four rhetors whose work I examine in this book each took such a risk; they were compelled to write—to take this kind of agency by publicly claiming an aspect or aspects of their humanity that dominant culture was determined to deny them, and the approaches they took suggest a range of practices that may be useful for others who want to follow their examples in other contexts.

Write Like a Man

"Write like a man" is an odd way to start this review of alternative rhetoric practices, but it's a fairly apt description of what Sarah Grimké did. Indeed, Grimké's case suggests that what is alternative in the practice of rhetoric may, at times, just be *who* is doing it more than it is *how* it is done. In some instances of creating a counterpublic, the oppressed or marginalized taking a voice is the primary issue for the practice of alternative rhetoric no matter what genre or discourse practices are used in such an act. A more nuanced statement of this principle is to use the features of a discourse that have been previously denied to you, but "write like a man" gets fairly close to the heart of the matter.

As my readings of Grimké's work illustrates, speaking from the margins may involve appropriating the discourses of power for a purpose that works against the interests of those in power. There are a couple of dangers in such a position. First, enabling the disenfranchised to appropriate the discourses of power to use for their own purposes cannot be the only goal of alternative rhetoric or we risk simply requiring assimilation to the discourses of power as the price of joining the conversation. Second, as Grimké's case illustrates, using the discourses of power for one's own purposes without exploring one's own opacity may involve a complicated dance in which one may deploy identity-based rhetorical moves in the service of troubling others' pejorative use of such moves. Given that the many faces of hegemony cannot be swept away in any single rhetorical exchange, such tactical use of essentializing moves may, at times, be necessary and even efficacious. However, such moves can also serve to reify the very kinds of problematic identity binaries that those who use them seek to unseat.

Tell Your Story

As I have already argued, narrating one's experiences is not a guarantee that one has substantively explored one's subjectivity. However, telling a story that brings aspects of the systematic inequities in our society into focus is a potentially powerful way to make the oppressed copresent in discourse. Like Grimké, Frederick Douglass used binary relationships of power (master/slave, black/white) to expose underlying systems of oppression in American society, and, unlike Grimké, he did not rely primarily on extended logical reasoning as his primary tool. Although he proved himself adept at traditional argument, one of Douglass's most powerful rhetorical tools was his ability to describe the dehumanization he experienced because of slavery, and after emancipation because of lingering racism in American society. In short, Douglass's narrative accounts of his experiences with slavery and other forms of racism provide one of the most powerful examples in American history of using alternative rhetoric to challenge a societal ill primarily through talk and writing that embodies one's own experiences.

Douglass's case also suggests that telling one's story is not a simple matter. For example, we see small glimpses of the complexities of intersectionality in his conflict with women's suffragists about the ratification of the fifteenth amendment, and Douglass's accounts of his struggles with his white abolitionist sponsors suggest the problematic nature of sponsorship of the oppressed by privileged people who, despite good intentions, perpetuate subtle forms of racism because they have not accounted for their own privilege. Both Grimké's and Douglass's accounts of their struggles to find voice illustrate the importance of sponsorship by those in power for the disenfranchised but also the dangers of such sponsorship.

Untame Your Tongue

More than any of the other authors examined in this book, Gloria Anzaldúa can be read as pressing the practice of alternative rhetoric beyond remaking the master's tools for other purposes and as directly challenging problematic values in dominant culture. Her work invites us to see that identity is multiple and contingent, and, thus, an alternative theory of rhetoric must move beyond simple notions of identity and demand an accounting not only of one's position but also one's relative privilege as the beginning point for participating in responsible social discourse. Some of the work we need to do may fall largely within existing argument structures, using the master's tools to challenge a particular cultural/moral value that needs to be unseated and exposing the specific cultural means used to keep those discriminatory values in place. However, as rhetorical theorists and teachers we must also recognize that much of the work necessary will require the kinds of sweeping changes that Anzaldúa envisions—changes not only to such fundamentally "American" concepts as citizenship, free speech, and equal opportunity, but also to the linguistic and rhetorical practices we teach. As her own writing so vividly illustrates, engaging in this work will likely mean untaming our tongues, resisting dominant cultural values and the discourse practices that support them.

Don't Be So Serious All the Time

This is the hardest one for me. Indeed, one of the reasons I always use a Sedaris book in my writing courses is that his voice is so relaxed and playful compared to my own often overly serious and sincere voice. As I have already argued, this is not to say that Sedaris's writing does not do serious work, as identity issues in Sedaris's work are nearly as multiple and complex as those in Anzaldúa's writing, and, like Douglass, Sedaris embodies various kinds of oppression in his memoir writing. However, unlike Anzaldúa and Douglass, Sedaris does not look to challenge oppression explicitly; instead, he creates the copresence of the other by presuming the normality of such things as homosexuality, obsessive-compulsive disorders, and drug and alcohol addiction. Of course, Sedaris can take this "cool" stance toward his own and others' oppression largely because of his gender, race, and economic privilege, but his use of confession, apology, and other forms of self-deprecation allow him to account for his positions of privilege in more substantive ways than Grimké, Douglass, or Anzaldúa, even though he must be seen as engaging in a rhetoric of indirection.

WHO WILL DO THIS WORK?

Given the complexities and potential dangers of engaging in such forms of alternative rhetoric as I have examined in this book, the crucial question which with I begin this chapter is Who would choose to take up this task–who would choose to risk himself or herself unless facing the kind of direct prejudice and discrimination faced by Grimké, Douglass, and Anzaldúa? One obvious answer to this question is that those who are marginalized in society by systems of oppression continue to have a decided stake in taking such risks. Indeed, those whose differences from the presumed norms are immediately visible usually have no choice but to do so, and those who experience a version of closeting must, at some point, decide to make claim to a problematized identity. However, as I argued in chapter one, the agency basic to alternative rhetoric requires a further risk for all who engage in it: we must act despite opacity—despite the fact that we cannot fully understand our own positionality or all it means for us to take agency within the system that gives our words and actions meaning. Further, we must take responsibility for such agency, not only in terms of our intent but also in terms of sets of relationships with others that are, to some degree, beyond our understanding and control. Butler explains the essential conundrum of such opacity:

> If I try to give an account of myself, if I try to make myself recognizable and understandable, then I might begin with a narrative account of my life. But this narrative will be disoriented by what is not mine, or not mine alone. And I will, to some degree, have to make myself substitutable in order to make myself recognizable. (2005, 37)

Butler's words ring true to me; for far too many years I substituted heterosexuality as a critical aspect of who I was. At some level I knew this was wrong; as early as the third grade, I knew this narrative did not fit me when the first inklings of sexual desire began bubbling up and were directed toward the smart cute boy who sat in the front of the row next to me and who seemed to get all the teacher's attention. But it was twenty-eight years later before I could find the words to say to someone who mattered in my life that I did not fit into the heteronormative narrative of courtship, marriage, parenthood, and widowhood. My dearly departed friend, Wendy Bishop, finally asked me because I couldn't tell her, because she knew I needed to say it—sitting on a hard cement wall in the bright Phoenix sun, moments stolen from her busy CCCC schedule–private moments in a public street–my tears, her stories of disappointing would-be lesbian lovers after she ditched the asshole husband, and her scores on their gaydar.

My graduate training in rhetoric and composition had, in part, prepared me for that moment by helping me develop an understanding of texts, context, and interpretation that allowed me to gain distance from the evangelical Christian version of the Bible of my youth that declared homosexuality an unnatural abomination. However, that training did not give me anything like Butler's notion of substitutability that might have helped me see that the performative nature of all discourse—that language and identity are constituted by previous practice but also depend on continued practice for their continued existence—means we are all always substituting conventions for self to some extent. That is, the only way we can make ourselves intelligible is to represent our experiences and perspectives in language and other symbol systems that carry with them baggage we cannot fully control or understand. For people like me whose identities have been systematically problematized within dominant discursive practices, the question of how much substitutability to tolerate before one challenges the underlying discursive system is often faced multiple times a day and cannot be avoided, and the relevant question becomes when does substitutability move beyond necessity, become too costly, too overdetermined by social convention, too misrepresentative of one's self? For those in positions of privilege, this substitutability may seem unproblematic; indeed, it may go unnoticed. However, Butler's larger point is that we are all implicated, simply by existing, in the underlying values that drive the system: any attempt to articulate ourselves within the system implicates us within that system. And I would add to this position that even those who experience marginalization on one or more axes of difference must still work to account for our relative positions of privilege on other axes of difference.

At this point, the part of me who spent his youth in evangelical churches and camp meetings being indoctrinated with missionary zeal wants to stand on a soapbox and shout out that we must all engage in such reflection about our relative positions of power and disenfranchisement simply because it is the right thing to do; it is our responsibility as humans. However, the more practical me recognizes that this is hard work and that people need to have real motivations to do so. For that reason, I pause before I launch into my discussion of how we might engage in the teaching of alternative rhetoric to share some remarkably candid observations from Patrick, a student in one of my recent writing classes, about why he chose to decline my efforts to entice him into engaging in the kind of writing that might lead him to articulate some aspects of his identity that had the discursive power to explain himself to others. In his final journal entry of the course, Patrick began:

> I think my favorite part of this class is a shining example of my priorities in life as a lazy bum only giving effort in those activities that genuinely interest me. As english is not one of those interests, my favorite part of the course is how well it fits the "slide by method." This involves putting in a minimal effort to pass the class and be on your way.

Patrick continued to explain that although his "slide by method" was not a good approach for all courses, "it works great for those pesky courses you hate to be forced into." In some of the most engaged writing he did for me all semester, Patrick further explained that the modified portfolio grading system I used allowed him to take the "continue revising" credit I give for all reasonable drafts and to decline my invitations for further revision that might have dramatically improved his grade (and his writing): "type up some garbage, print out the garbage, turn in the garbage, get a continue revising, rinse and repeat. . . . Easy peasy lemon squeezy take your 'C' and get the hell out."

It would be easy to read Patrick simply as a relatively privileged white guy who waited until he was a senior to take the second course in the required first-year composition sequence, and who was moderately interested in his computer science courses but only passionately engaged by the band in which he played drums. And such a reading has some merit; however, his journal reflects a bit more thoughtfulness than this in that he understood the opportunity he was choosing not to take:

> Now don't let this seem like I am bashing or making fun of your class. For those that aspire to greatness you are always available to lend support and advice. I believe that this class becomes what you make it, and in that regard I loved it. It let me finish my general education requirements easily and painlessly allowing me to spend time on things I love. Thank you.

It may seem odd to launch a discussion about applying alternative rhetoric in composition pedagogy with what is arguably my most spectacular pedagogical failure of late, but I do so because it is important that such discussions be grounded in the bread and butter of our profession—college writing courses—because if these ideas are to work they need to be made accessible to students like Patrick, who may have little interest in writing instruction in general and even less in understanding their relative privilege within dominant cultural values and the discourse practices that support them.

Before I proceed, I should note that Patrick is notable not only for his frankness but also because he is unusual in my courses. The vast majority of my students eventually take up the opportunities I provide for revision and make significant progress as writers during the course, and a smaller percentage write pieces in which they bring aspects of their lives and identities into at least some critical conversation with those of others or with dominant cultural values. In this sense, my approach to alternative rhetoric in my courses aims more for the kind of memoir pieces Douglass and Sedaris write than for the more overt arguments of Grimké and Anzaldúa. Although I believe that moving beyond acknowledging our own opacity to actively taking responsibility for the agency we exercise is beneficial for us all, I recognize that many in our field, and perhaps the majority of our students, will see little immediate need to do so, and thus, we must think carefully about how to engage others in such dialogue. As Anzaldúa suggests, although there may be a time for shouting across the river, we also need a wider range of strategies to engage others.

As a starting point in this task, I turn once more to Butler, who argues that we need the other in order to address the fundamental opacity in ourselves, in a sense to understand those parts of us inaccessible to us except in dialogue with others:

"If we are formed in the context of relations that become partially irrecoverable to us, then that opacity seems built into our formation and follows from our status as beings who are formed in relations of dependency" (2005, 20). Here I see Butler arguing for a different understanding of the function of authorship—that accounting for our own opacity is the only way we can get access to the self and, further, that we need to be deconstructed in some sense by others to understand ourselves (in extreme cases we need counselors and psychoanalysts to continue interactions in the world). In essence, I have argued in this book that each of the four rhetors whose work I examine were engaging in this kind of task, in articulating themselves in response to others, and this is the task I see as fundamental to all of rhetorical practice and its attendant pedagogy, whether we realize it or not. What alternative rhetoric and its attendant pedagogy require is that we embrace this fundamental tension in identity as the only generative place from which to engage in real authorship. And this is what eventually hooks most of my students when they realize—without all of the theoretical trappings—that articulating themselves in the context of clashes of values in dominant culture gives them something worth saying, something their classmates, friends, and family might really want to read.

THE PAPER THAT CHANGED MY TEACHING

Can we really do this? Can we exercise in our own speech and writing alternative rhetoric that accounts for our relative privilege and opacity, and can we help students learn to do so? I can think of many reasons to throw up our hands and declare this an impossible goal:

1. The work is conceptually hard: as Anzaldúa notes, unless a person has experienced some systemic marginalization, it will be difficult to see how identity is constructed by dominant culture and how language, rhetoric, and culture are themselves discursive.

2. Engaging in alternative rhetoric will likely mean expanding the curriculum of rhetoric and composition to include and support the learning of a wider range of discourse practices.

3. We will likely need to give up the myth that composition courses can and should provide all students with the same basic set of skills for academic and professional writing—the very reason most of our institutions presume is the basis for our existence.

4. We, as teachers and theorists, will have to engage in the same kind of identity negotiations we ask our students to explore.

5. The other will need to be substantively present in our classes, and our classrooms are likely to be become real "contact zones" in which we and our students move beyond detached critiques of discourse and culture and engage in the kinds of substantive negotiations of identity and culture that Mary Louise Pratt (1991) had in mind when she proposed the term.

6. The majority of people who teach first-year composition do so under circumstances that make engaging in such challenging pedagogical work difficult, both because of the workload involved and because of a lack of real opportunities for engaging in larger disciplinary discussions.

Given all these potential problems, why should we take on such a daunting task? Two reasons. First, as I argued in chapter one, it is not enough to proclaim to our students that language and rhetoric are not simply neutral tools and to offer them a set of liberal values to offset the ways in which traditional rhetoric has been part and parcel of the dominant social values and discourse practices that have systematically marginalized some groups of people in our society. Nor is it enough to provide students with a new set of supposedly neutral tools by which they can understand the discursive nature of language and rhetoric, tools they can use to deconstruct culture if they wish or to expand the canon of acceptable practices to include a few discourse practices from non-dominant strains of our society. Second, our students can do it. I believe there is hope that we can do this because of a paper one of my students wrote for me ten years ago. Before I even knew how to ask students for alternative rhetoric, Sarah gave it to me and provided the impetus for me to see how the issues I had been struggling with as a writer and a teacher could be addressed in first-year composition courses.

Segment 1
   Hate them cuz they will get everything
   Hate them cuz they will win and I won't
   Who are THEY?
   Mommy and Daddy are rich
   They won when they were young
   They don't know what they are missing
   They party and drink

"Gee lets go into that store!" says a high falsetto voice, making fun of the nasal voice that all geeks are supposed to have. I hear them all laugh and I hang my head. These people could never be my friends, because they wear Abercrombie and Fitch, because they wear leather and two hundred dollar shoes and skirts with designer labels. These people spend their money on better cars and better clothing, while I spend mine on books; games and sometimes I even pay rent.

Sarah's first draft of this paper was dominated by the lengthy version of the "Hate them" poem that sat long and indigestible between two prose sections that also ranted at some length about all the injustices she had experienced in the first nineteen years of her life. We both knew it wasn't very good, but we also knew she had something important to say. She was angry, and neither of us was interested in tempering her anger. As I talked with her about her draft, I instinctively rejected the advice from my teacher training as a PhD student about helping students develop Rogerian-style arguments in which they carefully consider the differences between their position and that of their intended audience and seek a strategy that builds common ground between the two. Instead, I focused on content and organization, asking Sarah to sort out more clearly the three difference issues that seemed to be competing for attention in the piece and to temper some of the ranting with more detailed descriptions of scenes that would allow readers to witness more directly what she had experienced.

Segment 2
    Hate them cuz they have the right answers on god
    Hate them cuz they are right and I am not
    It's so easy to believe what you are taught
    Religion . . .
    Why are they right?
    Why am I wrong?
    Who cares about their one god?
    I am told I go
    I can't
    I'm not like them.
    "Fucking Satanist!"

A push by someone, I can't tell who. Someone in the hallway, and another harsh sting as I get slammed into a locker, I can taste the metallic tang of blood as I try to get my footing on the newly polished floor. Finally I can speak, even though people keep pushing me on. I can't let them think that I am evil; all I want is to worship in peace. So I shout:
    "I am a Wiccan!" But no one cares.
    "I am not a Satanist!" But no one cares.
    "I don't even believe in Satan!" I have to shout because of the laughter and the sounds of fists on lockers and my head smashing into the wall. Finally relief in the form of a teacher. I say that I am all right and that they were just joking

around, but both she and I know the truth. She takes my pentacle in her hand and says: "Maybe you shouldn't wear that." And from then on I don't, it's just not worth it. I felt like I was betraying my faith, but I didn't have a choice. I wasn't like them and they knew it, things would never be good again.

The semester Sarah wrote this paper, I was a recently tenured associate professor at a large midwestern university in rural Iowa teaching two sections of first-year composition. I was just emerging from the closet myself, but I wasn't really out at work yet. The focus of my research was on race and gender—trying to understand what it meant for African American students, many of whom were recruited to our rural campus from urban centers, to find an identity and a voice on our predominantly white campus and why my eighteen- and nineteen-year old women students thought their gender didn't matter. Through these efforts, I was coming to understand my own privilege as a tall, thin, middle-class white man who had recently taken on his first mortgage. I was just discovering Judith Butler, Eve Sedgwick, and queer theory and starting to forge relationships with other queer scholars and allies that would eventually enable me to make the arguments I have made in this book. Also, I had never confirmed for my students what I'm sure most of them suspected: that I am gay. As a writer, I was experimenting with narrative seriously for the first time, mostly writing pieces about my mother and cooking as a means of grieving the loss of her as a living presence in my life.

The critical conference with Sarah happened at the end of class on a workshop day when most of the other students had already finished their work and left. It was her second or third draft, and the three themes were starting to emerge more clearly because we'd found the basic poem/story/poem/story/poem/story/poem structure we wanted to use. But the prose sections were still too preachy. I wanted Sarah to learn to trust the stories themselves, to show first—as the creative writing pedagogy commonplace goes—and tell later, and then only if necessary. "Let's try this in your next draft. Try to just let the poem sections do the explaining and just show in the prose examples." Sarah liked this idea, and we worked through the Wiccan example, cutting out the opening explanation of setting, and jumping in with direct dialogue. "You can backtrack and explain the setting later if you need to, after you grab your readers' attention." Sarah liked this technique, too; she's smart and a good writer, and her next draft pulled it all off, needing only minor editing.

Segment 3
> Hate them cuz they just don't care
> Hate them cuz they hurt me
> Xenophobia
> Homophobia
> Ageism
> Sexism
> Racism
> Classism
> It's all condoned and no one cares.

"Hey weren't you in the Daily [campus newspaper]?"

Its night on campus, and I was coming back from a late test as a voice pierces the darkness. I have to search for the sound and I find it, in three very large guys standing by an old building that bears the scars of thousands.

"Probably." I answer back. It was National Coming Out Days and I was the president of the [LGBT] Alliance. I walked towards them, and I wasn't sure if I knew the one in the middle or not.

"You faggots are ruining this place you know that?" It was the one on the right; he had blond hair if I remember correctly, and had an ISU jacket on.

"Yeah, we should kill all you fucking fags." I knew that it was probably time to go; the murder of Mathew Shepard wasn't all that long ago and the thoughts of hanging on a fence somewhere doesn't appeal to me. The one in the middle stepped towards me, his face shrouded and undistinguishable from the night that was bearing down upon me.

I was glad that I have martial arts training or the punch that he threw could have really hurt. He aimed for my gut, and I think he was surprised when I dodged. Then I just wasn't there anymore. I ran like a scared little girl I am sorry to say. I wasn't brave like I always told myself I was going to be. I had always told myself that I wasn't going to run, that I was going to stand and fight. Things don't always work out the way I want them to.

> Hate them cuz they hate me
> Hate them cuz they hate what I love
> Games and theory
> Guns and swords
> Philosophy
> Religion
> History
> Mythology
> They don't KNOW anything

> They keep themselves
> Dumb and Uncaring
> I am not like them
> I care
> I am
> I . . .

One of the students in Sarah's writing group was from her high school; he couldn't believe the Wiccan incident happened at his school. Sarah's writing group decided to give her paper to the class on the day their group was in charge of choosing the reading for class discussion. I talked with them about the risks involved with using a paper written by a student in the class, particularly given that they didn't want to tell the class initially that Sarah had written the paper, but they decided to do it anyway. The class admired the structure and power of the paper. With a little prompting from me, they could see how it balanced showing and telling neatly in a genre none of them had ever seen before. But they were disturbed too; some were put off by the obvious anger, offended because they often wore clothes from Abercrombie and Fitch, and skeptical that all these things could really have happened to one person in friendly Central Iowa. The discussion changed quickly when Sarah revealed herself as the author of the piece: "Those guys were really going to hit you?"

I have used Sarah's paper with every writing class I have taught since then, but I have never been able to recreate the effect of that moment of revelation—when Sarah sat in a room full of mostly white, middle-class, privileged classmates and showed them that systemic marginalization existed in their communities and schools and claimed authorship of her paper. Earlier in the semester, two male students in Sarah's class had written papers with clearly homophobic passages, and in my response to their drafts I had asked them to consider the effects on gay members of their audience, of whom I was one, but it wasn't until after Sarah took a stand as a working-class Wiccan lesbian that I also found an opportunity to be out to the class—the first time I had ever publicly claimed my homosexuality with my students.

I have written this lengthy example in part because I believe in giving my students voice in my writing about pedagogy, and, in Sarah's case, I need to acknowledge the considerable debt I owe her as both a writer and a writing teacher. Also, I think it is important to practice what I preach about alternative rhetoric—to account, in as concrete terms as possible, what it meant for me to come to the kind of understanding I believe is necessary for responsible rhetorical practice and composition pedagogy. However, my primary motivation in telling this story is to demonstrate that the kind of pedagogy I propose in this book is possible—that it can be accomplished and that some of our students will be our natural allies in doing so if we can only see ways to help them find their voices. Perhaps most importantly, though, I want to illustrate what it looks like when students in composition courses practice alternative rhetoric.

Sarah's piece is like Anzaldúa's *Borderlands* in that it is clearly intersectional and angry; its unstated purpose is to expose some of the means by which dominant culture marginalizes others and bear witness to the ways she herself as been marginalized. However, missing in Sarah's piece is any substantive discussion of her own opacity, of the limits of her own understanding and consideration that she might have participated in some forms of marginalization. We do not get the connections to larger social issues that Anzaldúa makes or the reflections about how stories are being told that Sedaris often provides. Granted, this would be a lot to expect in a three-page paper written by a first-year composition student, and the hundreds of students to whom I have read Sarah's paper have found it challenging for its blending of genres and disturbing because of its vivid representation of the oppression she experienced, even though some are put off by the relentless anger in the piece. For good or ill, I choose to read Sarah's paper in light of Audre Lorde's argument that anger has its uses when it is given honestly and substantively: "We cannot allow our fear of anger to deflect us nor seduce us into settling for anything less than the hard work of excavating honesty" (1984, 128). However, in light of the arguments I have developed in this book, I wonder if I failed to push Sarah far enough. Even in retrospect, I don't think I could have asked Sarah for more than she gave in this paper, but as I review other papers in the file I have kept of her writing, I don't see any indication that I pushed her to a more nuanced understanding of her own position in relationship to others. Her skill as a writer, and my delight in her willingness to bring what had previously been unspoken into public view in my class, were enough for me, and now I suspect Sarah was capable of more if I had been able to ask her for it.

UNPACKING PRIVILEGE

The complement to finding voices in response to oppressive systems is accounting for one's own privilege. The potential trap in speaking back to oppression, even when accounting for multiple aspects of that oppression, is that it can limit our voices to angry shouts across the river. Few of us enjoy complete social and economic privilege in all aspects of our lives or experience oppression in all aspects and contexts of our lives; therefore, taking an intersectional perspective on the complexities of our identities can allow for a more nuanced voice that can create the basis for shared understanding with less chance of overlooking the important inequities that mar our societies and our lives. I don't mean to suggest that such accountings of privilege should pit one form of oppression against another as measured by some oppression meter. Rather, the act of understanding the limits of one's own experiences and understandings is the critical issue, but it is important to recognize that doing so is likely to be difficult work for all.

The work involved in accounting for one's own privilege is perhaps most difficult and most important for those who have led lives of relative sociocultural and economic privilege, as it can be painful to come to an understanding that one has participated in the oppression of others (even unwittingly) and to an understanding that one's educational and economic privilege may rely on things other than one's own merit. However, without such work we are not likely to move beyond shallow efforts at multiculturalism to address the deeper issues in our society. It is also important to consider how difficult it may be for those of us who have experienced some form of systemic oppression to sort out our privilege as well. Simply coming to a voice that refuses to be silenced or marginalized by the racism, sexism, heterosexism, ableism, and other forms of oppression that many of us have faced and continue to face is an accomplishment in and of itself, and it may not leave much energy for other kinds of struggle. However, if we decline to do so, we miss an opportunity to build the kinds of understanding that could help us move beyond binary notions of difference issues, with their inherent dangers of shoring up the very problematic designations of difference they seek to challenge.

Again, I am aware that I ask much of us as individuals and as a discipline. Why would anyone want to take up this hard work, and what is to be gained, particularly for those for whom dominant cultural values and their attendant discourse practices are not particularly problematic? I answer this question with a second paper in which a student of relative privilege takes an unflinching look at his own attitudes about sexual identity, gender, and race.

One of the most frequent responses from my students of relative privilege to Sarah's paper, and to other papers I have collected that show the operation of systemic oppression, is a bit of dismay:"Nothing like that has ever happened to me, I have nothing important to write about." I am always struck by the irony of this complaint, as if I am supposed to have sympathy for those whose lives have been so privileged they don't have an oppression story to tell. One of my responses to such concerns is that plenty can be usefully written about experiences that do not involve a dramatic clash of cultural values; I provide examples of such papers as starting points for their writing and ask them to write about aspects of their heritage or to create the kind of tribute piece Sedaris writes about his foul-mouthed brother who enjoys a special relationship with Sedaris's father. My other response to such concerns is to acknowledge that there is some truth in them, that these students are at a disadvantage in terms of the kind of authorship I am trying to encourage them to take up—using one's experiences to expose the clash of cultural values. The larger point here is that those who have experienced systemic marginalization in one form or another have an advantage in the reverse economy of alternative rhetoric and other forms of critical awareness that seek to deconstruct the sociocultural values and discourse practices that create and maintain systems of oppression. As I have argued throughout this book, those who have experienced marginalization do not automatically have access to understanding their own opacity; indeed, I believe we must all be prepared to account for our relative positions of marginalization and oppression along a number of the axes of difference in our culture, no matter how oppressed or privileged we have been along any given single axis. But those of us who have experienced systemic oppression based on at least one of these axes have often been forced to consider the implications of cultural values on a daily basis and to develop a form of DuBois's "double consciousness," which provides us with the means for cultural deconstruction and reconstruction unless, as Anzaldúa notes, we have been "brutalized into insensitivity" by those experiences (1987, 60).

To rephrase a question I posed earlier, why would anyone, but particularly those for whom dominant culture is relatively unproblematic, choose to engage in the difficult work of unpacking their own privilege and then seek means to take responsibility for it in their interactions with others? Is it reasonable to expect anyone without a direct stake in moving toward social justice to engage in such self reflection? For example, why would a tall, thin, straight, white, middle-class, athletic honors student choose to represent his own cultural privilege, and could he pull it off if he chose to do so?

Segment 1
I am the all American boy.
I do my homework on time.
I tell the truth and follow the rules.
I go to church and believe in God.

"Great game tonight, John." I look up, acknowledge the compliment, and then finish peeling off my game pants and shoulder pads. Showers turn on and steam billows through the locker room. Andy sits in the corner facing the wall, waiting for others to leave before he will change his clothes. "What's the matter, faggot? Too afraid you'll get a boner in the shower?" someone yells at him. Laughter comes from the shower. I laugh, too. Stay away from me, fag, I think.

This was the best piece this student, whom I will call John, wrote for me, in part because he wrote it late in the semester, and in part because he was inspired by Sarah's paper, borrowing her poem/story/poem/ story/poem/story/poem structure. In our conference, he was a bit shy about showing it to me, worrying that he was taking too much risk, but I encouraged him to be brutally honest, and, much like in Sarah's conference, I sat with him and showed him how to cull all the explanation in the prose portion and just let the story speak for itself in response to the poem-ish section that preceded it.

Segment 2
I am the all American boy.
I exercise and stay healthy.
I respect my elders.
I am going to college so I can improve my future.

"And that is the derivative of the function." I look up, finish my notes, and run the problem through my mind. "Now, let's do a practice problem. Carrie, can you tell me what the derivative of this is?" Carrie giggles, twists her hair around her index finger, and blows a bubble. Carrie's group of girl friends giggles with her. I wonder why girls are even allowed into advanced math classes. Why don't they stick to something they'll use later in life as moms, like food and nutrition? Besides, girls aren't good at math anyway.

When I have read John's paper to subsequent classes, I have often seen puzzled looks on my students' faces; my students wonder why their liberal teacher is using this homophobic and sexist paper, particularly when they see it is obviously a kind of response to Sarah's paper, which I always read to them before I show them this one. By this point in the semester they are well accustomed to this practice. I put a former student's text up on the overhead projector or document camera and read it to them. I ask them first for their gut reaction to the piece (does it work for them or not and what aspects of it are particularly well written or could be done differently?) and then we move into a more detailed analysis of structure and techniques. They know I only show them student examples I think are well done. Indeed, one or two of my more insightful students invariably point out that John adheres even more strictly to the show, don't tell rule in his prose sections than Sarah does but that his poem-ish sections aren't as good as hers. But as I read this text, there is almost always an uneasiness in the room that mirrors the tension created when I read Sarah's paper.

Segment 3
   I am the all American boy.
   I look up to my father with respect.
   I play sports and watch them on TV.
   I like working on cars.

A black girl is standing in front of me in the lunch line, loudly voicing her opinion about the quality of food to anyone nearby. I pretend to ignore her and try not to catch her eyes. I really don't want to get involved in that conversation. She blabs with the girls in front of her and cackles at something. Why can't she just talk quietly like everyone else in the cafeteria? I think it's probably because she's black and wants attention. She continues to talk loudly with bad grammar. And they wonder why they are seen as uneducated thugs.

   I am racist.
   I am sexist.
   I am homophobic.
   I loathe these things about me.
   But I cannot deny any of them.
   So much for being all American.

Of course, the room relaxes when I get to the final stanza. In fact, many students say they like John's paper more than Sarah's, and I can understand why they admire John's willingness to bear witness to his participation in systems of oppression as well as his refusal to temper his stark portrayals of his own prejudice. Some students also like the simplicity of John's paper with its confessional turn that provides a kind of positive ending. Sarah's piece offers no new insight, no respite from the anger that leaves her speechless in the end, trailing off and unable to continue articulating herself in response to the many faces of oppression she has experienced.

I usually end up arguing that Sarah's is technically the better paper and that she deserves more credit than John as a writer because she created the structure he imitated, but I also agree with my students that John is more reflective about his position and his actions than is Sarah. He moves closer to the kind of accounting for opacity that Butler demands because the most powerful move at his disposal for joining the dialogue that Sarah and I offer him is confession. And in the end, I admire him as a writer for not complicating the final move of his paper with a request for forgiveness or a call for change.

My purpose in offering Sarah's paper as a kind of call and John's as a kind of response is to suggest the broad parameters of the problem that alternative rhetoric poses, both for our disciplinary practice and for composition pedagogy, as well as the basic challenges we face in engaging in such work. Sarah's case suggests that for those who have been brutalized by dominant culture along one or more of the axes of difference in our society, finding the voice to bear witness to that marginalization is an important and useful contribution, but that the effort necessary to do so may leave little energy for reflecting in more nuanced terms about other aspects of one's identity in which one might enjoy considerable privilege (race and physical ableness in Sarah's case). In both our disciplinary practice and our pedagogy, we must work to make places for those who have been marginalized to help others understand those experiences, recognizing and seeking to mitigate the risks involved for the oppressed to do so. However, we must also recognize that those who do so must also stand ready to account for the limits of their accounts, recognizing that while anger and outrage have important uses, they cannot be the only contributions made by the oppressed to social justice dialogues.

John's case suggests that a first move for those who enjoy positions of relative privilege in both society at large and in the practice and pedagogy of rhetoric may be a form of confession and apology based on a substantive accounting of their own participation—even if unwitting—in those systems of oppression. In John's case, a simple confession was appropriate because, I believe, that was where he was at the moment; Sarah's paper provided the impetus for him to think about his identity in a new way, and in this sense I believe he is a useful model for many composition students in similar circumstances. However, we need to set a higher standard for those of us who teach composition and an even higher standard for those of us who have had the opportunity to consider and debate the appropriate response to feminist, postmodern, postcolonial, queer, and other calls to rethink the complicity of rhetorical theory and pedagogical practice in the maintenance of systems of oppression.

One of my most basic arguments in this book is that as purveyors of rhetoric we bear a particular responsibility to teach and model the wide range of rhetorical practices because our discipline is by nature complicit in the systems of oppression embedded within the discourses of power that we teach. Thus, I contend we need alternative rhetoric that not only expands the genres and discourse moves seen as relevant to academic and professional discourses, but that also requires interlocutors to substantively account for their positions within the discourses of power. Of course I recognize that the term *alternative rhetoric* itself could eventually become meaningless if the kinds of change it advocates become the norm and if the underlying systems of inequity were dismantled. However, given the continuing sociocultural problems based on race, gender, class, sexual identity, religion, and other axes of difference in American culture, it is unlikely this utopia will emerge any time soon. Further, I am not so naïve as to believe that teaching alternative rhetoric in college composition courses will be the major social force that can move our society toward that change. However, we have an important opportunity and considerable responsibility to help students of all identities to understand their place within such a system and what it means to take a responsible voice. Thus, alternative rhetorics are likely to be necessary for quite some time.

Further, to enact such a rhetoric and pedagogy we must move beyond acknowledging and even celebrating discursive subjectivity if we are to engage in rhetoric and pedagogy that is alternative in practice. Of course, we should not seek to be alternative just for the sake of novelty or for a sense of being avant garde. Rather, the very concept of alternative rhetoric presupposes that systemic injustices exist and that the discourses of power must constantly be critiqued to sort out the ways in which they perpetuate those injustices. As I have argued, this sorting process is itself discursive in that it is dependent on the interplay of such factors as the conventional/transgressive nature of the discourse practices used, the intent of the originating interlocutor, the contexts for the discursive acts, and the varied perspectives and experiences of those involved in the acts. However, the examples I have drawn from the work of Grimké, Douglass, Anzaldúa, Sedaris, and my student Sarah illustrate that these theoretical complexities need not be debilitating—that it is possible to speak/write from the margins. Thus, I suggest three steps we might take to begin moving toward developing alternative rhetorics and their attendant progressive pedagogies.

Step One: Piercing the Veil of Fairness

Perhaps the chief obstacle to moving beyond the presumption that we must acculturate the discursively disenfranchised to the discourses of power is our collective inability to unseat the notion that "standard" English (and other discourses of power) provides equal opportunity for social and economic advancement in our society. Our field has struggled with this issue for more than thirty years despite the fact that postmodern, postcolonial, and feminist theories (among other approaches) offer us powerful means for understanding the constructed nature of language and culture. Of course, one problem is that our students and our colleagues in the institutions in which we work have not embraced a discursive understanding of language and culture, and, in some sense, we undermine our own authority as the purveyors of "correct usage" when we attempt to build theory and pedagogy that does so. Yet we must put this privilege at risk; indeed, in our work with students, administrators, colleagues, and workplace professionals, piercing the veil of fairness is a critical first step in creating understandings of language and discourse that might make our theory and practice a real force for equality in American society.

Step Two: Envisioning New Goals for Rhetoric and Writing Instruction

If we are successful in piercing the veil of fairness in our composition and rhetoric programs for our students, colleagues and superiors, then we must also stand ready to articulate new goals for rhetoric and for writing instruction that reflect a discursive understanding of writing and rhetoric. Part of our problem in doing so is that, as a discipline, we have taken as our primary mission the challenging task of making the discourses of power accessible to our students. Here I do not intend to demean the important work that has been done to demystify the discourses of power and make them available to groups who have been historically excluded from them. But if we are to move beyond an updated version of Hugh Blair's calls for teaching good taste, then we must envision a different basic goal for our theory and pedagogy. That goal, I propose, is to develop voices that allow us and our students to speak in and to the discourses of power. Such a goal can make use of the considerable work done to identify and taxonomize the discourses of power, but it also commits our field to developing theory and pedagogy that envisions roles beyond assimilation for our students and ourselves. I am proposing here that teaching cultural critique based on additive models of multiculturalism is not enough—that we must embrace transformation as an explicit goal and also explicitly identify a wider range of roles and the attendant rhetorical practices that support those roles. Embracing such a goal does not mean change must be immediate and wholesale; the rhetorical traditions many of us have grown up with and have spent considerable parts of our professional lives developing will remain relevant, but as one important component of rhetorical practice rather than as all the rhetoric worth knowing.

Step Three: Substantively Accounting for Our Own Subjectivities, Particularly Our Own Privilege

The work I propose in steps one and two is difficult, in part because it requires individual and collective accountings of participation in oppression. In a society that prizes its sense of fairness, deeper understandings of culpability in such systems of marginalization are painful: no one enjoys learning he or she has participated in sexist, racist, heterosexist, classist, ageist, or ableist systems of oppression, even if it was without conscious intent. Thus, we must recognize that if we hope to be real advocates for change, we must begin with the hard work of sorting out our own participation in such systems of oppression, and we must substantively account for our own privilege.

For example, as I read Douglass's *Narrative* for this book and chose passages to summarize, I was keenly aware that I was both aided and limited in doing so by my own subjectivity. The particular set of experiences I have had as a queer academic from working-class roots shaped my reading in particular ways. For example, when Douglass describes his sense of isolation and helplessness when he first escapes to New York, I accept his statement that only another escaped slave could fully appreciate the experience he describes. Yet, I also recognize a kindred sense of isolation and powerlessness I have experienced in my own coming out as a gay man. This experience directs my reading, creating a hunger to see a connection between Douglass's experiences and my own. Doubtless other readers would be directed by their unique subjectivities, and this engagement of subjectivities is at the heart of a discursive understanding of language, rhetoric, and culture. However, it would be a mistake, I think, to end this investigation, as too many postmodern rhetorical theorists do, with the always unique interactions of subjectivities. To stop here is to be in danger of invoking a dangerous form of individualism that allows one to invoke the potential powers of deconstruction without accepting the attendant responsibility to assess one's own participation in systems of oppression. As I argued in chapter one, alternative rhetoric begins at the point where one moves beyond the recognition (and perhaps celebration) of discursive subjectivity to exploring (and accepting one's participation in) systems of power that use language and rhetoric both to disenfranchise and to liberate.

COMPOSITION PEDAGOGY AS AN INTRODUCTION TO AUTHORSHIP

I conclude this book with a call to see writing as authorship and to see composition pedagogy as an introduction to authorship. In doing so, I join a number of scholars in our field who call for us to understand our basic purpose differently. As mentioned earlier in this chapter, Matsuda counsels that the primary aim of rhetoric and composition should no longer be "to produce English that is unmarked in the eyes of teachers who are custodians of privileged varieties of English" (2006, 640). Similarly, Min-zhan Lu argues that moving away from a monolithic understanding of English and toward an understanding of English as living, as continually evolving, means we must problematize what has been the central objective of composition: "Writing *in* or *across* the disciplines or professions." Instead, teachers and researchers "must continue to challenge ourselves to construct a global perspective on the politics of 'nonliterary' uses of English" (2006, 616). Working from a different strand of composition theory and research, Doug Downs and Elizabeth Wardle have made a similar argument about the need to change the basic goal of composition. Like Lu and Matsuda, Downs and Wardle see the goal of "teaching students 'how to write in college' in one or two semesters" (2007, 553) as problematic, in part because it is unreachable, citing decades of writing research demonstrating that "writing is neither basic nor universal but content- and context-contingent and irreducibly complex" (558).

Taken together, these calls suggest that one reason rhetoric and composition pedagogy has largely failed to implement what we have learned from our own theory and research, to some extent, is that we have not been willing or able to reimagine our basic task, our reason for existence. The question of how to do so is a complex one, and Matsuda suggests that it entails such complex issues as how the "perpetuation of the myth of linguistic homogeneity in U.S. college composition has been facilitated by the concomitant policy of linguistic containment that has kept language differences invisible in the required composition course and in the discourse of composition studies" (2006, 641). Lu suggests that one means for change is to encourage nonidiomatic uses of English (á la Chinua Achebe), and Downs and Wardle argue for recasting composition as an introduction to writing studies enterprise which conceptualizes "research writing much more like expert scholarly researchers do, as turns in a conversation or contributions to addressing an open question" (2007, 573).

I agree wholeheartedly with the substance of these critiques, and there is merit in the actions proposed, largely because they break with the status quo and suggest concrete means by which we can build on what we have learned about what it means to teach and learn composition. My own approach, however, begins with a different assumption about what it means to unseat the dominant goal of composition as training students for academic and professional writing. One way to take up alternative rhetoric, as I have sketched it in this book, is to recast the college composition course as an introduction to authorship—as a course that focuses on helping students understand what it means for them to take voice in culture and that seeks to expand their repertoires of discourse strategies as opposed to preparing them to participate within the discourses of power.

The central assumption of the pedagogical approach I outline in the remainder of this chapter is that negotiating identity cannot and should not be avoided in composition pedagogy; indeed, the negotiation of identity is critical to authorship. I mean to challenge the many

ways thoughtful colleagues in the field have argued that we can provide students with more sophisticated sets of skills that are somehow
neutral within the supposed safe spaces of our classrooms—that skills
take on sociopolitical import only as students choose or choose not to
employ them in other contexts. If we believe language matters—that
it is central to the construction and maintenance of cultural practices
and values—then we must do more than acknowledge the possible
sociocultural import of our own pedagogical discourses. We must, as
others have argued, understand that we are doing more than helping
students understand what it means for them to attempt to engage in
the discourses of power that dominate academic and professional discourse in America.

Creating a pedagogy that embraces alternative rhetoric means facing
two fundamental challenges: (1) helping students learn to be in conversation with the discourses of power (and with other discourses) without
presuming they will all be assimilated to the values and the linguistic
practices of dominant culture, and (2) giving up on the goal that all
students will master or attempt to master the same set of genres and discourse practices—whether those genres and discourse practices are traditional or transgressive. To be sure, addressing these challenges means
reconceiving composition pedagogy in terms that run contrary to dominant notions of college curricula as defined bodies of knowledge and/
or skills that serve as building for further work. However, let me be clear
here; I am not proposing that we shirk our disciplinary responsibility to
prepare students to participate in the discourses of the academy or professional life or that we ignore what we have learned in 2,500 years of rhetorical theory and practice. Instead, I want to suggest that we make our
primary goal to aid students in understanding what it means for them to
take voice and to expand their options for doing so. To that end, I conclude this book by posing not a single pedagogy that everyone should use
to accomplish this goal but a set of six principles as guides for developing
pedagogy that encourages the practice of alternative rhetoric.

Principle #1: Teach Composition as if What Students Have to Say Really Matters

More than 150 years ago, rhetorician Richard Whately argued, for
pragmatic reasons, that the beginning place for composition pedagogy
was the things students already know:

The teacher should frequently recall to his own mind these two considerations; first, that since the benefit proposed does not consist in the intrinsic value of the composition, but in the *exercise* to the pupil's mind, it matters not how insignificant the subject may be, if it will but interest him, and thereby afford him such exercise; secondly, that the younger and backwarder each student is, the more unfit he will be for *abstract* speculations; and the less remote must be the subjects proposed from those *individual* objects and occurrences which always form the first beginnings of the furniture of the youthful mind. (2001, 1014)

In one sense, the point from Richard Whately's *Elements of Rhetoric* quoted above reflects an approach to the pedagogy of rhetoric that is very forward thinking. Indeed, its underlying premise—that real learning begins with students' knowledge and experiences—has surfaced in a number of ways in education: it is a central assumption in John Dewey's pragmatism, in Lev Vygotsky's zone of proximal development, and in Stephen Krashen's I+1 second language-acquisition model. If we embrace the goal of helping all students to learn (as opposed to screening the so-called underprepared out of higher education), then beginning where students are is the only sensible starting point for education. Much like current advocates of using popular culture in composition teaching, Whately argues, for pragmatic reasons, that the subjects of composition pedagogy must "be *interesting* to the student, and on which he has (or may, with pleasure, and without much toil, acquire) sufficient information" or we risk the sort of writing that induces a student to "string together vague general expressions, conveying no distinct ideas of his own mind, and second-hand sentiments which he does not feel" (2001, 1013).

Whately's apt description of the kinds of voiceless writing students produce when they are not connected to their topics speaks to the perennial problem of engaging students actively in the subject of composition pedagogy. I want to argue that beyond pragmatism, students' interests and experiences are important beginning places for learning because who they are, what they know, and what discourse practices they already know how to use are critical for engaging in the work of helping them to understand what it means to engage with the discourses of power and to expand their repertoires for doing so. Unlike Whately, who grudgingly accepts "backwarder" students' interests and abilities, I propose that we must embrace what our students bring to us as a critical part of our pedagogical project. Of course, another critical part of the

232 COMPELLED TO WRITE

pedagogical project is what we have to offer students beyond their previous knowledge and experiences. Indeed, school makes no sense as an
institution if students do not learn something they have not learned elsewhere. But what I propose here is that in pedagogy that takes alternative rhetoric seriously, what each student gets will be different, not only
for the pragmatic reason that he or she brings a unique set experiences
and abilities to the composition class, but also because our primary goal
should not be to ensure that as many of our students master as much of
a particular set of discourse practices as possible, but that each has the
opportunity to further develop his or her writing repertoire in ways he
or she sees as relevant.

One of the challenges of moving students from such starting points
toward taking up authorship is that students often have no idea what
kinds of additional discourse abilities will be relevant. However, such
pedagogy may usefully begin with valuing students' discourse abilities,
knowledges, and life experiences beyond Whately's notion of them as
simply a vehicle for learning new discourse practices. In my writing
courses, I refuse to separate what students have to say from learning
about what it means to say it, and my primary aim is for students is to
begin to understand what it means to take authorship by using their own
experiences, observations, and interests as the basis for finding something worth saying—something that will engage and challenge others.
Like many proponents of alternative rhetoric, I seek to break down the
distinction between the personal and the professional, and I encourage
students to explore hybrid genres that mix narrative, descriptive, and
expository elements. I encourage my students to tell stories and to analyze them. Although my writing courses provide students with the opportunity to learn important writing skills, my primary goal is not my students' mastery of a particular set of discourse practices but helping them
to take up a larger task: understanding what it means for them to articulate themselves in society and to learn some new means for doing so.

Principle #2: Make Genres Accessible to Students

Although I have been critical in this book of Joseph Harris's attempts
to limit the negotiation of identity in composition pedagogy, I believe he
is absolutely right that the primary focus of composition courses should
be teaching the material practices of writing—that students have much
to learn about how to use the kinds of discourse practices that will "make
writing work toward their own ends" (2003, 591). In simple terms, a

writing course is not a writing course unless students learn some genres and discourse practices they did not know how to handle, or handle well, before they entered the course. My point here is rather fine; certainly we should not simply reinvent the five-paragraph theme or the comparison-and-contrast essay as master genres that all students should learn in writing courses; yet, if we do not make some genres accessible to students, we are not doing our jobs. Downs and Wardle's solution to this problem is to argue that the primary purpose of college composition courses should be to start students on a larger path, in their case learning what it means to engage in academic scholarship and to engage in the varied discourse practices necessary for such work (2007). Their primary goal moves sensibly away from the unreachable goal of laying the basis for students to participate in all kinds of academic discourse, and their pedagogy is also notable because it attempts to demystify the production of knowledge by engaging students in primary research projects and the discourse practices related to them. A writing course must teach writing, and genre features are a critical part of what it means to write.

My own approach to this problem is to introduce students to a set of discourse practices common in the humanities—memoir and other forms of nonfiction writing—to demystify the production of such texts and to provide students with tools by which they can begin to see what it means to represent their own and other experiences along with more traditional sources of information in genres common in American life (e.g., Op-Ed pieces, reports, stories with a point). However, my primary purpose moves farther away from the genres and values of the academy than does Downs and Wardle's approach, and this distance is critical because pedagogy that seeks to enact alternative rhetoric as I have defined it must provide the means for articulating where one stands in regard to the cultural values that support systemic oppression in our society, as well as providing students with the tools to begin to understand what it means to participate in the discourse practices that can reinforce or challenge those values.

Of course, the memoir, Op-Ed, and other genres I use in my courses are not inherently progressive, and engaging in them is not a guarantee that critical reflection about one's positionality within the discourse of power will follow. However, beyond the pragmatic reason Whately provides for beginning with students' experiences and interests, doing so also invites students to ground their understandings of what it means to participate in new genres and contexts for writing in their life experiences. This emphasis on the personal nature of knowledge and knowing runs contrary to the dominant notion of detachment and objectivity in the academy and provides a starting point for functional understanding of subjectivity. Even within our own field, many have cast the focus on the personal as indulgent or unethical, failing to see, I contend, that helping students understand what it means to articulate their experiences in a wider set of genres and contexts may be the most substantive and practical starting point for the difficult work of alternative rhetoric. When it comes to applying what we have learned from postmodern theory, feminist theory, and other forms of cultural criticism, our theory has outstripped our pedagogy. And I think Judith Harris (2001) is right that one reason for this is that we have defined the personal as outside the realm of academic writing rather than considering how it can and must be included. It is ludicrous to assume that the cultural critiques we invite, even require, students to engage in will not have implications for their lives, and it is adding insult to injury to define these personal implications as outside the writing acceptable in the very academic settings in which they are invited to find those insights.

Principle #3: We Need to Model the Kinds of Writing/Thinking/Living We Want Our Students to Do

One of the chief obstacles to enacting a pedagogy of alternative rhetoric is that we must practice what we preach. What if we were present as writers as well as teachers in our classes? Indeed, central to the kind of pedagogy I envision for enacting alternative rhetoric is a relationship with the teacher that extends beyond the usual detached, impersonal teacher role—an expansion of the teacher role beyond designer and manager of class activities and assignments and evaluator of students' writing to include the teacher as a writer addressing the same kinds of authorship issues students face. My favorite among the many good things the National Writing Project does for writing students and teachers is its emphasis on the need for writing teachers to be writers themselves and to share their writing with their students. Adapting the basic principle that teachers must be writers themselves to my version of alternative writing pedagogy means teachers must do the same kinds of work students are asked to do. Specifically, we must account for our positions within the discourses of power, and we must illustrate to our students how we attempt to do so in the kinds of genres we ask students to learn to use.

In my own teaching, this means I include several of my own pieces in the mix of professional and student texts I use as examples in my courses. I do this for three main reasons. First, I want to be present as a writer with my students, to show them what it means for me to engage in the kinds of challenges I ask them to take up. Second, I share my writing with my students to illustrate the difference between reading pieces written by those unknown to the class and pieces by someone who is in the room. I want my students to understand by my own example that placing one's own experience in play involves risk and that one must be willing to take criticism about the effectiveness of one's attempts to do so. Third, sharing my writing with my students makes me somewhat vulnerable to them. Indeed, in addition to a couple of fairly standard and safe pieces, I always choose something current, something unfinished, to share with my students. Some in our field find such a practice problematic; for example Geoffrey Sirc dubs teachers' use of their personal experiences in writing classes as just an excuse to work out "a complicated inner drama" (2001, 522). Of course, we should not be using our students as captive audiences for the purposes of stroking our egos or working out serious emotional issues. Also, as a tall, thin, white male, I realize that being vulnerable with my students is a different act than it might be for other teachers. However, the critical issue here is turning Sirc's value judgment around to embrace teachers' willingness to share their own struggles with the problematic ways dominant culture has defined them or to account for their own privilege within the discourse of power. Such work always needs to be done in the service of inviting students to explore similar experiences, and it is a tricky business, even if done thoughtfully, when it exposes the problematic values and conventions that support systemic oppression in our society.

The larger issue here is how to manage personal revelations while maintaining a stance as teacher. My best answer to how I do so is that I want all my students to succeed, want to see all of them grow as writers and as people, and that I realize I cannot predict in advance what that will mean for each of them. Of course my job is to introduce them to genres and discourse strategies that will help them get heard/read in the world, but equally important is my willingness to be surprised by their ability to twist genres and tweak conventions to do something I would have not thought possible.

In short, then, I propose that the extent to which students are able to substantively explore problematic constructions of culture in their writing depends, in part, on the extent to which their teachers make themselves accessible as writers doing the same thing. I must also add here that one of my biggest concerns about implementing the kind of pedagogy I propose in composition programs is that the vast majority of those who teach composition courses do not have the leisure to develop as writers themselves and/or they are in more vulnerable positions than I am. The work of creating disciplinary practices, genres, and staff development opportunities that will allow such pedagogy to be implemented on a large scale is considerable. Yet, as Downs and Wardle (2007) argue, if we fail to engage in the work of training specialists in writing pedagogy who can engage in the kinds of teaching we believe needs to occur, then we are tacitly acceding to the position that writing skills are so detached and general that virtually anyone can teach our courses (575).

Principle #4: Structure Courses in Ways that Balance Support and Evaluation

As I have already argued, it is not enough to change our goals for composition, to invite students to take up larger authorship roles, and even modeling such authorship for them will not magically impart the underlying discourse skills students need to take up such invitations. Students need practice; they need to experiment and take chances and get feedback about how their writing works or fails to work. These opportunities for exploration and feedback are particularly important for those learning to engage in alternative rhetoric, as they must often engage in complex identity negotiations and try out new discourse practices in doing so. Creating a context for such explorations requires a careful balance of support and evaluation to encourage students to learn about writing through revision.

My experience teaching composition and training composition teachers at two large state-sponsored universities leads me to suspect that what we have learned from the process movement about what it means to teach and learn writing too often devolves into encouraging students to revise but providing limited help for them to do so through peer review, and teacher input given largely to justify the grade given to texts which students will not revise any further. There have been some interesting attempts to move beyond this model, such as having students write a series of assignments on a single topic that they research throughout the semester, having a class edit a journal that publishes the best of their own writing, or having students submit a final portfolio of their work for grading, but I believe we have not yet affected the pedagogical practice of the bulk of our discipline, nor have we developed models that allow for students and teachers to substantively negotiate what disciplinary expectations mean as they are enforced in the evaluation criteria teachers use to grade students' writing.

My own approach to solving this problem begins with attempts to engage my students in writing about topics of interest to them through starting points for writing. However, pairing the starting point procedure with an approach to the evaluation of student papers that has the express purpose of encouraging revision is equally important. This practice grew out of my own frustration with writing evaluative comments whose main purpose seemed to be to justify why a paper was B+ instead of an A-. The immediate impetus for change was a colloquium in which several new teaching assistants I was helping to supervise reported on a modified portfolio grading system they discovered in which students are allowed to revise and resubmit their papers as many times as they like. They receive one of three evaluations each time a paper is submitted: "continue revising" (for any reasonable draft), "satisfactory" for a solid paper, and "outstanding" for truly remarkable papers that have something to say and are well crafted. In my version of this procedure, students must submit at least four different papers once each, they may revise each of those papers as many times as they like to try to get a higher evaluation, and they may have as many as six different papers in the revision process. The highest evaluations they receive on four of their papers determine their grade for the lion's share of the course (e.g., four "continue revising" papers equals a C-; to get a B, four papers must receive "satisfactory" evaluations; an A requires at least two "outstanding" papers).

Since I have adopted this teaching practice, I have been able to manage much more productively one of the fundamental tensions of being a writing teacher: the need to serve as an evaluator of students' writing and the need to be a coach and cheerleader, trying to help them find ways to improve their pieces. When I respond to a student paper now, I am trying to give the student a realistic assessment of where the piece stands as well as provide some input about how it could be improved. To be honest, my students find this process frustrating at first; at midterm, it is not unusual for my students to think I am the hardest grader they have ever had and that my standards are so high no one in the class will ever get an "outstanding" evaluation. My larger point in this example is that we must marry our egalitarian efforts in teaching alternative rhetoric with careful consideration of how to enact what we have learned from thirty years of research about writing pedagogy; we must create courses that move beyond calls for critique and actually provide students with realistic opportunities to learn how to enact such calls in writing that engages them. Of course, the examples from my own pedagogical practice are not the only way to do so, but unless we are willing to reconsider the basic goals of our pedagogy, to reconsider the range of genres and discourse practices we see as relevant to composition pedagogy, and to carefully apply what we have learned about the mechanics of the effective teaching of writing in our own research, then we have little chance of engaging our students in the arduous task of learning to articulate themselves meaningfully.

Principle #5: Create a Community of Writers

Beyond serving as a model of writing and balancing support and evaluation in the classroom, writing teachers also need to create a community of writers to help students in the process of learning what it means to take authorship. Although the teacher's voice is an important voice in this process, it should not be the only voice. However, as most writing teachers know, getting students to give each other honest and useful feedback is a difficult business. Too often, peer review is a make-work task in which students use teachers' generic prompts to provide perfunctory responses about their peers' work. To be honest, at the beginning of my writing courses, the majority of my students are not very good at peer review because we have not yet engaged the set of reading and writing activities that will help them develop more informed understandings of what it means to press their writing further. However, following the example set by Robert Brooke (1991), I commit to writing groups in my classes, building a sense of community in the groups through in-class activities, several out-of-class meetings (for which I cancel several class meetings), and advocacy statements. Each time a student turns in a new paper or a revision, he or she must include a self-evaluation of the paper and an advocacy statement written by someone in his or her writing group. The purpose of these self-evaluations and advocacy statements is twofold. First, I want to create some kind of discussion with my students about what distinguishes a "continue revising" paper from a "satisfactory" paper or a "satisfactory" paper from an "outstanding" one. Again, early on, most of my students are not very good at advocacy statements, but as the semester moves along they become increasingly good advocates for each other.

A second reason I use the advocacy statement procedure is that I want my students reading each other's papers; I want them to see how their classmates are interpreting the starting points and to see what it means for others in the class to take voice. After midterm, the advocacy statements usually become much more substantive; occasionally an advocacy statement writer does most of the work of responding to the paper for me; more often, I frame my comments against what the advocacy statement writer has said, agreeing with some points and disagreeing with others. As one of my recent students noted in an end-of-semester course evaluation: "The advocacy statement thing confused and/or annoyed me at first, but I suppose it was there as the only surefire way for us to read each others' papers and give feedback." Although I retain the role of evaluator and decide what evaluation each paper deserves, the writing group/advocacy statement process forces my students to be involved, at least to some degree, in conversations with me and with their classmates about what constitutes good writing. To encourage this participation, I require reports of students' out-of-class writing group meetings, and I keep track of how many advocacy statements students write for their classmates and count these toward class participation that makes up a small portion of the students' final grades. As I have already mentioned, my students are often frustrated by their evaluations at midterm; it is not unusual for there to be a slight us-against-him dynamic midcourse. However, the self-evaluation/advocacy statement procedure forces students to move beyond general complaints about my tough grading and to articulate particular reasons why a particular new submission or revision deserves a higher evaluation. A further benefit of this procedure is that when students do achieve "outstanding" work, their groups know it; they see what that kind of work entails, that such excellence can be accomplished, and what kind of underlying talent and/or hard work is necessary to pull it off.

Principle #6: Embrace Imperfection

Each semester, I ask my students' permission to copy any outstanding papers that are produced, and in addition to the long-time favorite papers, I try to include some new papers in the next class I teach. I am often surprised as we read these papers together that the pieces have occasional spelling errors and syntax problems I overlooked when I gave the paper an "outstanding" evaluation, and my current students are often much more critical of these depersonalized examples than they are of their current classmates' work. The underlying issue here, as most writing teachers know, is that it is much easier to be critical of the work of a writer who is not present. However, post hoc, I am often surprised at the generosity of my reading of these former students' texts—surprised at my willingness to embrace what others would likely see as imperfect work because a student has convinced me that he or she has something important to say or because a student took a risk or experimented with an innovative genre. These moments in which I discovered I had been blind to imperfections in "outstanding" papers bothered me until I realized that what I was rewarding were significant steps students took in their journey to finding voice.

Most of the papers my students produce are also imperfect, as reflected by the "continue revising" or "satisfactory" evaluations they receive, and, as I have noted, some imperfections even slip into "outstanding" papers. However, most of my students write something they are really proud of during the semester—something they and their classmates see as significant. One reason for this is that the apparatus to support their development as writers can be delivered in a semester-long course because most of the time students have the material for their writing ready at hand as well as having the relevant cultural knowledge to be able to engage in the necessary analysis. These simplifying assumptions make it easier to focus on the difficulties of learning techniques such as storytelling and analysis. But, ultimately I think it is my belief in my students that enables them, my surety that they all have something worth saying if they are willing to work on it and that they can learn some new ways to tell their stories so they can say what they need to say.

As I have argued in this chapter, one important aspect of mounting pedagogy that enables students to take up such tasks in ways meaningful to them is in understanding alternative rhetoric as a means to embrace subjectivity, as requiring a set of discourse practices that move beyond the usual detached roles of academic readers and writers to allow writers to account for their positions within the discourses of power. Doing so requires not just opening the practice of rhetoric and composition to a wider range of discourse practices but also moving beyond our pedagogies of neutrality. I readily admit this is difficult work; it took me over fifteen years to figure out how to be an authentic presence in my own writing classes, to use who I am as a person and a writer to engage my students in ways that challenge them to be authors of their own lives. I recognize that my unique identity, abilities, and limitations as a writer greatly affect the kinds of invitations I can extend to my students as well as the kinds of support I can give. Further, I cannot specify exactly what engaging in such a process means for others who choose to take it up. I can say, however, that if we are serious about substantively accounting for the differences that still mark our culture at large, our rhetorical theory, and our composition pedagogy, then we must engage in such work if we hope to move beyond the shallow generosity of tolerance.

Interchapter

GOD
ABHORS
YOU

the sign read, and the first letter of each word was printed in bright yellow to insure that readers would see exactly who its bearer believed god abhors. The sign was carried by a member of group of evangelical Christians protesting the Southern Decadence Parade. I first saw them the previous Friday evening, strategically positioned between Oz and the Pub, the two big gay bars on the corner of Bourbon and St. Ann Streets. The group of mostly men stood in a loose circle dripping in the humid New Orleans heat, all under the watchful eyes of several New Orleans police officers who stood off slightly to the side. Throughout the weekend, the group moved up and down Bourdon Street visually accosting revelers, who mostly ignored them. The God Abhors You sign was an addition for the Sunday version of the group that had come to protest the gay pride parade, as was a man with a small loudspeaker clipped to his belt and a microphone in his hand who preached to the crowd. Police officers were handy again, and so was a single man walking a yard behind the group and carrying a bullhorn through which he repeated over and over "stop the hate, stop the hate, stop the hate."

As a former evangelical Christian, I understood that the protestors believed they were doing God's work, that their presence with Bible verses on large signs was an act of devotion and a missionary presence in what they saw as the very heart of depravity. As a gay man, I was stunned that the bearer of the "God Abhors You" sign had given up even the pretense of the usual "love the sinner, hate the sin" stance, and I was grateful to the man who dogged the group giving literal voice to what most of us in the crowd were thinking: "This is hate speech." As a rhetorical theorist trying to take a break from work in one of the most gay-friendly places in the country, I found myself amazed to see what Gloria Anzaldúa calls a "borderland" physically incarnated and walking down the street in front of me. As an American, I felt a strange pride in the exercise of free speech, that law enforcement officials were present to ensure both that the protestors were allowed to peacefully present their message and that they did not interfere with the pride parade—a moment for uninhibited celebration of sexual identities and gender expressions that are still too closeted in many aspects of American society.

In the end, I think this event clearly illustrates how rhetorical acts are motivated, are situated in belief systems that are in conflict, and how it is the job of those of us who teach rhetoric and composition to do more than stand back as the police officers did. We must ensure the rights of all to receive a hearing but we must also sort out the underlying moral claims and how they conflict. Although I have profound respect for the practice of freedom of speech in American culture, the teaching and practice of rhetoric must aspire to more than just neutrality.

REFERENCES

Anzaldúa, Gloria. 1981. Speaking in tongues: A letter to 3rd world women writers. In Moraga and Anzaldúa.

———. 1983. La Prieta. In Moraga and Anzaldúa.

———. 1987. *Borderlands* la frontera: *The new mestiza*, 3rd ed. San Francisco: Aunt Lute Books.

———, ed. 1990a. *Making face, making soul/haciendo caras: Creative and critical perspectives by feminists of color.* San Francisco: Aunt Lute Books.

———. 1990b. Haciendo caras, una entrada. In Anzaldúa.

———. 2002a. now let us shift . . . the path of conocimiento . . . inner work, public acts. In Anzaldúa and Keating.

———. 2002b. Preface: (un)natural bridges, (un)safe spaces. In Anzaldúa and Keating.

———, and AnaLouise Keating, eds. 2002. *This bridge we call home: Radical visions for transformation.* New York: Routledge.

Baca, Damián. 2008. *Mestiz@ scripts, digital migrations, and the territories of writing.* New York: Palgrave/Macmillan.

Bahri, Deepika. 1998. Terms of engagement: Postcolonialism, transnationalism, and composition studies. *JAC: A Journal of Composition Theory* 18 (1): 29–44.

Bartlett, Elizabeth Ann, ed. 1988. *Sarah Grimké: Letters on the equality of the sexes and other essays.* New Haven: Yale University Press.

Bartlett, Elizabeth Ann. 1994. *Liberty, equality, sorority: The origins and interpretation of American feminist thought: Frances Wright, Sarah Grimke, and Margaret Fuller.* Brooklyn, NY: Carlson.

Bartholomae, David. 1985. Inventing the university. In *When a writer can't write*, edited by Mike Rose, 134–65. New York: Guilford.

Bergquist, Kathie. 2000. David Sedaris: La maison de mes dents. *Publishers Weekly*, June 19, 54–55.

Bishop, Wendy. 2003. Suddenly sexy: Creative nonfiction rear-ends composition. *College English* 65: 257–75.

———, ed. 1997. *Elements of alternate style: Essays on writing and revision.* Portsmouth, NH: Boynton/Cook.

Bizzell, Patricia. 1990. Beyond anti-foundationalism to rhetorical authority: Problems defining "cultural literacy." *College English* 52: 661–75.

Bizzell, Patricia, and Bruce Herzberg, eds. 2001. *The rhetorical tradition*, 2nd ed. Boston: Bedford/St. Martin's.

Bradford, Vivian. 2006. Neoliberal epideictic: Rhetorical form and commemorative politics on September 11, 2002. *Quarterly Journal of Speech* 92 (1): 1–26.

Brandt, Deborah. 2001. Sponsors of literacy. In *Literacy: A critical sourcebook*, edited by Ellen Cushman, Eugene R. Kintgen, Barry M. Kroll and Mike Rose. Boston: Bedford/St. Martin's.

Brooke, Robert E. 1991. *Writing and a sense of self.* Urbana, IL: National Council of Teachers of English.

Browdy de Hernandez, Jennifer. 1998. Mothering the self: Writing through the lesbian sublime in Audre Lorde's *Zami* and Gloria Anzaldúa's *Borderlands/la frontera.* In Stanley.

Butler, Judith. 2005. *Giving an account of oneself.* New York: Fordham University Press.

Carlacio, Jami. 2002. "Ye knew your duty, but you did it not:" The epistolary rhetoric of Sarah Grimké. *Rhetoric Review* 21.3: 247-63.

Cixous, Hélène. 1976. The laugh of the Medusa. Translated by Keith Cohen and Paula Cohen. *Signs: Journal of Women in Culture and Society* 1 (4): 875–93.

Collins, Daniel F. 2001. Audience in Afrocentric rhetoric: Promoting human agency and social change. In Gray-Rosendale and Gruber.

Crenshaw, Kimberle Williams. 1993. Beyond racism and misogyny: Black feminism and 2 Live Crew. In *Words that wound: Critical race theory, assaultive speech, and the first amendment*, edited by Mari J. Matsuda, Charles R. Lawrence, Richard Delgado, and Kimberle Williams Crenshaw. Boulder, CO: Westview Press.

Cushman, Ellen. 2008. Toward a rhetoric of self-representation: Identity politics in Indian country and rhetoric and composition. *College Composition and Communication* 60 (2): 320–65.

Daly, Brenda. 1998. *Authoring a life: A woman's survival in and through literacy studies.* Albany: State University of New York Press.

Daniell, Beth. 2003. *A community of friendship: Literacy, spiritual practice, and women in recovery.* Carbondale: Southern Illinois University Press.

Dehann, Kathleen A. 2001. "Wooden shoes and mantle clocks:" Letter writing as a rhetorical forum for the transforming immigrant identity. In Gray-Rosendale and Gruber.

DePeter, Ronald A. 1997. Fractured narratives: Explorations in style. In Bishop.

Dobrin, Sidney I. 2002. A problem with writing (about) "alternative discourse." In Schroeder, Fox, and Bizzell.

Douglass, Frederick. 1960. *Narrative of the life of Frederick Douglass: An American slave,* edited by Benjamin Quarles. Cambridge, MA: The Belknap Press of Harvard University Press.

———.1962. *Life and Times of Frederick Douglass: Written by Himself.* New York: Bonanza Books.

———. 2003. *My Bondage and my freedom.* Edited by John David Smith. New York: Penquin Books.

Dow, Bonnie J. 1989. The function of epideictic and deliberative strategies in presidential crisis rhetoric. *Western Journal of Speech Communication* 53 : 294–310.

Downs, Douglas, and Elizabeth Wardle. 2007. Teaching about writing, righting misconceptions: (Re)envisioning "first-year composition" as "introduction to writing studies." *College Composition and Communication* 58 (4): 552–84.

Elbow, Peter. 2002. Vernacular Englishes in the writing classroom? Probing the culture of literacy. In Schroeder, Fox, and Bizzell.

Espinoza, Dionne. 1998. Women of color and identity politics. In Stanley.

Fishkin, Shelley Fisher, and Carla L. Peterson. 1991. "We hold these truths to be self-evident:" The rhetoric of Frederick Douglass's journalism. In Sundquist.

Foner, Philip S., ed. 1976. *Frederick Douglass on women's rights.* Westport, CN: Greenwood Press.

Foster, Frances Smith. 1985. Adding color and contour to early American self-portraitures: Autobiographical writings of Afro-American women. In *Conjuring black women, fiction, and literary tradition,* edited by Marjorie Pryse and Hortense J. Spillers. Bloomington: Indiana University Press.

Franklin, Cynthia G. 1997. *Writing women's communities: The politics and poetics of contemporary multi-genre anthologies.* Madison: University of Wisconsin Press.

Frost, Elisabeth, and Cynthia Hogue. 2006a. *Innovative women poets: An anthology of contemporary poetry and interviews.* Iowa City: University of Iowa Press.

———. 2006b. Gloria Evangelina Anzaldúa: Introduction. In Frost and Hogue.

Fulkerson, Gerald. 1996. Frederick Douglass (1818–1895), abolitionist, reformer. In *African-American orators: A bio-critical sourcebook,* edited by Richard W. Leeman. Westport, CT: Greenwood Press.

Garrison, William Lloyd. 1960. Preface to *Narrative of the life of Frederick Douglass: An American slave*, by Frederick Douglass, edited by Benjamin Quarles. Cambridge, MA: The Belknap Press of Harvard University Press.

Gates, Henry Louis, Jr. 1991. From Wheatley to Douglass: The politics of displacement. In Sundquist.

Gee, James Paul. 1989. Literacy, discourse, and linguistics: Introduction. *Journal of Education* 171 (1): 5–17.

George, Diana, and Mariolina Rizzi Salvatori. 2008. Holy cards/immaginette: The extraordinary literacy of vernacular religion. *College Composition and Communication* 60 (2): 250–84.

Gray-Rosendale, Laura. 2001. Geographies of resistance: Rhetorics of race and mobility in Arna Bontemps' *Sad-faced boy* (1937). In Gray-Rosendale and Gruber.

———, and Sibylle Gruber, eds. 2001. *Alternative rhetorics: Challenges to the rhetorical tradition.* Albany: State University of New York Press.

Grimke, Sarah M. 1838. *Letters on the equality of the sexes and the condition of women (addressed to Mary S. Parker, president of the Boston Female Anti-Slavery Society).* 1970. Reprint, New York: Burt Franklin.

Harris, Joseph. 2003. Opinion: Revision as a critical practice. *College English* 65 (6): 577–592.

Harris, Judith. 2001. Re-writing the subject: Psychoanalytic approaches to creative writing and composition pedagogy. *College English* 64 (2): 175–204.

Heard, Alex. 2007. This American lie: A midget guitar teacher, a Macy's elf, and the truth about David Sedaris. *The New Republic,* March 19, 35–38.

Hindman, Jane. 2002. Writing an important body of scholarship: A proposal for an embodied rhetoric of professional practice. *JAC 22* (1): 93–118.

Hoffman, David C. 1997. Play, epideictic and argument. Paper presented at 83rd conference of the National Communication Association, November 19–23, at Chicago, IL. ERIC : ED 416 557

Japp, Phyllis M. 1993. Angelina Grimké Weld. In Kohrs Campbell.

Keating, AnaLouise. 1996. *Women reading women writing: Self-invention in Paula Gunn Allen, Gloria Anzaldúa and Audre Lorde.* Philadelphia: Temple University Press.

———. 1998. (De)centering the margins? Identity politics and tactical re(naming). In Stanley.

———. 2000. *Gloria E. Anzaldúa: Interviews/entrevistas.* New York: Routledge.

———. 2006. An interview with Gloria Evangelina Anzaldúa. In Frost and Hogue.

Killoran, John B. 2001. @ home among the .coms: Virtual rhetoric in the agora of the web. In Gray-Rosendale and Gruber.

Kirsch, Gesa. 1993. *Women writing the academy: Audience, authority, and transformation.* Carbondale: Southern Illinois University Press.

Knight, Lania. 2007. A conversation with David Sedaris. *The Missouri Review* 30 (1): 72–89.

Knox, Edward C. 2003. I see France: Priorities in nonfiction. *Twentieth Century Literature: A Scholarly and Critical Journal* 41 (1): 12–31

Kohrs Campbell, Karlyn. 1989. *Man cannot speak for her: Volume 1: A critical study of early feminist rhetoric.* New York: Greenwood Press.

———, ed. 1993, *Women public speakers in the United States, 1800–1925: A bio-critical sourcebook.* Westport, CT: Greenwood Press.

Kopelson, Karen. 2002. Dis/integrating the gay/queer binary: "Reconstructing identity politics" for a performative pedagogy. *College English* 65 (1): 17–35.

Kopelson, Kevin. 2007. *Sedaris.* Minneapolis: University of Minnesota Press.

kynard, carmen. 2002. "New life in this dormant creature": Notes on social consciousness, language, and learning in a college classroom. In Schroeder, Fox, and Bizzell.

Lerner, Gerda. 1967. *The Grimké sisters from South Carolina: Pioneers for women's rights and abolition.* New York: Schocken Books.

———. 1998. *The feminist thought of Sarah Grimké.* New York: Oxford.

Linden, Mary Ann. 2004. Breaking the ice with winter stories: Using short stories to introduce the narrative essay in first-year composition. *Eureka Studies in Teaching Short Fiction* 4 (2): 102–6.

Lorde, Audre. 1984. *Sister outsider: Essays and speeches.* Freedom, CA: The Crossing Press.

Lu, Min-Zhan. 2006. Living-English work. *College English* 68 (6): 605–18.

Lunsford, Andrea. 1998. Toward a mestiza rhetoric: Gloria Anzaldúa on composition and postcoloniality. *JAC: A Journal of Composition Theory* 18 (1): 1–27.

Lyons, Scott. 2000. Rhetorical sovereignty: What do American Indians want from writing? *College Composition and Communication* 51 (3): 447–68.

Mairs, Nancy. 1986. On being a cripple. In *Uncommon threads,* edited by Robert D. Newman, Jean Bohner, and Melissa Carol Johnson. New York: Longman.

Mao, LuMing. 2002. Re-clustering traditional academic discourse: Alternating the Confucian discourse. In Schroeder, Fox, and Bizzell.

Martin, Waldo E. Jr. 1984. *The mind of Frederick Douglass.* Chapel Hill: University of North Carolina Press.

Matsuda, Paul Kei. 2002. Alternative discourses: A synthesis. In Schroeder, Fox, and Bizzell.

———. 2006. The myth of linguistic homogeneity in U.S. college composition. *College English* 68 (6): 637–51.

McFeely, William S. 1991. *Frederick Douglass.* New York: W.W. Norton & Company.

McIntosh, Peggy. 1988. White privilege and male privilege: A personal account of coming to see correspondences through work in women's studies (working paper 189, Wellesley College Center for Research on Women, Wellesley, MA).

Moraga, Cherria, and Gloria Anzaldúa, eds. 1983. *This bridge called my back: Writings by radical women of color.* New York: Kitchen Table: Women of Color Press.

Moses, Wilson J. 1991. Writing freely? Frederick Douglass and the constraints of racialized writing. In Sundquist.

Muñoz, José Esteban. 1999. *Disidentification: Queers of color and the performance of politics.* Minneapolis: University of Minnesota Press.

Nies, Judith. 1977. *Seven women: Portraits from the American radical tradition.* New York: Viking Press.

Ouyang, Huining. 2001. Rewriting the butterfly story: Tricksterism in Onoto Watanna's *A Japanese nightingale* and Sui Sin Far's "The smuggling of Tie Co." In Gray-Rosendale and Gruber.

Patterson, Anita. 1999. Doing more than Patrick Henry: Douglass's *Narrative* and nineteenth-century American protest writing. In *Approaches to teaching* Narrative of the life of Frederick Douglass, edited by James C. Hall. New York: Modern Language Association.

Perelman, Chaim, and Olbrechts-Tyteca, Lucie. 1969. *The new rhetoric: A treatise on argumentation,* Translated by John Wilkinson and Purcell Weaver. Notre Dame, IN: University of Notre Dame Press.

Poulakos, Takis. 1987. Isocrates's use of narrative in the *Evagoras:* Epideictic rhetoric and moral action. *Quarterly Journal of Speech* 73: 317–28.

———. 1988. Toward a cultural understanding of classical epideictic rhetoric. *Pre/Text* 9 (3–4): 147–66.

Powell, Malea. 2002. Listening to ghosts: an alternative (non)argument. In Schroeder, Fox and Bizzell.

Pratt, Mary Louise. 1991. The arts of the contact zone. *Profession 91*: 33–40.

Pugh, Tison, and David L. Wallace. 2006. Heteronormative heroism and queering the school story in J.K. Rowling's *Harry Potter* series. *Children's Literature Association Quarterly* 31 (3): 260–81.

———. 2008. A postscript to "Heteronormative heroism and queering the school story in J.K. Rowling's *Harry Potter* series." *Children's Literature Association Quarterly* 33 (2): 188–92.

Quarles, Benjamin. 1960. Introduction to *Narrative of the Life of Frederick Douglass: An American slave, written by himself,* by Frederick Douglass. Cambridge, MA: The Belknap Press of Harvard University Press.

Royster, Jacqueline Jones. 2002. Academic discourses or small boats on a big sea. In Schroeder, Fox, and Bizzell.

Ryan, Pat. 1996. Epideictic discourse as a bridge to argumentation: A rhetorically based strategy for teaching the arts of persuasion. Paper read at 48th Annual Conference on College Composition and Communication, March 27, Phoenix, AZ. (ERIC 402 630)

Schiappa, Edward. 1995. Gorgias's *Helen* revisited. *Quarterly Journal of Speech* 81: 310–24.

Schonberg, Jeff. 2001. When worlds collide: Rhetorics of profit, rhetorics of loss in Chinese culture. In Gray-Rosendale and Gruber.

Schroeder, Christopher. 2002. From the inside out (or the outside in, depending). In Schroeder, Fox, and Bizzell.

———, Helen Fox, and Patricia Bizzell, eds. 2002. *ALT DIS: Alternative discourses and the academy.* Portsmouth, NH: Boyton/Cook.

———. Sedaris, David. 1994. *Barrel fever: Stories and essays.* Boston: Little Brown and Company.

Sedaris, David. 1997a. *Holidays on ice.* Boston: Little, Brown and Company.

Sedaris, David. 1997b. *Naked.* Boston: Little, Brown and Company.

Sedaris, David. 2000. *Me talk pretty one day.* Boston: Little, Brown and Company.

Sedaris, David. 2004. *Dress your family in corduroy and denim.* New York: Little, Brown and Company.

Sedaris, David. 2005, ed. *Children playing before a statue of Hercules.* New York: Simon & Schuster.

Sedaris, David. 2008. *When you are engulfed in flames.* New York: Little, Brown and Company.

Sedgwick, Eve Kosofsky. 1990. *Epistemology of the closet.* Berkeley: University of California Press.

Shaughnessy, Mina. 1977. *Errors and expectations: A Guide for the teacher of basic writing.* New York: Oxford University Press.

Sheard, Cynthia Miecznikowski. 1996. The public value of epideictic rhetoric. *College English* 58 (7): 765–94.

Spigelman, Candace. 2001. Argument and evidence in the case of the personal. *College English* 64 (1): 63–87.

Sirc, Geoffrey. 2001. Review: *The schoolmaster in the bookshelf. College English* 63 (4): 517–29.

Spivak, Gayatri Chakravorty. 1988. Can the subaltern speak? In *Marxism and the interpretation of culture,* edited by Cary Nelson and Lawrence Grossberg. Urbana: University of Illinois Press.

Stanley, Sandra Kumamoto, ed. 1998. *Other sisterhoods: Literary theory and U.S.women of color.* Urbana: University of Illinois Press.

Sundquist, Eric J., ed. 1991. *Frederick Douglass: New literary and historical essays.* Cambridge: Cambridge University Press.

Tobin, Lad. 1997. The case for double-voiced discourse. In Bishop. Trimbur, John. 2006. Linguistic memory and the politics of U.S. English. *College English* 68 (6): 575–88.

Vonnegut, Kristin S. 1993. Sarah M. Grimké. In Kohrs Campbell.

Wallace, David. L. 2004–2005. Shallow literacy, timid teaching, and cultural impotence. *Journal of the Assembly for Expanded Perspectives on Learning,* 10: 14–26.

———, and Jonathan Alexander. 2009. Queer rhetorical agency: Questioning narratives of heteronormativity. *JAC: A Journal of Composition Theory* 29 (4): 793–819.

Warner, Michael. 2002. *Publics and counterpublics.* New York: Zone Books.

Whately, Richard. 2001. From *Elements of rhetoric*. In *The rhetorical tradition: Readings from classical times to the present*, 2nd ed. Edited by Patricia Bizzell and Bruce Herzberg. Boston: Bedford/St. Martins.

Worsham, Lynn. 1991. Writing against writing: The predicament of *écriture féminine* in composition studies. In *Contending with words: Composition and rhetoric in a postmodern age*, edited by Patricia Harkin and John Schilb. New York: Modern Language Association.

Young, Morris. 2004. *Minor re/visions: Asian American literacy narratives as a rhetoric of citizenship*. Carbondale: Southern Illinois University Press.

Zaeske, Susan. 1995. The "promiscuous audience" controversy and the emergence of the early woman's rights movement. *Quarterly Journal of Speech* 81: 191–207.

INDEX

abled (-ness) 8, 18, 22, 26, 29, 37, 131, 147, 149, 177, 178, 184, 224

ableism (-ist) 193, 194, 200, 220, 227

abolition (-ism, -ist, -ists) 27, 36, 37, 38, 42, 46, 47, 48, 52, 53, 55, 56, 57, 59, 60, 74, 77, 78, 79, 80, 92, 93, 94, 98, 99, 100, 102, 104, 105, 207

Abrego, Carmen 143

Adams, Nehemiah 47

addict (-ed) 165, 184, 193, 198

addiction 37, 165, 166, 178, 193, 197, 198, 200, 208

additive 14, 147, 227

advocacy statements 238, 239

aesthetic (-s) 140, 165, 166, 167, 168, 170, 176, 185, 187

African American (-s) 26, 55, 72, 76, 79, 80, 103, 109, 110, 112, 132, 136, 216

African American (Black) Vernacular English: 12, 26, 139

ageist (-ism) 217, 227

agency 4, 5, 6, 7, 15, 16, 20, 23, 24, 27, 28, 31, 32, 34, 38, 43, 45, 50, 52, 59, 73, 74, 76, 81, 95, 109, 111, 135, 136, 152, 153, 157, 158, 163, 184, 196, 205, 206, 209, 212

alcoholic 171, 198

Alexander, Jonathan 1, 15, 22, 137

Alger, Horatio 74, 80, 95, 121

anger 113, 146, 151, 155, 156, 171, 215, 217, 218, 224

Anglo (-s) 17, 18, 119, 120, 122, 133, 141, 144, Anglocentric 121

Anzaldúa, Gloria 17, 36, 37, 38, Chapter 4, 162, 163, 165, 183, 200, 209, 212, 213, 219, 221, 226, 242

apology 105, 165, 187, 197, 199, 200, 209, 225

apostolic 60, 61

Aristotle 164, 165, 167

Asian American 6, 18, 113, 114

assimilate (-d) 9, 145, 230

assimilation (-ist) 12, 91, 109, 110, 124, 137, 138, 139, 146, 147, 206, 227

Auld, Hugh 73, 98

Auld, Sophia 87, 88

authorship 196, 212, 213, 218, 221, 228, 229, 232, 234, 236, 238

autobiography (-cal, -ies) 12, 18, 36, 38, 73, 76, 77, 78, 96, 100, 127, 171

axis (-es) of difference or oppresson 5, 16, 17, 22, 23, 44, 91, 93, 112, 114, 120, 148, 184, 210, 221, 224, 225

Baca, Damian 16, 17, 18, 119, 120, 125

Bacon, Sir Francis 77, 168

Bahri, Deepika 28, 29

Bartholomae, David 9

Bartlett, Elzabeth Ann 42, 46, 48, 49, 53, 54, 56, 62

Berquist, Kathie 162

Bible (-ical) 44, 45, 49, 51, 54, 60, 68, 159, 210

binary (-ies) 5, 26, 27, 28, 29, 32, 33, 44, 64, 109, 129, 147, 152, 163, 182, 192, 207, 220

bisexual (-s, -ity) 25, 30, 72, 112

Bishop, Wendy 1, 11, 12, 13, 210

bitch 33, 179, 186, 191, 192, 196, 200

Bizzell, Patricia 7, 12, 48, 76

black (-s) 21, 26, 27, 75, 76, 78, 79, 80, 88, 90, 96, 100, 105, 109, 110, 137, 139, 207, 223

Blake, Debbie 143

border (s) 129, 131, 132, 166,

borderland (-s) 17, 36, 38, 121, 126, 127, 129, 131, 132, 133, 135, 136, 137, 141, 144, 145, 146, 150, 154, 156, 219, 242

bourgeois 32, 48, 176, 179, 180, 184, 190

Bradford, Vivian 168

Brandt, Deborah 97

bridge (-s) 124, 125, 127, 149, 150

Briggs, Governor George N. 108

Brooke, Robert 1, 238

Browdy de Hernandez, Jennifer 127, 142

Burke, Kenneth 16, 167

Butler, Judith 1, 3, 6, 10, 11, 12, 19, 23, 24, 26, 31, 32, 33, 42, 73, 74, 77, 119, 120, 136, 162, 163, 174, 182, 183, 212, 205, 206, 209, 210, 216, 224

canon (-s) 11, 15, 19, 43, 119, 127, 163, 214

Carlacio, Jami 60, 61

Cartesian 127, 128, 140

Catholic 94, 140, 194
Cherokee 20
Chicano/a (-os, -as) 17, 21, 36, 122, 123, 133, 134, 138, 139, 140, 141, 153, 154
Christian (-anity, -s) 8, 20, 45, 49, 62, 68, 89, 125, 131, 140, 210, 242
church (-es) 46, 47, 54, 68, 70, 89, 95, 96, 140, 159, 160, 210, 222
citizen (-s, -ship) 14, 18, 72, 132, 208
civil rights 26, 106, 124
Cixous, Hèléne 34, 35, 97, 127, 128
Clarke, Edward 54
class (-es, -ism, -ist) 8, 20, 23, 26, 37, 58, 64, 72, 73, 83, 85, 90, 97, 101, 102, 105, 106, 107, 108, 109, 110, 112, 119, 120, 121, 122, 124, 125, 126, 128, 130, 131, 135, 138, 139, 149, 152, 153, 168, 184, 189, 190, 216, 217, 218, 222, 225, 227
clergy 47, 54, 55, 56, 61
Clifford, Colonel John Henry 108
Clinton, Hillary 26
Coatlalopeuh, María 140
Coatlicue 129, 130, 131, 142, 143, 145, 153, 161
cocksucker 186
code-switch (-es, -ing) 11, 14, 38, 91, 110, 111, 119, 125, 127, 139, 144, 146, 147, 151, 154
Collins, Daniel F. 13
Collins, John A. 27, 92, 98, 99
colonial (-ist) 16, 17, 18, 65, 132
color (-ed, -s) 20, 21, 22, 38, 53, 89, 90, 104, 108, 109, 114, 119, 125, 126, 128, 134, 138, 139, 147, 148, 149, 157
Columbian Orator 93, 98
Compelled to write/speak 3, 36, 42, 52, 103, 116, 118, 121, 162, 206
Conference on College Composition and Communication/CCCC 112, 113, 123, 210
confession (-s) 104, 165, 184, 187, 196, 197, 198, 199, 200, 209, 224, 225
Connor, Robert 16
conocimiento 127, 128, 129, 143, 153
copresence 31, 32, 33, 34, 43, 45, 63, 74, 120, 130, 134, 142, 146, 163, 183, 184, 200, 208
copresent 33, 61, 63, 207
Covey, Edward 95
counterpublic (-s) 27, 28, 32, 43, 52, 58, 92, 94, 183, 206
Crenshaw, Kimberlé Williams 5
cripple 184
crossing (-s)/travesía 96, 142, 143, 144, 145, 147, 153

Cushman 20, 21, 22, 29

Daniell, Beth 196, 197
Dehannn, Kathleen A 13
dehumanize (-d, -ation, -ed, -ing) 72, 73, 74, 79, 81, 82, 83, 84, 85, 87, 89, 90, 100, 102, 207
deliberative 164, 165, 167, 169
DePeter, Ronald A 13
depression 142, 198
descriptive 119, 154, 232
discrimination (-atory) 18, 61, 73, 90, 105, 106, 107, 110, 113, 114, 120, 123, 162, 208, 209
disabled 113, 147, 184
disablity (-ies) 112, 200
disidentification 33, 34, 35, 36, 43, 45, 103, 105, 120, 142, 186, 193
disidentify 34, 62, 104
diverse (-ity) 9, 37, 112, 113, 114, 124, 127
Dobrin, Sidney 7, 8
Double consciousness 71, 136, 221
Douglass, Anna 96
Douglass, Frederick 27, 36, 37, 38, chapter 4, 119, 121, 124, 132, 162, 163, 200, 206, 207, 208, 209, 212, 226, 227, 228
Dow, Bonnie J. 169
Down, Doug 228, 229, 233, 236
drunk (-ard, -s) 135, 173, 198
DuBois, W.E.B. 136, 221
Dumbledore, Albus 30, 31
Dumond, Dwight L. 47

Edwards, Jonathan 50, 57
Elbow, Peter 14
Elkin, Burt Jr. 39, 40, 41
embody (-ied, -ing, -iment) 4, 11, 12, 32, 34, 35, 38, 73, 77, 79, 81, 111, 154, 155, 183, 192, 200, 207
Encomium for Helen 164
Enlightenment 17, 140
enthymemic 167, 169
epideictic 163, 162, 165, 166, 167, 168, 169, 170, 171, 172, 176, 181, 187
epistemology of the closet 25, 29, 30, 81, 120, 127, 131, 142
ériciture feminine 34, 35, 127
Espinoza, Dionne 154
essentialist (-ism, -izing) 63, 64, 65, 207
ethnic (-ity) 125, 138, 139, 154, 184
ethos 38, 77, 92
Eurocentric 16, 119, 140
European 16, 17, 140
Evagoras 169, 170
evangelical 68, 210, 242

ABOUT THE AUTHOR

DAVID L. WALLACE is professor of Rhetoric and Composition and chair of the Department of Writing and Rhetoric at the University of Central Florida. When he's not swamped with payroll, annual evaluations, and approving electronic personal action files, he teaches first-year composition and other undergraduate writing courses as well as graduate courses in rhetorical history and theory, literacy theory, and research methods. With Helen Rothschild Ewald, he is author of *Mutuality in the Rhetoric and Composition Classroom*, and he has authored numerous articles and chapters about substantively addressing diversity issues both in pedagogy and disciplinary practice. Outside the academy, he's a decent setter for his volleyball team and makes pie crust that is almost as flakey as his mother's.